058965

HEROIN, DEVIANCE and MORALITY

Volume 112, Sage Library of Social Research

SAGE LIBRARY OF SOCIAL RESEARCH

HEROIN, DEVIANCE and MORALITY

CHARLES W. LIDZ and ANDREW L. WALKER

with the assistance of
Leroy C. Gould

Volume 112
SAGE LIBRARY OF
SOCIAL RESEARCH

SAGE PUBLICATIONS   Beverly Hills   London

For information address:

SAGE Publications, Inc.
275 South Beverly Drive
Beverly Hills, California 90212

SAGE Publications Ltd
28 Banner Street
London EC1Y 8QE, England

Printed in the United States of America

Library of Congress Cataloging in Publication Data

Lidz, Charles W.
    Heroin, deviance and morality.

    (Sage library of social research ; v. 112)
    Bibliography: p.
    1. Drug-abuse—United States. 2. United
States—Moral conditions. 3. Deviant behavior.
I. Walker, Andrew L., joint author. II. Gould,
Leroy C. III. Title.
HV5825.L46   362.2'93'0973   80-23327
ISBN 0-8039-1549-7
ISBN 0-8039-1550-0 (pbk.)

FIRST PRINTING

This is dedicated to our
predecessors
and
successors

Clara Heard Wooddy
and
James and Heather Carwile

CONTENTS

ACKNOWLEDGMENTS

The image of the ivory-tower scholar conjuring up solitary visions does not, of course, apply to us. This was a joint production. Almost equally important, however, are the contributions made by friends, colleagues, and informants.

As anyone who has ever done field work knows, one owes an enormous debt to those whom one is researching. Much of this volume is based on our field work in a city we call Riverdale. Without the aid and willing cooperation of these people, our field work could not have been done. We also owe a lot to members of our research staff who helped orient us to the addicts' world: Ernest Badger, Michael Figueroa, the Rev. E. Benjamin LaFrazier, Robert Logan, and especially Thomas Muskelley and the late Delores Outlaw. Barbara Clinton, a former methadone nurse, made a large contribution to our understanding of staff-patient relationships.

Mostly, however, this is a book of analysis and theory. As such, it developed out of almost endless discussions with our colleagues. Originally, this book was to have been written jointly with Leroy Gould, Steven H. Lewis, and Lansing E. Crane. Other tasks claimed them, but many of the original ideas were developed jointly with them. Leroy Gould persisted long enough to draft much of the early part of Chapter 2. Many of Steve Lewis's ideas are also contained in that chapter. Lanse Crane's ideas were the basis for Chapter 6. We owe them a heavy debt.

We also received good advice and counsel from a group we designated our Research Advisers: Albert Cohen, Abraham Goldstein, Stanislav Kasl, Stanton Wheeler, Gerald Klerman, Thomas Levin, and especially Egon Bittner and Kai Erikson. They provided guidance, wisdom, and encouragement during the darker periods of the research.

A large number of people have read this manuscript and have offered thoughts and suggestions that have helped. We particularly want to thank Mary Ashley, Rainer Baum, Joanne Brown, the late Jim Burkhart, Kai Erikson, Leroy Gould, Bennie Ruth Gilbert, Geoffrey Guest, Frank Hainer, Jane Isay, Christine Lidz, Lynn Lidz, Ken Magoon, Alan Meisel, John Nelson, Katie Walker, and Eviatar Zerubavel.

We must thank two teachers who influenced us jointly: the late Talcott Parsons and Howard Schwartz. Both supervised our work during the initial period of analysis and were extremely helpful.

We also owe an enormous debt to Florita Cohen, Betty Evans, and particularly Betty Brenneman for typing and sometimes editing seemingly endless drafts.

Thanks also is due Herbert Kleber for support of the project and the National Institute of Mental Health which, through Narcotic Addict Treatment Program Grant No. 1H17 MH16356, partially supported the data gathering and analysis contained in this book.

Finally, Chuck Lidz wants to thank the Department of Psychiatry of the University of Pittsburgh, and particularly its chairman, Thomas Detre, and Loren Roth, Director of the Law and Psychiatry Program, for support and encouragement in the production of this volume. A special debt of gratitude is owed to Victor Lidz, brother and colleague, whose advice and support were indispensable.

PREFACE

The late 1960s and early 1970s were years of great turmoil in the United States. They were years of black power and hippies, of riots and draft evasions, of war and drugs—things that most Americans have by now forgotten, just as one day they will also forget about Watergate, the oil embargo, Iran, and the other crises that have occurred since then. As the public forgets, however, sociologists and historians should not, for there are lessons to be learned from these hectic years that have relevance for both sociological and historical theories of deviance, morality, and social change.

This book, in the first instance, is about crises—in particular, the Drug Crisis of the late 1960s and early 1970s. In the second instance, however, it is also a book about the activities of drug addicts and social control agents. In traditional sociological parlance, it would be called a book about culture conflict, deviance, and social control, subjects that the authors refer to more colorfully, and perhaps more descriptively, as "doing morality" and "using morality."

The origins of the book trace to the year 1969, when I became research director for a drug treatment clinic that had opened the previous year as part of a new, federally sponsored, national effort to stem what appeared then to be a rapidly rising tide of drug abuse. Lidz and Walker, fresh out of graduate school, joined me the following year. Like most researchers who were then being sucked into the drug world, we knew little about drugs or drug users and even less about drug treatment or drug law enforcement. What we did know, moreover, came almost exclusively from the literature then extant on drugs (e.g. Lindesmith, 1947; Schur, 1962; Becker, 1963; Chein et al., 1964) or on deviance and social control more generally (e.g. Merton,1968; Cloward and Ohlin, 1960; Matza, 1964). Nevertheless, we assumed that we would have little difficulty getting to know drug users and that writing an account of drugs would involve little more than establishing what kinds of data would be theoretically relevant, generating data sets, and applying traditional forms of data analysis and interpretation. We were particularly hopeful that the then emerging "labeling" theory of deviance and social control (cf. Lemert, 1967; Becker, 1963) would serve as a sufficient paradigm for explaining the drug phenomenon.

We discovered quickly, however, that "labeling theory," as well as other more traditional theories of deviance and control, could not answer several questions that pressed themselves upon us. Why, for example, was drug use apparently increasing so rapidly? Why had society suddenly become so concerned about drugs? Why did the United States resurrect a program of medical intervention abandoned a half-century earlier to supplement law-enforcement efforts?

Since traditional theories did not give answers to these questions, we began to explore the idea that drug use and control in "crisis" times might be different from what it is in other times. This idea was reinforced as we reread Lindesmith's (1947 and 1965), Schur's (1962) and Becker's (1963) accounts of the rhetoric and activities that led to the Harrison Act of 1914 that controled opiates and the Marijuana Tax Act of 1937 that outlawed marijuana. What became clear, and was later reinforced by Musto (1973), was that these eras had more in common with the late 1960s and early 1970s than they did with any of the intervening years.

We were aware of only two sociologists who had discussed such "epidemics" of deviance and social control. Durkheim, in a few almost parenthetical comments in *The Rules of Sociological Method* (1964) and *The Division of Labor in Society* (1933), differentiated between "normal" and "pathological" deviance, and Erikson (1966) described and analyzed three "crime waves" in seventeenth-century Massachusetts. Both authors agreed that deviance can take crisis forms and that these crises probably have more to do with the state of the society at the time than with individual deviants. Since Durkheim and Erikson provided no guide to doing nonhistorical research on deviants and control agents caught up in a "crime wave," however, we were left with something of a dilemma. Traditional theories, which were designed to explain deviance and control in "normal" times, gave us no guide as to how to study the Drug Crisis from society's perspective, yet theories of social "crises" gave us no guide as to how to study the behavior of deviants and control agents during a "crisis."

Our solution to this dilemma was decidedly pragmatic. First, we divided into three teams to construct ethnographic accounts of the core activities. Walker led a team that studied the perspective of drug users. Lidz led a team that studied drug-law enforcement as understood by policemen, prosecutors, defense attorneys, and other members of the criminal justice community. Gould led a team that studied drug control from the perspective of those who were responsible for drug treatment. *Connections: Notes from the Heroin World* (1974) contains an account of this effort.

During this phase of our research we worked on the assumption that no one would be in a better position to understand the Drug Crisis at its micro level than those who were intimately involved in the day-to-day activities that made up what was then commonly called the "drug scene." We did not assume, however, that these actors—doctors, lawyers, junkies, cops— were in a privileged position to describe the phenomenon at its macro or societal level. To grasp the phenomenon at this level, we had to analyze the kinds of second-hand accounts that were then readily available to citizens and policy makers. Thus we subscribed to a clipping service that gave us a compilation of local newspaper articles dealing with drugs or their control and gathered data from national sources on the number and content

of articles dealing with the crisis that appeared in popular
magazines and professional journals. We monitored the number
of drug arrests, both local and national, and charted trends in
local and federal support to law enforcement and treatment
agencies. Like everyone else, we also watched television and
listened attentively to politicians and other pundits as they
described the horrors of drugs and the demise of our honored
way of life.

Early in 1971, I noticed the first evidence that the Drug
Crisis, at least locally, might have reached its peak. The evidence
was so slim, consisting only of a three-month drop in the
number of drug arrests, that the other members of my research
staff were unwilling to believe that it was anything more than a
random statistical fluctuation. Nevertheless, I warned the clinic
for which we worked that a decline in drug activity might be in
the offing. The suggestion was roundly dismissed. Not until the
next year, when admissions also began to drop (see figure 5),
did the clinical staff take cognizance of my hypothesis and even
then few were willing to accord it any validity. My research
staff, on the other hand, had by then become more or less
convinced, as arrest rates had continued to decline throughout
the year.

The ebbing of the crisis had several ramifications, not the
least of which was the potential erosion of the treatment clinic's
economic foundations. Like any threatened organization, it
fought back. "Everyone knows," the clinic's director told the
press and a Senate hearing, "that drug use is increasing. The
decline in drug arrests is just a sign that law enforcement
agencies are not doing their proper job." Local arrests for drugs
(marijuana and other nonopiate drugs, but not heroin) increased
the following year, and admissions to the clinic went up the
year following that. Both resumed their decline in subsequent
years.

This and similar episodes made it clear that the macro and
micro elements of the Drug Crisis indeed did affect each other.
Without the activities of drug users and social control agents,
the crisis would have had no empirical referent, yet without the

crisis atmosphere generated by society, drug users and control agents would not have had the extraordinary moral climate that came to define drug-related activities in those years. Because of this, Lidz and Walker have concluded that the key to understanding crises of this kind lies in a dynamic concept of morality—that is, in the socially based schema operating at the time that determines the rightness and wrongness of acts, actors, interactions, and settings.

Since Durkheim's decisive analysis of social solidarity (1933), sociologists have been aware that shared morality is a critical foundation for social integration. Nevertheless, twentieth-century sociology transformed Durkheim's generative concept of morality into the more static concepts of culture, norms, folkways, and mores, concepts which are not nearly as satisfactory as Durkheim's for explaining solidarity, particularly the solidarity of highly differentiated social systems.

This volume begins, then, with Durkheim's thesis that morality provides points of common orientation that make sustained interaction possible, particularly interaction between people whose socially recognized "self-interests" are divergent. It is the same view that Erikson takes when he suggests (1977: 82) that the term "culture" be applied, "not only to the customary ways in which people induce conformity in behavior and outlook but also to the customary ways in which they organize diversity."

So stated, however, an immense question remains: how are new moral schemes developed, tested, and maintained? To answer this, Lidz and Walker follow a path similar to that taken by Erikson in his further remarks about the inherent *"axis of variation* that cuts through the center of a culture's space and draws attention to the diversities arrayed along it" (1977: 82).

> The forms of contrast experienced by a particular people are one of the identifying motifs of their culture, and if one wants to understand how any given culture works, one should inquire into its characteristic counterpoints as well as its central values. The axes of variation cutting across a culture are not only sources of tension but gradients along which responses to social change are likely to take place. When individual persons or groups of people undergo what

appear to be dramatic shifts in character, skidding across the entire spectrum of human experience from one extreme to the other, it is only reasonable to suspect that the potential had been there all along—hidden away in the folds of the culture, perhaps, but an intensive element of the larger pattern nonetheless. Such shifts do not represent a drastic change of heart, not a total reversal of form, but a simple slide along one of the axes of variation characteristic of that social setting [1977: 83-84].

Within this context, I am inclined to view the 1960s and 1970s not as rents in the fabric of society but as a temporary unfolding of its moral garments. Black militants and Flower Children, Green Berets and draft resisters, ghetto rioters and drug addicts are seen thus not as aberrant cultural forms but as temporary outposts on the axes of variation that have always defined American cultural space.

The social climate today is less hectic than it was ten years ago and probably looks to most people to have more in common with 1960 than with 1970. I do not share this view, contending instead that all three eras had more continuity than is apparent on the surface. The continuity was that moral core, in all its dimensions and complexity, that defines American culture. What appeared to be diversity was simply a particular epoch during which underlying moral schemes were exposed and iterated. Whether or not the moral core itself changed in subtle ways during these years is not so clear. I suspect, however, that it may have, making possible what now appear to be several rather permanent social changes: changes in the status of blacks, women, and other minorities; changes in sex roles and the composition of families; and changes also, perhaps, in the concern Americans show for their bodies and their physical environment.

These, however, are speculations that go well beyond this volume, which is addressed more modestly to but one of the "crises" that occured in the turbulent years of the late 1960s and early 1970s. By analyzing this crisis within a dynamic concept of morality, the authors show that the drugs were not an orthogonal event brought on by a sudden and mysterious epidemic of drug use, but rather a "normal" social episode that played an integral role in the ongoing and dynamic process of cultural integration. To explain this episode in full, the authors apply their concept of morality to both the macro level of society and the micro level of the actors who made it all possible—that is, at both the level of culture and at the level of the drug users and social control agents who played out society's moral drama.

—Leroy C. Gould

Chapter 1

INTRODUCTION

It is no closely kept sociological secret that the processes of deviance and control are intimately related to the ways in which people define the rightness or wrongness of acts, actors, intentions, and settings, i.e., to morality. This is a connection that sociological theorists of deviance of all schools have long recognized. However, in spite of the general agreement, sociology has had a great deal of difficulty in constructing a productive theoretical formulation of deviance which explicates its relationship to morality. A brief review of several approaches to deviance might be helpful in understanding the nature of this difficulty.

Over the years, issues concerning deviance and social control have been continually important to sociology. There are probably two distinct reasons why sociologists have sustained an interest in these matters. First, since the "problem of social order" has been paradigmatically central to sociology, problems of disorder have always been theoretically relevant. Second, deviance is a matter of intense practical concern to ordinary people, and they have continually turned to sociology for solutions to the everyday problems of crime, delinquency, alcoholism, and so on. Thus deviance presents itself as a problem in two senses: a phenomenon that any scientifically adequate theory of society must confront, and an everyday phenomenon that ordinary people must face.

Since early in this century, criminology has tried to understand deviance in a manner that would satisfy the practical demands of ordinary people. The dominant theoretical concerns were why other people engaged in deviant behavior, and what social control strategies will decrease or eliminate deviance. From this, we can say that most traditional criminology was etiological in focus and correctionist in intent. (Matza, 1969). With the advantage of hindsight, we can easily see that early criminology compromised its "scientific" value by accepting ordinary moral concerns and judgments as the unexamined presuppositions of its analysis. The "badness" of deviance was a fundamental analytic assumption. The "goodness" of social control was equally taken for granted (except where agents of control were "corrupt," in which case they became "bad," and just another type of deviance).

Numerous criticisms can be (and have been) offered of the traditional criminological approach (Matza, 1969; Taylor et al., 1973), but the most salient for the present purposes is that while criminology had quite a bit to say about offenders, it had relatively little to say about either deviance as a class of social phenomena, or the sociological significance of social control. Again, with the advantage of hindsight, it is easy to see that these omissions resulted from the common-sense moral presuppositions and concerns of the early criminologists, but they certainly limited the compatibility of criminology with the rest of sociological thinking.

Beginning in the late 1950s, a new wave of sociologists attacked the problem of deviance. Recognizing the basic flaw in traditional criminology, they rejected common-sense moral presuppositions and focused attention on the process by which the "badness" of deviants and their behavior is discovered. Under the guidance of symbolic interactionism, they undertook the analysis of the "social construction of deviance" in order to avoid the problems of their predecessors. Of course, one of the major benefits of this approach is that they were able to extend their analysis to cover the part played by control agents in the whole phenomenon. This extension produced a much more balanced view of deviance and social control as a transpersonal, transactional process rather than a character trait. The symbolic interactionists were able to demonstrate and theoretically account for what some people had suspected all along—that the identification of deviance depends on a host of factors in addition to the question, "who did it?" To put it another way, they began the process of creating a sociology of deviance that went beyond a study of role recruitment.

In large measure, the successes of the symbolic interactionists resulted from their stripping away the "moral certainty" which imbues common-sense discussion of deviance; they were able to see that the "rightness and wrongness" of various activities and participants in the deviance and control process depends on the social (and moral) perspective from which they are viewed. For instance, to some drug users, illicit drugs are morally good (Szasz, 1974, speaks of them as "holy" to some users), while to various anti-drug crusaders they are clearly evil (describing marijuana as the "devil weed," for instance).

However, while the symbolic interactionists were able to uncover brilliantly the social *construction* of deviance, they were largely at a loss to explain the social *significance* of the whole process. They realized the moral relativity characteristic of the process, but they could not explain the "stake" the larger society has in the outcome of the negotiations between deviants and agents of control. Without an articulated theory of morality, they could only note, again and again, the moral nature of the phenomenon they sought to explain. This is a particular problem because deviance seems to be a phenomenon common to all groups. The interactionists's observation that deviance was a social construction did not provide an answer to the question of why society should bother to construct deviance and deviants.

Kai Erikson has recognized some of these problems and, in *Wayward Puritans* (1966), pointed a way to their solution by forging a link between symbolic interactionism and functionalism. In order to do this, he turned to the original Durkheimian concepts of morality. As Gould has noted, in modern sociology the concept of morality has coalesced around the concept of "norm" and has largely been taken over by the structuralists, who used it in a somewhat mechanistic way to ground their notion of social structure as a stable pattern of interrelationships in equilibrium. Erikson reemphasized the *symbolic function* in fixing the "moral identity" of the community. For Erikson, morality and its acceptance are crucial elements in the identification of the individual with the community. That is, morality does not just provide direction, it imbues life with moral meaning which is equally essential to the community and the individual.

Following this reasoning, Erikson was able to conclude that as the community changed—for whatever reason—the normative symbolic system would also change. But these symbol system changes could only be verified in their actual application to the behavior of members. Thus deviance (in the sense of actual events which are publicly labeled and responded to as "wrong") serves the function of verifying what it presupposes: the moral "contours" of the community. In brief, Erikson's work opens up a whole new area in the sociology of deviance and control. It encourages us to focus on the moral schemas that the deviance exemplifies and how the creation of the deviance, both from the point of view of the deviants and the control agents, is tied to those moral schemas and conflicts concerning them.

There are, however, several limitations to Erikson's accomplishments. However intriguing his case studies may be, his theoretical formulations do not really go beyond Durkheim's functional hypotheses. There is little discussion of the dynamics by which deviance is actually generated at problematic points in the community's normative boundaries, and no theoretical discussion at all of the patterns of interaction between deviants and agents of control. These limitations result, perhaps, from Erikson's necessary reliance on historical data which do not permit the sociologist to actually observe the interaction which constitutes the deviance in question.

In this volume, we will refine and add to Erikson's analysis in two ways. First, we will specify in greater detail the theoretical relationship between deviance and morality; and second, we will apply these theoretical formulations to various data pertinent to the Drug Crisis, some of which were generated by direct participant observation. Right now, we must turn to a discussion of the sociology of morality.

Morality: A Definition

Perhaps it would be best to begin by clarifying what we mean by the term "morality," for our definition differs somewhat from convention. By morality we simply mean the process of defining any object in the world as good or evil or any similar evaluative dualism (e.g., kind-mean, free-enslaved, smart-stupid, and so on)[1] Obviously, we do not mean to imply that any particular moral judgment necessarily is correct, that it is based on any cosmic system of good and evil, or that the moral schema is acceptable to all other people. Using our definition, Adolf Hitler was probably every bit as actively moral as Mahatma Gandhi. We realize this use of the term is somewhat divergent from popular usage, but it is important to keep this definition in mind throughout the argument that follows.

Most sociologists, implicitly or explicitly following Durkheim (1933) and Parsons (1937), have tended to view morality as regulating only acts and the ends toward which acts are oriented. This reflects the general concern with the role of morality in maintaining the social order and the assumption that this involves largely the regulation of overt acts. We believe that this is too narrow a view of the role of morality in social life. Any society's moral order inevitably involves evaluations of persons, groups of persons, and settings of activities as well as acts and purposes (Lidz, 1981). Indeed, as we will show in the next chapter, the Drug Crisis primarily focused on the moral constitution of groups, not acts.

Using Morality

Morality is essential to the practical accomplishment of everyday life. It must be emphasized that we are not talking about the "burning moral issues of our day." We want to discuss the definitions of good and evil inherent in the routine assumptions of everyday life.

Consider, for example, the morality of housework. Whether done by the traditional housewife, a maid, a "liberated" woman, or an even more "liberated" househusband, the core morality is the same. There is a fundamental commitment in doing housework to the morality of cleanliness and order and the immorality of dirt and disorder. Without a moral commitment to order and cleanliness, housework becomes a nonsensical enterprise. The judgments of when the house "needs" cleaning, what is orderly, and when the house is "clean enough" and housework can be stopped vary from one individual to another, but almost everyone employs these moral concepts to organize his or her housework. Similarly, Durkheim's (1933) analysis of noncontractual elements of contracts demonstrates quite clearly that even the most basically self-interested economic transactions depend on shared moral groundings. Perhaps even more interesting is that "self-interest" itself is a complex moral schema.

Indeed, all social activities seem to be dependent on the actors using a moral schema specific to that activity as well as the situation in which it takes place. This is true for several reasons. Most critical is the fact that social action is oriented toward goals, or to put it another way, it is intentional (Schutz, 1967). But ends cannot be chosen on a purely instrumental basis. At some point, the actor must decide that one future state is better than another. While he may choose his means to ends purely on the basis of "rational" criteria, the ends of action cannot be selected on such a basis (Parsons, 1937). At a social level, any sort of coordinated activity depends on the development of some coordination of ends. Thus social organization depends on its ability to achieve a considerable degree of consensus about the appropriate ends for the behavior of people in various roles.

Morality functions as the orienting factor in social action. Decisions about what acts are good, desirable, or pleasant, who is nice, perceptive, or useful, what ends are holy, sexy, or proper, and what settings are safe, good to grow up in, comfortable, or disgusting allow us to make decisions about our actions and provide meaning to our lives. Most of the time, moral schemas act as the "ground" against which the "figure" of the particular decision is made. Under these circumstances, the moral schemas can be described as unquestioned and unattended to.

However, moral schemas are not unquestionable. What is the ground of action can, by a shift in focus, be turned into the focus of attention. Moral schemas can thus be best described as "typically unquestioned but always open to question." We do not usually open moral schemas up for question unless pressed to, since these moral schemas are the basis for the habits, routines, commitments, relationships, and hopes that make up our everyday life. But the man who comes home and finds his wife in bed with his best friend may find himself with little choice but to call some of his assumptions into question. Likewise, as we will see, the moral schema that portrayed American youth as younger versions of their elders was called into question in the late 1960s.

Doing Morality

All action depends on moral orientations. We must use morality in order to act. Unfortunately, however, we are not born with a morality. Nor can morality simply be given to us by society in a series of maxims to be memorized. The social world is much too complex. Punching someone in the stomach may be aggravated assault in one case and heroism in another. A woman making identical small talk with two men at a party may find that her words are taken as charming and engrossing by one and insulting and perverse by another. Indeed, we spend much of our lives defining and refining our knowledge of the moral universe. It is a process of considerable cognitive complexity which we will not detail here.

For our purposes, however, two things are critical. First, in order for the morality that we "use" to be shared, it must be *socially* created. If we wish our evaluations to be sympathetically received by others and persuasive in orienting their actions toward us, there must be some elements in common between our morality and theirs. Morality must, to some degree, be done or accomplished collectively. In order to know about the moral world jointly, we must moralize together. Second, we tend to do our moralizing on real events and people or on accounts which purport to accurately represent real people and events. Precisely why this is so is not completely clear, but one factor is probably that there is no other way to provide sufficient moral complexity to the stories. Furthermore, if the moralizing is not done on reality or something that is thought to "stand for" reality (i.e., novels, T.V. programs, etc.), the "relevance" of the moralizing is brought into question. We wish to suggest that this process of "doing morality" is the essential process in deviance and control and that, to a large extent, it is the function of deviant acts and their apprehension to provide society with a basis for "doing morality."[2]

Doing morality, even of the most routine type, involves a shift of figure and ground from ordinary instrumental activity. It involves focusing on the moral schemas that are usually taken for granted. In doing morality, standards that are usually implicit are made explicit by illustration. This involves two separate but related processes. First, doing morality involves the moral placement of the persons and events in question. In the criminal courts, this involves the establishment that the accused is, indeed, guilty. The second aspect is, for our purposes, even more important. It is the "review" of all of the properties of the instance at hand which demonstrates the evil of the deviant. This involves an implicit development of the moral schema of *that type* of thing. The case at hand is made to stand, "more or less," for all cases of that type. The moral evaluation of the deviant tends to spread to those things with which he is associated. Thus hearing about the childhood of a particular deviant tends to tell us about the moral character of child rearing techniques, the nature of the environment in which he grew up, etc. We learn more from the discussion of deviance than we are told.

Doing morality is the stuff of everyday life. It is present in court work (Garfinkel, 1956), psychiatric hospitals (Goffman, 1961), gossip, T.V. shows, great novels, pornographic stories, and innumerable other activities. The pervasiveness of this moralizing process probably reflects the complexity of the functions that doing morality performs for social actors. To begin with, the complexity of social life is such that even the formal law, with its relatively simple universalistic standards of decision making, must have "case law." Judges and lawyers routinely find that no set of legal statutes, no matter how clear, provides enough guidance to determine how a decision should be made. Thus, in every area of law, past decisions and commentary serve to elaborate the law itself. Similarly, in everyday life moral stories provide elaboration and clarification of moral rules. Even if this were not the case, doing morality would still serve an important socializing function. New role incumbents, be they children or adults playing new roles, need to be socialized into the moral schemas of the new systems. While it might perhaps be possible in formal organizations to socialize individuals totally in a differentiated subsystem of the organization, this is clearly impossible in all of the various informal groups which compose the bulk of our social world.

Finally, doing morality becomes a way of clarifying the boundaries of solidarity groups. The moral heterogeneity of the society is both a reflection of and the source of diverse solidarities. Doing subgroup morality both clarifies membership in these groups and clarifies their moral content. Doing morality is a constant aspect of social interaction and as such will never be far from our analysis of the core processes of the Drug Crisis.

Moral Heterogeneity

Morality, like almost all subjectively meaningful behavior, is grounded in language. We both create and express our moral schemas in the medium of language. As Chomsky and the tranformational linguists have so clearly demonstrated, language is creative or, as they call it, "generative." What they have noted is that with the logical structures of grammars it is possible to generate new sentences, meanings, and ideas that one has never before heard. Morality, like language, is generative. No moral dogma can ever be free from challenge, because new positions can always be created. Given that people in different social positions in society will view the world differently, there must always be diversity in the moral universe of any society. Furthermore, any effort to coerce a uniform moral consensus may well widen the differences in perspective between the coerced and the coercing.

Equally important, different aspects of a complex society require different moralities, which can be called subgroup moralities. The moralizing winemakers do about wine will be likely to emphasize its positive aspects. They will claim that it is good for the digestion, a nice way to unwind from the day's tensions, and the love object of the gourmet. The social worker who treats alcoholism on skid row will likely see other sides to wine and winemakers. Likewise, the "businessmen" who spend the day trying to buy low and sell high will probably have a different view of the "natural" place of self-interest in the moral universe than will the consumer of the goods whose price is higher because of the "speculators' " activities. Indeed, in the Preface to the second edition of the *Division of Labor in Society,* Emile Durkheim argued that the very existence of social order in a modern highly differentiated "organically" integrated society depends on the existence of such subgroup moralities.

The Moral Structure of Deviance and Control

Before we outline the ways in which deviance and social control are morally structured, it will help to return to the classical origins of this sort of analysis and review briefly Emile Durkheim's vision of the moral structure of a society. Although we have disagreed with what we believe is Durkheim's excessively narrow definition of morality and will depart from his analysis in other places, the core of this book is an effort to describe one aspect of our society—that aspect that has to do with the deviance and control of drugs—in a manner consistent with Durkheim's theory.[3]

For Durkheim, the essential core of any society was what he called the *conscience collective.* While in his initial works the content of this structure was somewhat broader, as his studies of modern society developed this came increasingly to mean a core of *values* which belonged to the whole society. The collective conscience is everybody's, while belonging to no one in particular. In primitive societies, the collective conscience is quite specific and regulates the behavior of all members of society; in modern societies, the collective conscience becomes progressively more general and distant from the day-to-day activities of the members of the society, while continuing to provide the ultimate justification and orientation for the society's institutions.

As societies develop, the individual's behavior becomes increasingly freed from the "mechanical" solidarity which focuses on the prescriptions of the collective conscience and increasingly regulated by "organic" solidarities in which the individual is tied to the society, not because he is identical to other members as he is in a primitive society, but because he is a highly differentiated individual who cannot exist and whose identity does not have any meaning without the reciprocal roles of the other members of the society.

The prototype of the relationships in an organically integrated society is the relationship of contract. A buyer and a seller may interact quite anonymously, but their roles and the meaning of their roles are mutually dependent. Durkheim's important insight here was his analysis of the "non-contractual elements of contract." The core of this insight was that relations between individuals in organically integrated societies are morally regulated by the imposition of societally specified norms. One cannot contract for whatever one wants in whatever manner one wants to. Contract law is filled with regulations about the permissible forms of contracts, contents of contracts, and the ways in which contracts can be made. Prohibitions against slavery and child labor, as well as all of the law regulating labor contracts, restrict the purchase and sale of labor.

Parallel normative restrictions regulate the relations between every set of institutionalized roles in the society.

Durkheim's vision of the moral structure of modern society was rounded out in his Preface to the second edition of the *Division of Labor in Society*. In it he observed that each occupational group must have its own collective conscience which specified the meaning and appropriate values for the differentiated subgroups. The prototypical examples of this are, of course, the ethical systems of the various professions, but, as we will see, such collective consciences are not limited to the professions.

Let us now return to the problem of the moral structure of deviance and control. If we want to understand the social organization of deviance and control, and if etiology of deviance or role recruitment procedures is not a central topic, then what do we want to know about the moral organization of deviance and control? Durkheim provides us with an excellent guide. First, we want to know what elements of the collective conscience are involved with the particular type of deviance. This means that we must at least explicate the value context in which the activity takes place. As we will see, other moral elements of what Durkheim called the collective conscience were also involved in the Drug Crisis, not just values. Next we must try to explicate the moral schemas of the groups involved in the production of the social phenomenon of deviance, what Durkheim called their occupational moralities and we will call their ideologies. Finally, we must describe the structure of the moral schemas shared by the deviants and control agents which partially corresponds to what Durkheim would call the noncontractual elements of contract. The remainder of this volume is devoted to this task. Although we have not used Durkheim's terminology, we think the reader will have little trouble recognizing that Chapter 2 is devoted to showing that the drug crisis was a crisis in the collective conscience and explicating the elements of it, that Chapter 3 lays out the "occupational" moralities, and Chapters 4-6 are concerned with the nature of the organic solidarities that tie deviant to control agent.

Study Setting and Method

While the goal of this book is to elaborate a theoretical description of the ways in which the moral order functions and the place in which deviant behavior and its control plays in that functioning, we will do this through the analysis of empirical data. That data was largely gathered in an ethnographic study of the patterns of heroin use and control in a small American city between 1969 and 1973. While the design of that study, as well as its general ethnographic results, were published in a previous volume (Gould et al., 1974), a brief review of the setting and method will be helpful to the reader.

Riverdale[4] is a city of about 150,000 population which is the core of a small metropolitan region of about 400,000. The area as a whole is located at the outer edge of a very large urban metropolis. It has a broad economic base, including manufacturing, education, and transportation. The population is stable and includes large populations from several older ethnic groups as well as substantial Black and Spanish-speaking populations.

The core events of the Drug Crisis in Riverdale, as elsewhere, involved three "groups" on whom our study concentrated: a loosely integrated community of drug users, law enforcement agents (including, of course, "officers of the court"), and various members of the medical community and their professional and paraprofessional assistants.

At any one time during the Drug Crisis, there were never more than several thousand heroin users in the Riverdale area, with the actual figure probably fluctuating between 1000 and 2000, depending on how "heroin user" is defined. There were probably roughly an equal number of black and white heroin users and a much smaller group of Spanish-speaking users. The entire heroin-using population was somewhat transient, but the black users constituted a more stable group than either the white or Spanish groups.

There was no highly centralized heroin distribution system in Riverdale. Proximity to much larger urban centers meant that many, but not all, serious users maintained "connections" in these larger cities and thus supplied small dealing networks. So heroin came into Riverdale in a roughly constant flow of small amounts and through many channels rather than through periodic large shipments from major dealers. Most heroin users supported themselves by means of either legitimate occupations or the usual assortment of small time hustles: prostitution, shoplifting, burglary, selling drugs, and so on. Riverdale was neither "the big time" nor the "sticks." For most heroin users it was not a particularly good place to live, but most succeeded in living fairly comfortably.

Most law enforcement efforts were organized by the Riverdale Vice Squad, which comprised eight detectives, both black and white. Several suburban police units were also involved in heroin arrests, but only sporadically. While there was a great deal of talk about forming a regional narcotics squad, it became operational only at the very end of the crisis period. As the name implies, the vice squad did not concentrate its efforts solely on narcotics, but also worked on gambling and prostitution, although these areas were definitely relegated to a subsidiary status during the years of our study.

Arrests were heard first in the Riverdale District Court. Prosecution of cases was directed by a Prosecuting Attorney with a team of six assistants (most of whom were half time). The defense was almost invariably managed by one of two Public Defenders, several local Legal Aid lawyers, or various "court regular" private attorneys. Serious cases were "bound over" to the Superior Court (the felony court) for disposition, but most "drug-related" cases were disposed of in the lower court.

The medical community's involvement in the Drug Crisis was largely channeled through the Riverdale Mental Health Center, and more specifically through the Narcotics Addiction Unit (N.A.U.). The N.A.U. was created at the initiative of the National Institute of Mental Health in 1968, although part of the funding was from the state in which Riverdale was located. Between 1968 and 1973, over 1400 "drug users" applied for treatment at the N.A.U., although not all of these were heroin users, and not all of them did actually receive any treatment.

Organizationally, the N.A.U. was composed of five divisions: administration, research, a methadone program, a "therapeutic community," and an out-patient clinic. The director of the N.A.U. was a psychiatrist, and the senior personnel in each of the clinical divisions (except the therapeutic community) were psychiatrists, clinical psychologists, psychiatrically oriented social workers, physicians, and nurses. With a few exceptions, the senior clinicians held positions on the faculty of the medical school that was affiliated with the Riverdale Mental Health Center. Most of the lower-level clinical staff were ex-addicts who had been successfully "rehabilitated," generally at the N.A.U. While there was considerable staff turnover during the period of study, the clinical staff generally numbered between twenty and thirty-five.

While criteria of clinical success are somewhat ambiguous in the field of drug-abuse treatment, the N.A.U. was nationally recognized as one of the leading drug-abuse treatment programs in the country. The director became known as a national expert on drug abuse, and the N.A.U. claimed to have successfully treated a fairly large number of "drug abusers." In Riverdale, the hegemony of the N.A.U. over drug-abuse treatment was never seriously questioned, and its medical legitimacy was consistently respected.

The research division comprised three sociologists (including the present authors), an attorney, three ex-addicts, and a nurse who had been on the staff of the methadone program. Our mandate was to evaluate the impact of a drug-treatment clinic on the system of heroin use and control in Riverdale. While this might conceivably be accomplished in purely quantitative terms (How many addicts were cured? How many hours of court work were saved?), we chose instead to develop a qualitative approach, focusing on the question, "How does the *system* of heroin use and control operate in Riverdale?" While various sets of quantitative data were appropriate to this question (e.g., arrest and conviction rates, incidence/prevalence rates, measures of treatment activities, and so on), it also required an ethnographic investigation into the social organization of the system.

The primary component of the research strategy was a three-part participant-observation study of the social reality of heroin use and control. Separate teams studied that reality from the perspective of the addicts, the law enforcement personnel, and the medical community. Each team first constructed an account of the social organization of its subjects (as reported in Gould et al., 1974), then the separate accounts were integrated into an analysis of the system as a whole (reported in this volume). While the organization of the separate constituents could be reported in ethnographic, descriptive terms, the system as a whole is so abstract that it requires analytic, rather than descriptive, consideration. In a sense, the analytical problem that gives shape to this entire piece is that our observation showed that the system is based on well-established patterns of interaction which are significantly different from participants' accounts of how those interactions should and do proceed.

As was mentioned above, though, we found that the operation of the system as a whole was pervasively influenced by the Drug Crisis. So, before we can focus on the patterns of interaction characteristic of the empirical system of heroin use and control in Riverdale, we must first examine the symbolic context of drugs during this time. The following chapter considers the social construction of the Drug Crisis.

NOTES

1. Obviously, whether or not a category is a moral term is a matter of degree, not of absolutes. Equally obviously, the moral meaning of a particular term is situationally specific. For instance, addicts we studied often used the word "bad" to mean something close to "good" as that term is commonly used (e.g., conveying approval through the phrase "He is a really bad dude.")

2. This raises the question of why we do our moralizing primarily about examples of evil rather than of good. Why do we need deviance at all? The answer is certainly complex, but at least part of it relates to status considerations. As Garfinkel (1956) has noted, the person denouncing the behavior of someone to an audience is elevating his status and that of the audience vis-à-vis the deviant. One who praises someone to an audience implicitly degrades himself and the audience vis-à-vis the praised person. Indeed, most of our positive moralizing is done about ourselves or our audience.

3. Rather than footnote specific passages of Durkheim's works to support each of our statements, we will simply refer the reader to three excellent discussions of his work: Parsons (1937), Bellah (1973), and especially Ernest Wallwork's excellent review of Durkheim's ideas on morality (Wallwork, 1972).

Chapter 2

THE "DRUG CRISIS": Doing Morality as a Societal Process

Although the term "moral crisis" is new to sociology, sociology has long been concerned with the events to which we refer when we use the term. In the last few decades, American society has generated many such events to which the label moral crisis can be appropriately applied. These include the McCarthy Era concern with communists in the government, the intense concern with juvenile delinquency in the late fifties and early sixties, the war against poverty, the concern with ecological disaster, the Watergate scandal, and concern about the decline of American business. In this chapter, however, we want to describe and analyze the "heroin epidemic" of the late sixties and early seventies.

We are not without considerable counsel from our sociological colleagues in analyzing these events. Sociologists, lay and professional, have always had a special affinity for moral crises. Indeed, as a profession, we have played an increasingly impor-

---

AUTHORS' NOTE: This chapter was coauthored by Leroy C. Gould, Ph.D.

tant part in elaborating the meanings of specific moral crises and acting as spokespersons for various points of view on them. Most colleges have courses on "social problems," and these largely consist of discussion of the foci of current and past moral crises.

Two major viewpoints on moral crises have developed within sociology which closely parallel the correctionalist and labeling theories of deviance. (Matza, 1969) The first treats the reality of the crisis as basic and seeks to understand the origins of the evil. Such analyses have tried to locate the cause of crime increases, ecological destruction, political immorality, and other crises in contemporary social structures. The second approach has treated the reality of the problem as problematic and largely blamed it on the efforts of a dominant group to maintain control of the society. To slightly oversimplify, this latter group has argued that these crises are "symbolic" and not "real" (Gusfield, 1963). Among the important works in this tradition is, of course, Erikson's (1966) important effort to try to link the collective phenomena which calls "crime waves," i.e., epidemic outbursts of a specific type of deviance, to what he calls "boundary problems" in the normative structure of society. A second, related development is a series of efforts to reformulate traditional social problems theory along the lines of labeling. Blumer (1971a, 1971b) and Kitsuse and Spector (1973, 1975) have tried to show that a social problem is roughly a collective version of a deviant act and that labeling theory is equally applicable. The major issue then becomes the nature of the value structure and public processes which could account for the public "creation" of a social problem.

Our analysis of the heroin crisis of the late sixties and early seventies is certainly closer to the second school, but for our purposes the interesting properties of moral crises are twofold. First, any moral crisis involves rendering a moral schema problematic. It involves making credible the claim that something is wrong in the society that must be corrected. The moral elements of the organization of the schema may or may not end up modified, but the potential is clearly there. Second, inasmuch as moral crises involve focusing on and making highly visible a moral schema, they are an excellent opportunity for us to analyze the organization of moral schema and the process of doing morality.

The Origins of the Heroin Crisis

We have noted that there are two general theories of the origins of moral crises. The first argues that the crisis is caused by an increase of a troublesome fact. The second, while not necessarily denying an increase in the objective problem, argues that the definition of the event as a moral problem is the critical process. Blumer makes this fairly explicit (1971: 301-302):

> Social problems are not the result of an intrinsic malfunctioning of a society but are the result of a process of definition in which a given condition is picked out and identified as a social problem. A social problem does not exist for a society unless it is recognized by that society to exist.

Applying this perspective to the Drug Crisis of the last decade is, however, not without certain problems. Since the early part of this century, society has identified heroin and other drug "abuse" as one of its major evils (Musto, 1973; Schur, 1962). Although what constituted "drug abuse" was peculiarly defined if compared with the "objective" health problems of drug use—e.g., non-prescription use of amphetamines and barbiturates by middle-aged, middle-class people has never been successfully defined as a social problem—nonetheless, heroin and certain other drug use by lower-class and young people has been a "problem" since before the Harrison Act of 1914. Thus demonstrating a major increase in such drug abuse, followed by the definition of such an increase as a critical crisis, would not support, although neither would it totally disprove, the labeling theory perspective. It would, on the contrary, seem to support the idea that society responds relatively rationally and directly to "epidemics" of behavior that violate its values.

Thus, before we take up the moral character of the definition of drugs as a crisis, let us settle the issue of to what extent the massive increase in control was simply a rational response by the society to an increased use of heroin. However, even before we can get to that topic, it behooves us to describe briefly the evidence that a moral crisis arose around heroin, that is, the evidence that heroin and its use became the focus of unusual concern in the society.

Evidence for a Moral Epidemic

The striking data on which this chapter is largely based are the massive increase in public concern and discussion about heroin in the last decade. This can be seen in numerous indicators. A theoretically important measure of public concern is the rank of drugs as a social problem in the Gallup Poll. Unfortunately, Gallup did not even ask about drugs until 1970. While this indicates a relative lack of concern about the issue, it does not provide us with hard data. Table 1 shows the rankings of drugs and several other issues in the frequency that the problem was mentioned to Gallup pollsters over time.

Probably the most important measures of a crisis from the Durkheimian perspective that we will discuss later are those that concern the newspaper and magazine coverage of drug use (Erikson, 1966: 12). Since these institutions specialize in conveying and elaborating those shared beliefs and values that Durkheim called the collective conscience, we used three measures of the amount of press coverage of the Drug Crisis. The most general of these is the number of articles concerning heroin and narcotics appearing in the U.S. periodicals (Figure 1). This measure shows more than a tenfold increase between 1964 and 1971. The number of articles was roughly stable at a low level prior to 1965. At that point the massive increase began. The measure peaks in 1971 and declines more than 75% in the next four years.

The second measure is a measure of coverage in the New York *Times* (Figure 2), which is the closest thing that the

TABLE 1 Gallup Poll Rankings of "Most Important Problem Facing America"

Problem	1964	1965	1966	1967	1968	1969	1970	1971	1972	1973	1974	1975
Vietnam	2	2 *	1	1	1	1	1	1	1			
Crime & Lawlessness		4		4	2	2	4	4	4	3	5	6
Poverty (and Welfare)			5		5	6	6	9	8	11		
Drugs								6	3	2	8	
Pollution							8	7	6	6		

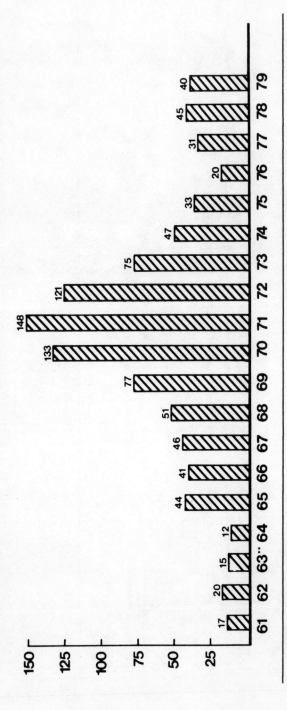

Figure 1: Number of Articles Appearing in U.S. Periodicals Dealing with Narcotics and Heroin, 1961-1979

SOURCE: Reader's Guide to Periodical Literature.

(Year in each case begins with March and runs through February of the following year in accordance with the practice of the Reader's Guide to Periodical Literature.)

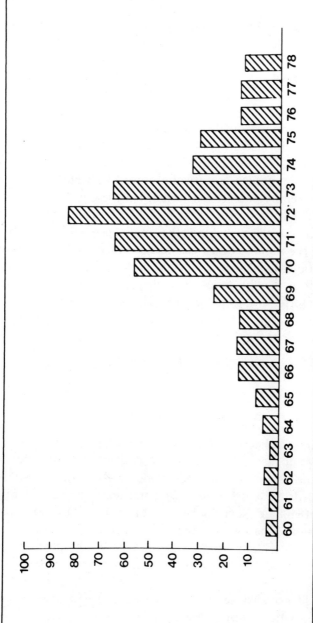

Figure 2: Columns in New York Times Index of Drug Addiction: "Abuse and Traffic" and "Therapy for Addicts"

*1971 and 1972 are weighted figures that correct for the fact that N.Y. Times Index columns were increased in length and averaged 40% more articles. In 1973, further changes returned typical column to previous number of articles.

41

United States has to a national newspaper. Once again the amount of coverage of the drug problem is relatively stable in the first half of the sixties and increases dramatically in the second, peaking in 1972. By 1975, the indicator has dropped almost 60%.

The final indicator is a much more specialized one and concerns the number of articles on heroin and heroin addiction in journals published by and for the medical profession (Figure 3). This indicator seems important because the mental health treatment community, a critical group of specialists for heroin control, generally publishes its articles in these journals.

Here the pattern of rise is the same, although it appears to lag three to four years behind the more general publications. Although the number of articles had stabilized by 1974, there is as yet little evidence of a substantial decline. This is probably because it generally takes several years to gather the data necessary to publish in these journals, and there is often a lag of another year or two between submission of an article and its publication.

The Control Crisis

Both of the current theories of moral crisis would assume an increase in social control efforts during this period. The realistic school would expect that social control would follow an increase in heroin use and public concern about it. The Erikson, Blumer, Kitsuse and Spector "societal reaction" school would argue that an increase in social control activity is the core of the phenomenon. Since we see the heightened interest in the moral schemas surrounding drug use as the core of the phenomenon, we would expect increased involvement from all sectors of society.

The evidence also clearly indicates a massive increase in social control activities followed by a decrease in the mid-seventies as the crisis in public concern receded. One set of interesting data consists of the levels of federal expenditures for treatment,

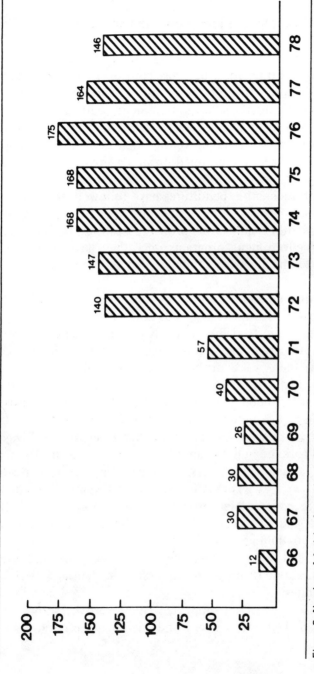

Figure 3: Number of Articles Appearing in Medical Journals Dealing with Heroin Addiction and "Diacetylmorphine," 1966-1978

SOURCE: Index Medicus.

NOTE: In 1977, Index Medicus began indexing articles from the Proceedings of the National Conference on Methadone Treatment, which had not previously been indexed. For comparison, these articles have not been counted.

research, education and prevention, and law enforcement (Table 2).

The figures show rather clearly that in the early seventies federal expenditures for drug abuse control skyrocketed. During President Nixon's first term in office, the expenditures for "Prevention"--which includes treatment, education, training, research, and planning—increased tenfold. Law enforcement increased sevenfold. Total prevention figures began dropping for fiscal 1975 and have continued dropping slowly (if inflation is taken into account).

Law enforcement expenditures have followed essentially the same pattern. The failure of federal expenditures to drop as quickly as other indicators probably testifies to the staying power of government programs once they have been created and also to the long lead time needed to prepare the federal budget.

Given that federal expenditures rose, it is not surprising that the number of treatment programs in the country also increased drastically. Prior to 1968, when N.I.M.H. funded its first six experimental programs largely directed toward treating heroin addiction, there were probably not more than a few dozen scattered treatment programs. The federal government had, for a long time, funded two federal hospitals for addiction treatment, one in Lexington and the other in Fort Worth. Synanon had met with considerable success in San Francisco, and Daytop in New York copied Synanon's methods. Vincent Dole and Marie Nyswander had been experimenting with methadone treatment in New York City for several years. Beyond that there were only isolated programs in state hospitals, mostly in California and New York State, which often treated addicts in the same program as alcoholics.

By the end of this period, there was at least one (and usually several) treatment programs in every substantial city in the United States.

Likewise, our data collected in Riverdale shows sharp increases in law enforcement and treatment activity. Figure 4

TABLE 2 Federal Drug Abuse Expenditures
Fiscal Years 1969 - 1977 (Millions of Dollars Obligated)

Category	1969	1970	1971	1972	1973	1974	1975	1976[a]	1977[a]
Drug Abuse Prevention	45.9	76.4	133.9	341.9	441.3	517.2	471.1	492.7	489.7
Law enforcement	35.5	52.6	81.6	164.1	221.7	264.8	294.6	308.7	296.2
Total Federal Expenditures	81.4	129.0	215.5	506.0	663.0	782.0	765.7	801.4	785.9

SOURCES: This table is consolidated from information contained in three monographs published by the Drug Abuse Council: Sybil Cline, Peter Goldberg, and Carl Akins, *Government Response to Drugs: Fiscal and Organizational*; Sybil Cline and Carl Akins, *Governmental Response to Drug Abuse: The 1976 Budget*; and Sybil Cline and Peter Goldberg, *Governmental Response to Drug Abuse: The 1977 Federal Budget*.
a. Estimated

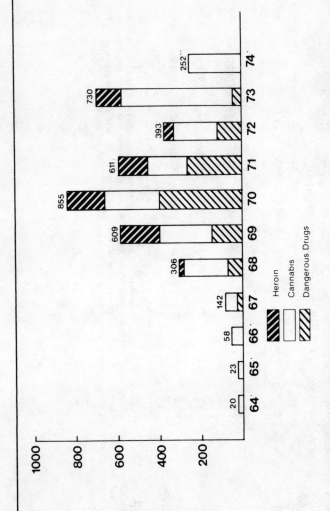

Figure 4: Drug Arrests in Riverdale, 1964-1974

*Breakdown by type of drug arrest not available.
**Projected from arrests for first half of 1974.

Legend: Heroin, Cannabis, Dangerous Drugs

64: 20
65: 23
66: 58
67: 142
68: 306
69: 609
70: 855
71: 611
72: 393
73: 730
74: 252**

shows that heroin arrests increased sharply in the late sixties, peaked in 1970, and dropped sharply by 1972.

Figure 5 charts applications to the N.A.U. showing the same pattern where first applications are concerned. Indeed, with a one year time lag, applications to the N.A.U. correlate highly (r = .95) with heroin arrests in Riverdale.

Was There a Heroin Epidemic?

That people become more concerned about a particular form of deviance in a given historical era and increase social control efforts to eliminate it does not mean necessarily that the prevalence of that behavior has increased. For example, the concern about opiate use in this country, which grew at the beginning of this century and eventually led to the Harrison Act and a number of drug treatment clinics, came about despite an apparent decrease in the consumption of opium. (Musto, 1973: 2) Similarly, there is little evidence that the increased concern about marijuana use some years later and its eventual legal ban was associated with a substantial increase in the use of the drug. (Becker, 1963) Other social scientists have also found considerable disparity between the prevalence of other forms of deviant behavior and the magnitude of the social responses, and have concluded that variations in social concern or social control are not necessarily associated with variations in the behaviors in question (Kitsuse and Cicourel, 1963; Erikson, 1966; Douglas, 1967; Gould, 1969). It is important, therefore, to examine the evidence concerning the heroin "crisis" of the late sixties and early seventies to determine whether or not, like its predecessors earlier in the century, it was an "epidemic" of social concern and of social control and not an "epidemic" of drug use.

Specifically, a number of epidemiological investigators, including Hunt and Chambers (1975) and Greene and DuPont (1974), have suggested that there was an epidemic growth of heroin use in the United States which peaked in 1970 or 1971 and declined sharply thereafter. In spite of wide public accep-

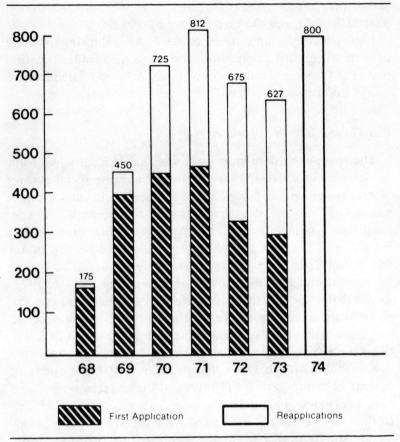

Figure 5: Applications for Drug Treatment of the N.A.U., 1968-1974
*Breakdown for first applications and reapplication not available.

tance of this viewpoint, it has been received with some skepticism in the literature (see particularly NIDA Research Monograph 16). What we want to do here is briefly review their data
and suggest an interpretation.

One difficulty with the epidemic hypothesis is that almost all
the indicators which have been used, by social scientists as well

as the public, to document the "epidemic" of heroin use are *derivative*. That is, they are not direct measures of the incidence or prevalence of drug use in the general population, but measures which infer such incidence or prevalence from various data gathered by law enforcement or medical agencies. Increases in drug arrests are an example. Whether or not an increase in arrests is a good indicator of increased use depends upon the relationship between arrests and use. If this relationship remains constant—that is, if the police arrest a constant proportion of all drug users each year—then arrests would be a good indicator of relative changes in the prevalence of drug use. If the relationship is not constant, however (for example, if police departments put more emphasis on drug arrests and consequently arrest increasingly larger proportions of users each year), then arrests would be a biased indicator of the prevalence of drug use, since number of arrests could increase more rapidly than prevalence. Given this potential for bias, an increase in arrests cannot be used uncritically to indicate an increase in drug use. Especially given the evidence in Table 2 of the increase in spending for drug law enforcement, it is not unreasonable to believe that, during this period of public concern about drugs, the police made more of an effort to arrest users.

Number of patients in drug treatment, for very similar reasons, is also a derived indicator of drug use and will accurately reflect trends in incidence or prevalence only if there is a constant relationship between the number of drug users in the community and the number of those who enter treatment. Given that the availability of treatment expanded so rapidly during this period, however, an increased number of drug patients could indicate nothing more than increased availability of treatment. Furthermore, the evidence we presented earlier seems to show that applications to treatment are a direct function of the number of arrests.

Recognizing these problems, some researchers have come to rely upon types of data which should be free, at least theoretically, from variations in social-control activity. Deaths due to drug overdose or admissions to hospitals for adverse drug reactions are examples. These indicators, however, are probably based upon an extremely small fraction of the total population of drug users and also are very sensitive to factors other than amount of drug use in the community, e.g., variations in the purity of drugs available on the street. Many investigators, therefore, have abandoned them as reliable indicators of changes in the relative size of the drug-using population (DuPont and Piemme, 1973).

The "purity" of heroin sold on the streets (that is, the percentage of heroin in the "bags" being sold) and the price of heroin are sometimes presented as indicators of heroin use. However, following classic supply and demand economic theory, the price of heroin, or its purity (reducing purity is one way of increasing price), will depend not only upon the number of people in the market for heroin and the amount each is willing or able to buy (demand), but also on the amount of heroin available to be sold and the costs of bringing that heroin to market (supply). So long as factors affecting supply are independent of demand and unknown, there is no way to know for certain whether changes in price reflect changes in supply or demand. In the late sixties and early seventies, both federal and local authorities made serious efforts to increase police pressure on supply and suppliers. This affected supply both because some drugs were confiscated and because the "costs" to suppliers increased in terms of greater likelihood of jail terms, the need for better organization, and other "hassles." The increased "costs" may have forced some suppliers out of the market, and others may have been "forcibly retired." We can never know for certain whether increased prices during this period reflected increased demand, diminished supply, or both, but increased prices do not seem to be adequate evidence of increased demand.

A presumably more direct measure of the relative incidence of heroin use based upon data gathered from drug users when they are admitted to treatment has been used by some researchers who purport to show an epidemic of heroin use

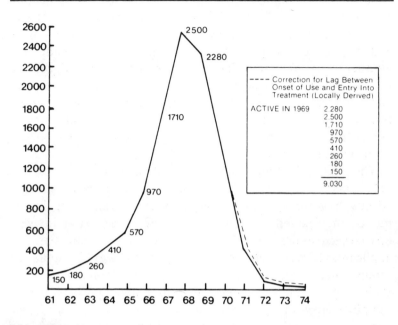

Figure 6: Year of First Heroin Use: Reports from First Admission to the NTA Treatment Program, 1961-1974

SOURCE: This figure after Leon Hunt (1977) "Prevalence of active heroin use in the United States," p. 80 in J. D. Rittenhouse (ed.) The Epidemiology of Heroin and Other Narcotics. NIDA Research Monograph 16, DHEW (ADAMHA). Washington, DC: Printing Office.

beginning in about 1965 and peaking out somewhere between 1968 and 1970 (Greene and DuPont, 1974; Hunt and Chambers, 1975). The technique involves the tabulation of intake interview responses to the question, "When did you begin using heroin?" Constructing a graph showing the relative proportions of all those who applied for treatment in a given time period who began using heroin in successively earlier calendar years results in a "relative incidence curve," according to these authors (Figure 6). Unfortunately, as others have shown (Gould

52 HEROIN, DEVIANCE AND MORALITY

et al., 1977; Richman, 1974), data analyzed in this manner cannot be successfully freed from two systematic biases. First, there is a bias built into the delay in entering treatment, since addicts are not as likely to enter treatment during the first months of use as they are later in their careers. Second, the risk that heroin users run of being removed from the population of addicts increases after the opening of a treatment center. Indeed, these two forms of bias combine to produce what would look like an "epidemic" curve even if no epidemic occurred at all (Gould et al., 1977).

The most direct source of primary data on the incidence and prevalence of drug use comes from community-based surveys. Although surveys are far from perfect data-gathering instruments, they nonetheless have distinct advantages over the various derived indicators and over data gathered from treatment applicants. Surveys can be conducted within normal population groups; and if they are based upon good sampling technique, their results can be generalized with known probabilities of sampling error to quite large populations. The results of such surveys, then, allow the direct construction of incidence and prevalence rates, something which cannot be done with derived indicators. When repeated at different points in time, results from surveys can show not only relative trends in drug use, but to the extent that the surveys are accurate, absolute trends.

The disadvantage of areawide surveys for measuring trends in drug use derives not from their being derived indicators but from their being expensive and subject to interview and nonresponse[1] bias. These biases are offset somewhat by the fact that areawide surveys are usually anonymous. Nevertheless, the potential for bias exists, and its magnitude is hard to measure. It is worth noting, however, that the efforts of Single et al. (1975) and O'Donnell et al. (1976) to measure the biases in these surveys show relatively high levels of reliability of responses.

However, the biggest problem with survey data for measuring changes in the incidence or prevalence of drug use during the past decade is that too few surveys were done during that period on the same or similar populations over time to allow the definitive plotting of clear trends. The literature, to be sure, is full of drug-use surveys, but almost all were conducted at one point in time. The questions asked or the populations studied were sufficiently different, moreover, to preclude reliable comparisons between studies.[2]

Gould et al. (1977) recently summarized all of the available drug use surveys on students which involved repeated measures of heroin use. Their table is repeated here as Table 3.

While the rates of heroin use in these studies are all quite low and it is difficult to tell whether the changes are due to random variation or real differences,[3] the overall picture is one of a slight increase in the early years and a small decrease in the later ones.

These studies, of course, are not representative of the American population as a whole and cover only 1963-1974. Nonetheless, they are not consistent with the epidemic hypothesis which the derived indicators seem to support.

A Crisis of Control or Deviation?

We now seem to be in a position to discuss tentatively whether an increase in heroin use was caused by the control crisis or vice versa. On the surface, the evidence seems to lean in the direction predicted by the labeling theorists. Most of the reasons to believe that heroin use increased during this period seem to be derivative of increased control activity. It is also possible that the increases in heroin could have occurred independently of the increase in control and concern about heroin use, but this hypothesis is not supported by the small amount of direct survey evidence. Thus, while the evidence does not conclusively prove the labeling theory hypothesis, it supports it better than the contrary hypothesis.

It is important to realize that this conclusion refers only to the changes in rates over time, not to the absolute amount of heroin use. We are not saying that there was not a lot of heroin use in America at this point. Indeed, a fairly substantial pool of heroin addicts was needed to generate the statistics. But

TABLE 3A   Trends in Opiate Use Reported in Surveys of High School and College Populations (in percentages)

Location	Source	School Grade or Age	Use Period	Drug
California	San Mateo County, 1974	11th G.	"past year"	Heroin
New Jersey				
Community A	Lavenhar & Sheffet, 1973	11th G.	"ever"	
Community B				
Florida	Glenn & Richards, 1974	11th G.	"ever"	Heroin or Morphine
Missouri	Glenn & Richards, 1974	11th G.	"past year"	"Opiates"
Connecticut	Berberian et al., 1975	11th G.	"ever"	Heroin
Maryland	Glenn & Richards 1974	Sr. Hi.	"ever"	Heroin
Toronto, Canada	Smart et al., 1973 and 1974	11th G.	"past six months"	"Opiates"
Halifax, Canada	Whitehead, 1971	11th G.	"past six months"	"Opiates"
Vancouver, Canada	Russell & Hollander, 1974	Ages 15-16	"ever"	Heroin
Arizona	Corder et al., 1974	College	"ever"	Heroin
Colorado	Corder et al., 1974	College	"ever"	Heroin
Pennsylvania	Corder et al., 1974	College	"ever"	Heroin
Tennessee	Corder et al., 1974	College	"ever"	Heroin
Eastern U.S.	Glenn & Richards, 1974	College	"last six months"	Heroin

it is also important to realize, as we will describe in more detail in later chapters, that the control system used some addicts many times in their statistics. Many addicts were arrested

TABLE 3B

| Sex | School Year: | | | | | | |
	1967 -68	1968 -69	1969 -70	1970 -71	1971 -72	1972 -73	1973 -74
M	--	--	--	4.9	3.8	3.8	3.5
F	--	--	--	3.3	2.9	2.7	2.5
M	--	--	3.0	--	3.6	--	--
F	--	--	0.9	--	4.0	--	--
M	--	--	3.9	--	--	6.3	--
F	--	--	5.3	--	--	1.3	--
M	--	--	--	4.5	5.7	--	--
F	--	--	--	2.1	4.2	--	--
M	--	--	--	8.3	8.0	--	--
F	--	--	--	4.4	6.4	--	--
M & F	--	--	--	3.5	2.7	2.2	--
M & F	--	6.5	--	--	1.1	--	--
M & F	1.8	--	5.8	--	5.0	--	3.9
M & F	--	2.7	3.3	--	--	--	--
M & F	--	--	--	1.9	--	--	1.9
M & F	--	--	--	1.0	--	--	1.0
M & F	--	--	--	1.0	--	--	3.0
M & F	--	--	--	2.0	--	--	2.0
M & F	--	--	--	1.0	--	--	1.5
M & F	--	--	3	4	--	--	--

SOURCE: This table taken from Gould et al. (1977), "Biasing factors in the measurement of trends in heroin use." Addictive Diseases: An International Journal 3, 2:156-157.

several times in the same year and applied for treatment several times. Moreover, the more the control system emphasized treatment rather than incarceration, the more available the addicts were for using in generating statistics. Addicts in outpatient treatment could be arrested repeatedly, whereas addicts in prison could not be.

Yet, if we accept this conclusion, we are simply led to another question. What caused the rise in control of and concern about heroin? The answer we propose is in some ways simpler than might be expected; a rise in marijuana use during the sixties. The evidence for this rise is overwhelming (Berberian et al., 1975; San Mateo County Department of Health, 1974). Furthermore, a review of newspaper reporting on early phases of the drug crisis reveals that a rise in perceived marijuana use was the focus of most feature reporting, and there were frequent articles on college marijuana use which evidenced such a rise. Indeed, the first major rise in the amount of reporting of drug use by the New York *Times* (Figure 2) which occurred in 1965 seems largely to involve articles about the growth of marijuana use. For example, on January 4, 1965, the New York *Times* published its first feature article of the sixties on drug use and for the first time argued that drug use was increasing, although it referred only to New York City. The claim that drug use was increasing, however, referred entirely to marijuana.[4]

This, however, leads us to the puzzle of why an increase in the use of marijuana should lead to a repression of heroin use. Later in this chapter we will discuss why an increase in marijuana and some associated phenomena should call for the panicky reaction that it did, but here we must ask why the two were related at all.

To begin with, heroin and marijuana share the same cultural moral category, "illegal drugs." They were both talked about as part of the same moral schema, "the drug problem." This pattern of moral organization is reflected in the fact that the same section of the police department—the narcotics squad or the vice squad—handles the enforcement of both laws. Often the legal statute that criminalized marijuana was the same one that criminalized heroin. The association of the two was brought about by the widespread belief that marijuana use "leads to" heroin use. Thus the New York *Times,* in the aforementioned 1965 feature article, stated that approximately one-third of marijuana users go on to become heroin addicts.[5]

This may seem perfectly natural to the reader who is accustomed to the association, but the association is hardly one of essential identity or experiential connection. Marijuana is pharmacologically categorized as a mild hallucinogen, not as an addicting depressant like heroin. Furthermore, although the evidence about whether or not marijuana "leads to" heroin is unclear, Gould et al. (1976) have recently shown that alcohol leads to heroin in precisely the same way. It is also interesting to note that methadone, which is pharmacologically almost identical to heroin, is morally classified as opposed to—i.e., as a treatment for—heroin.

Theoretically, this peculiarity in the relationship between deviance, control, and the heroin crisis is extremely important. *You cannot understand the origins of the heroin crisis without knowing the moral schema on which it was based.* The crisis of control is a response to an increase in deviance, but only via the moral schema that linked heroin and marijuana as part of the same phenomenon. More generally, *doing morality,* in this case the organization of a Drug Crisis, *requires using morality.* They are inextricably linked. Any theory of doing morality, including a theory of deviance verification such as labeling theory, will misunderstand the process if it insists, as labeling theory sometimes has, that moral schemas are too vague to be used in analyzing behavior (cf. Gibbs, 1966).

However, we are now faced with a new problem. The realistically minded reader may now justly ask whether all of the previous argument in the chapter might not have been a waste. Perhaps the response and concern were primarily related to marijuana use, and the concern about heroin use was largely peripheral. If this were so, then there would be little support for the labeling theory of social problems here, since once again the crises of control and concern would be a simple "realistic" response to the existence of a crisis of deviation.

However, there is much evidence to contradict this belief. To begin with, almost without exception, treatment facilities emphasized the treatment of heroin addicts, not marijuana users. Methadone was, and still is, the largest treatment modality in America, and it is, by federal regulation, available only for the treatment of opiate addicts. Furthermore, at least in Riverdale, the increase and subsequent decrease in arrests for drugs between 1969 and 1972 is largely accounted for by changes in the arrest rates for heroin (see Figure 4). Further evidence is provided by the rhetoric used to condemn "drug abuse." It was seen as accounting for the "serious rise in crime," which in turn was accounted for by the need for money to maintain an addiction. For example, on July 14, 1969, Richard Nixon sent a message to Congress which contained several interesting passages:

> A national awareness of the gravity of the situation is needed, a new urgency and concerned national policy are needed at the Federal level to begin to cope with this growing menace to the general welfare of the United States.

> Between the years 1960 and 1967, juvenile arrests, involving the use of drugs, rose by almost 800 per cent; half of those now being arrested for the illicit use of narcotics are under 21 years of age.

> It is doubtful that an American parent can send a son or daughter to college today without exposing the young man or woman to drug abuse. Parents must also be concerned about the availability and use of such drugs in our high schools and junior high schools.

> The habit of the narcotics addict is not only a danger to himself, but a threat to the community where he lives. Narcotics have been cited as a primary cause of the enormous increase in street crimes over the last decade.

> As the addict's tolerance for drugs increases, his demand for drugs rises, and the cost of his habit grows. It can easily reach hundreds of dollars a day. Since an underworld "fence" will give him only a fraction of the value of goods he steals, an addict can be forced to commit two or three burglaries a day to maintain his habit.

> Street robberies, prostitution, even the enticing of others into addiction to drugs—an addict will reduce himself to any offense, any degradation in order to acquire the drugs he craves.

The systematic mixing of college and high-school use of marijuana and other "nonnarcotic" drugs with the use of (and troubles associated with) heroin is apparent. Without this mixing, it would have been difficult, if not impossible, to justify the massive expenditures on heroin treatment and law enforcement programs. Mr. Nixon's use of nonopiate drug use to justify a war on drugs, on the grounds that they were similar to or led to heroin, was not unique, but typical of the rhetoric of that era.

It thus seems that neither simple model of the relationship between deviation and control can totally account for the data. On the one hand, the control epidemic was not a simple rational response to a growth in the use of heroin. On the other hand, it will not do to say that it was not a response to a growth in deviant behavior. Instead, the control "response" seems to have been an "irrational" response to a "real" change in the amount of one type of deviation. Yet, as we will see, even this account is too simple. The heroin moral crisis was not a response just to the increased use of marijuana, but to the use of marijuana as part of a more complex moral and—to a lesser extent—political movement.

The Heroin Crisis—A Social Fact Sui Generis

The argument that we have outlined above is complex. We believe that we can simplify the argument somewhat by reference to some of Emile Durkheim's ideas about the social order. Durkheim argued that society is its own reality. In his classic treatise, *Suicide,* he tried to argue that suicide rates are a societal fact independent of the motives of individuals and could be explained as such.[6]

What we wish to argue is that the increased rates in socially accepted indicators of heroin use are a reality in and of themselves. While there is some evidence that there may have been little or no increase in heroin use, the "real" rate of heroin use remains largely unknown. In many ways it is not important. The "social rate" of heroin use, the one which American society knew through its statistics, increased. Whether or not the "real rate" increased is immaterial. *The social rate could have increased simply through an increase in public concern,* through what Durkheim might have called the focusing of the collective conscience of the society on the problem. The rates reflect the public concern, not the activities of deviants.

Moreover, the rates are a social reality because they are part of that reality. Their production was part of the production of the crisis. The perception of the rates was used by the public, as lay sociologists, to understand the crisis and to argue its meaning. The rates were part of the meaning of the crisis. To fully understand them, we must now consider the meanings in which they were embedded and of which they were an integral part.

Moral and Political Context of the Crisis

Just as Erikson found that the three crises in Puritan Massachusetts had moral parameters which were not apparent from the overt justifications for the sanctioning of the deviants, we believe that the Drug Crisis had similar meanings which are only comprehensible to those who know the moral schemas in which drug use and its control occur. These moral aspects of the crisis, which largely determine the viewpoints of the public and the policymakers, were produced by factors very distant from the day-to-day interaction among law enforcement and legal officials, treatment personnel, and addicts which we will discuss in following chapters.

In the discussion that follows, we will make a series of statements about the structure of American values and other moral schemas. This can only be an overgeneral gloss.[7] However, if the undertaking is inherently dangerous, it is not an excuse to fail to undertake the task. Talcott Parsons was the master of this sort of analysis, and his description of the dominant pattern of the American value system is worth quoting (Parsons, 1967: 225-226):

> The value system of the contemporary United States centers on what may be called "instrumental activism." It is oriented to control the action situation in the interest of range and quality of adaptation, but with more economic than political emphasis. In goal definition it is highly indefinite and pluralistic, being committed to a rather general direction of progress for improvement, without any clearly defined terminal goal. Economic production is highly valued as the most immediate focus of adaptive capacity. Beyond that,

however, we value particularly technology and science as means to productivity and the maximization of opportunity for individuals and subcollectivities manifested above all in concern with health and education.

While such analysis is always extremely tricky, we believe that Parsons's analysis comes about as close to capturing the core of the dominant American value system as is possible. What Parsons called "instrumental activism" is important because of its focus on the support of the society's adaptive capacity. American society places tremendous emphasis on the development of diffusely useful facilities and relatively less emphasis on societal prescriptions of what those facilities are to be used for. For example, it is not particularly surprising that American society in the era between World War II and the Vietnam War developed a clear-cut societal commitment to being the "strongest nation in the world" but seemed unable to develop specific policies that would employ that strength. Even the concepts of freedom and individualism, which are so sacred in American belief systems, primarily emphasize the idea that control of our general resources should be left to subcollectivities and to the individual. Fitting in with this value schema are a fairly general consensus in the United States in favor of increasing productivity in business, the development of excellent educational facilities, and the corresponding high prestige of the technically oriented intelligentsia.

The culture of American society of that era placed a great deal of emphasis on a world view which might be called rational empiricism. It has emphasized the rational control of environment and knowledge which would be diffusely "useful." This has produced an emphasis on "this worldly" knowledge which, for related but separate reasons, has been organized heavily around systems of mathematical logic and strongly tends toward the positivistic and reductionistic positions in social thought. In the period following World War II, this sort of scientism was widely believed to be intimately tied to the collective salvation of the society. In several important ways, many traditionally religious questions about the ultimate meaning of existence and the purpose of individual existence were answered in part through this sort of philosophy. Meaning was to be found in this world, and largely through personal achievement as symbolized by the possession of material goods.

If we are to understand the Drug Crisis, another aspect of its setting that we must note is the relative internal peace and high level of consensus on major issues in American society in the fifties and early sixties. It is worth noting that in the Presidential election of 1960, the major issues which the Republican and Democratic candidates debated was whether or not Russia had more I.C.B.M.'s than the United States and which of the candidates would do more to "protect" two tiny fortified islands off the coast of mainland China. While other political issues divided the two candidates, none of these "captured the public imagination."

As C. Wright Mills noted (1956), there was a general belief in a convergent self-interest among major segments of the society, including government, the military, industry, and much of the labor union movement. The phrase "the public interest"[8] was widely used to provide a point of rhetorical orientation in policy discussion.

What is particularly important for our purposes is the deep involvement of the university-based intelligentsia in the leadership of the society during this period. This was particularly apparent in the early sixties with the Kennedy and Johnson administrations. As guardians of the quasi-sacred moral symbols of the society (Shils, 1969), the intelligentsia from the elite universities lent their ideas and prestige to the policies of both the Kennedy and early Johnson administrations. While there were obviously dissenters, in general the intellectuals, with their special role of preserving and elaborating the moral traditions of the society, became very involved in practical administration of the society. In doing so, they lent to the Kennedy administration the special air of being in close touch with the most highly valued moral symbols of the society. This special quality about the Kennedy administration was to lead to a widespread uneasiness that the deepest and finest traditions of this society were

somehow corrupt when political troubles of the late 1960s—
particularly (but not exclusively), the Vietnam War—and the
growing racial conflict descended upon the society. The
demoralization that resulted is an important reference point of
the drug crisis, although not particularly as a cause of drug use.

The military-industrial-educational complex which drew its
moral justification from instrumental activism was not without
its opposition, however, even within the general consensus of
the fifties and early sixties. Perhaps the most important could
be called expressive passivism. As a value core, this was in
dialectical opposition to the instrumental activism which dominated American society. Obviously, the elaboration of expressive passivism involves dramatic rituals of opposition to the
dominant moral schemas of instrumental activism. Inasmuch as
these values are implemented in specific overt actions, there are
likely to be rather serious conflicts over the "right" action to
take.

This expressive passivist position has roots in a variety of
sources in American tradition, the more important of which are
worth noting, if only to clarify the substance of this position.
One of the sources is idealist European philosophy, particularly
the existentialist variety. American science has been largely
Lockean in its epistemology. Most later European philosophy
has, on the other hand, rejected the materialistic determinism of
Locke (Whitehead, 1926). First Hegel and later his phenomenological and existential successors took much more "mystical"
and/or "personal" or subjectivist views of truth. While it is
obviously beyond the scope of this book to try to trace the
complexities of these arguments and why they lead to such
radically different positions on the nature of knowledge and the
procedures for gathering knowledge, it is important to note that
there existed in European philosophy grounds for doubting
many of the intellectual enterprises carried on in American
universities. This is particularly true in the "social sciences,"
where American intellectual thought turned reductionistic, positivistic, and objectivistic, while in Europe, the view of a person
as a freely choosing, nonobjectifiable, and holistic being tended

to dominate. While such statements are too general, the European tradition of the study of man emphasized "understanding," whereas the more pragmatic American tradition—following the general instrumental activism pattern—emphasized "prediction and control" of human behavior (Berger, 1963).

While the prestige of European thought declined in America during the post-World War II era, in the humanities (which had been largely left out of the postwar academic expansion in America, since they contributed relatively little to the material adaptive capacity of society), there remained something of a base of opposition to the heavily positivist forms of intellectual inquiry which dominated the American university. This opposition was fundamentally moral. Poets, novelists, ethicists, philosophers, and others were frequent and vocal in their denunciation of American society, even during the 1950s. This was probably more true of the intellectuals outside the university complex, i.e., clergy, artists, writers, "beatnik" poets, etc., than of those inside the universities, but even within the universities, criticism of the ethical and moral emptiness of many of the specifications of instrumental activism was frequent and persistent. While the "beatniks," and earlier the "bohemians" and transcendentalists, were the most visible groups in opposition to the instrumental activist positions, many intellectuals were quite critical of some aspects of it. (White, 1961; Roszak, 1969).

What led to a revival and expansion of this opposition into the "hippie" movement in the middle and late sixties is extremely complex and cannot be completely detailed here, but one of the most important origins of this movement was the opposition to the Vietnam War. Primarily because of the nature of the war itself, the Vietnam War developed opposition in the universities and among the cultural leadership of the society which previous twentieth-century wars had not. The dictatorial tendencies of the South Vietnamese regime, the absence of a clear-cut invasion (as in Korea), the absence of the U.N. mandate or general allied support, the relative resistance of the liberal administration to overt repression of early criticism of the war, and the absence of press censorship of the coverage of the war all contributed to this opposition (Reich, 1970; Slater, 1968).

The resistance to the war combined with the sense of mission which the younger generation had picked up from President Kennedy's relatively skillful use of the sacred symbols of the civil religion (Bellah, 1975) to mobilize commitment to political goals. When in his inaugural address Kennedy proclaimed that "the torch has passed to a new generation," he was referring to those who, like himself, came of age during world War II. However, many Americans much younger than that saw him as speaking for them. His dramatic style and intimate association with many of the nation's most eminent mind made him the closest thing to a charismatic political figure that much of the new generation had ever known. Like charismatic figures before him, Kennedy was able to mobilize diffuse commitments to moral symbols and to come to personify those symbols himself. He mobilized a generation to act in the name of the society's moral symbols and then was assassinated before his charisma could become routinized.

The "now generation," transforming the familiar American theme of the "chosen people" into the property of a generation, had relatively little tolerance for activities which did not accord with their interpretation of the basic values of the society. The persistence of the war and the refusal of both the Johnson and Nixon governments to give up the Vietnam policy led to very deep disillusionment with both political leadership and, later, when efforts to change leaders failed, with the entire political system. It is particularly critical that the intellectuals, as guardians of the moral traditions of the society, had committed themselves so deeply to the Kennedy and Johnson administrations, for when the prestige of the policy declined, the intelligentsia (and to some degree, rational empirical thought) was devalued. In the phrase of that era, they had "sold out" (Reich, 1970). This left a credibility vacuum which the expressive passivist intellectuals could fill. What had previously been a despised, disorganized, and almost unnoticed group of dissident intellectuals suddenly found itself in a position to mobilize a mass audience. The prominent spokesmen of this group varied tremendously both in background and in the specific issues that they addressed. They ranged from an ex-Harvard psychology professor whose panacea was a chemical hallucinogen to several groups of British, lower-class near-delinquents who had learned to play rock music. Between these extremes, a variety of different figures emerged with different types of criticisms of, and panaceas for, American society. Psychologists and yogis taught means of gaining intrapsychic peace, ex-radicals from the thirties and Kentucky poets talked of the glories of rural self-sufficiency, people invented new types of beds and new types of shoes and sold both as part of the movement.

Politically, the "hippie" movement was tied together by a dislike of war and racial repression. Expressively, its *major integrative symbol was the use of marijuana.* Anyone who had used marijuana was part of the movement, and anyone who hadn't could not claim full membership (Monroe, 1967: 55). While marijuana use was variously touted as a way of improving one's sex life, producing happiness, and putting one in touch with God (Hopkins, 1968, passim), its primary import was as a membership ritual for an otherwise very diffuse and disorganized group. The membership ritual was seen as expressing a strong commitment to the group precisely because it involved making oneself an outlaw from conventional society and because it was seen as entailing a risk. The importance of this ritual was reflected in the frequent discussions that we heard in the course of our observations of the great benefits which would accrue to civilization when all members of the society had smoked marijuana. However silly these claims may sound in retrospect, it is critical to note the central place of drug use in integrating the diverse moral schemas of this movement.

A critically important ramification of the expressive passivist movement is the threat that this movement posed to that aspect of American society which the movement's participants called "The Establishment." Timothy Leary's injunction to "turn on, tune in, and drop out" posed a serious threat because both the movement and the establishment perceived the movement as a developing and growing one.[9] If the movement were to take control of American society, the value commitments of the society and the distribution of power, wealth, and prestige would be radically altered. The threat that the movement posed was not simply to the war policy, the policy of industrial growth, or anything that specific. It posed a serious threat to the whole moral organization of the society around instrumental activist moral schemas. This is not to say that we believe that the United States was ever on the verge of a general revolution. The movement was never that strong, but in the late sixties, the possibility of revolution began to seem, if not immediate, at least no longer as impossible as it had seemed five years earlier.

Before we go on to discuss the role of the Drug Crisis and the repression of heroin in the struggle between the establishment and the expressive passivist movement, it is necessary to take a detour and talk about another threat to the establishment which came from a related but separate movement—that of the revolutionary black activists. One way of viewing the political situation in the late 1960s is to recognize that, even under the best of circumstances, the process of recognizing full citizenship for a caste that has long been excluded from society is not likely to be a particularly smooth process (Parsons, 1965). The end of formal legal exclusion of black Southerners from full participation in the society went relatively smoothly despite serious resistance from some white Southerners and the need for fairly massive intervention of the federal bureaucracy. However, from there, the problem became more complex. By the mid-sixties, there were essentially two competing moral schemas which were applied to the integration of blacks into the society. The first was that blacks, now no longer excluded from equal participation, should compete on an equal footing with whites for power, status, and other rewards that the society had to provide. In some ways, this was the major thrust of the civil-rights movement of the forties and fifties. In that sense, the civil-rights movement had been a "bourgeois" revolution (Marx, 1963). However, the status of blacks was not to be so easily resolved.

To begin with, the morality that had had to be done in order to produce the grass-roots black political action involved in the civil-rights movement had raised the expectation among the black community that the success of the movement would involve some substantial change in their way of life in the relatively immediate future. Many blacks, particularly in the North, did not feel that the ability to use the same restrooms as white Southerners was that sort of a change. Instead, they invoked a second moral schema that the society which had repressed them so long was required to provide some form of restitution and compensation. This vision of an integrated and just society involves a change in standards of the white society such that the society would include black cultural standards on the same level with traditional white standards (Pinkney 1975). The need for this revision came out of the dicovery that, even with the formal barriers removed, many of the lower-class blacks were not moving up in the hierarchy of reward distribution very quickly. It turned out that, contrary to the Horatio Alger-open society schemas, money, influence, and power were very important resources with which to gain more money, influence, and power. Thus, if blacks were to progress as a group, some fairly major structural changes would have to be made in American society.

The black revolutionary movement, led by such organizations as C.O.R.E., S.N.C.C., and the Black Panthers, did form some rather tentative alliances with the expressive passivists in the political realm. However, this was generally restricted to the political arena and produced a good deal of strain internal to black politics. The moral differences between the two movements remained substantial. The black movement was much more activist in its value orientation and rejected much of the passivism, including some of the drug-related activities, as remnants of the previously repressed status (Malcolm X, 1976).[10] Both sides of the alliance, however, shared a common enemy, and each used the other's complaints in its rhetoric as further evidence of the decay and immorality of the Establishment.

Thus, at the end of the sixties, the political and intellectual elites of the country were faced with a threat of some magnitude from two groups which challenged their legitimacy. It is certainly possible to overestimate the seriousness of that challenge. The Establishment had wide, relatively deep support within midwestern and southern areas of the country and throughout the middle-aged and older white population. Even within the more rebellious sectors of the population, commitment to at least some components of basic moral schemas such as democratic government, "free enterprise," and cognitively rational standards of knowledge was probably quite deep. Furthermore, the political disorganization of the expressive passivist group certainly made the idea of political revolution in the immediate future unlikely. Expressive passivist ideological commitments were a poor basis for effective political action. Likewise, while the black movement was probably sufficiently militant and clear about its goals to produce such a revolution, blacks constituted a relatively small minority in the country and, in spite of rhetoric and threat, were unable to produce such a revolution without substantial allies. Nonetheless, the riots of the late sixties and the spread of marijuana, long hair, and new patterns of sexual relationships among the youth did seem to constitute a serious threat to the central moral schemas of American society.

One way of understanding the political context of the drug crisis would be to consider the political situation after the 1968 elections, just prior to the massive buildup of the Drug Crisis. Richard Nixon, the newly elected President, came from a minority party which had been out of power almost continuously since the early 1930s. He did not, therefore, have the resources of a large army of intellectuals, loyal officials, and other appropriate people to fill top government positions. Nixon himself took control of his own party more or less by default after the party almost disappeared following Goldwater's defeat in 1964. He had relatively little personal support

and had almost managed what seemed to be the impossible task
of losing the election to a very badly splintered Democratic
Party.[11]

The Democratic Party, on the other hand, was in even worse
shape. The incumbent Democratic president had been forced
not to seek reelection when it became apparent that he could
not be renominated. The Democratic convention, usually a
vehicle for organizing the party to campaign for the presidency,
had broken up in the middle of a riot with much of the liberal
wing of the party, traditionally the source of most of the active
campaign workers, vowing not to support the party nominee.
The Vietnam War divided the party into two radically opposed
factions which apparently could not be reconciled.

The new president had a very brief "honeymoon." Having
consistently supported the war policy, he inherited the immediate opposition of a very large segment of the population and
the immediate suspicion of the press, which had been a major
source of opposition to the war.

Nixon clearly needed a way of rallying the country and of
extending his support beyond the confines of the business
community and the conservative midwestern and southern
Republicans. In particular, he needed a way of unifying the
political and social establishment of the country, which was
much more pluralistic than the radicals believed, into cohesive
opposition to the black radicals and the "hippies." In this
formidable task, he faced a number of obstacles, not the least of
which was that large sections of the Establishment sympathized
with both the black radicals and the antiwar movement, at least
inasmuch as they shared common goals with them. Furthermore, inasmuch as the new President claimed to be the leader
and personal symbol of any new unity among members of the
Establishment, he had to contend with many old hatreds for
him personally that went back as far as the late forties.

Previous efforts to mobilize this support and this type of
cohesiveness had been based on simple patriotic schemas. This
strategy, however, became increasingly problematic as it became
more and more apparent that large segments of the population

did not consider opposition to the war unpatriotic. On the other hand, the Establishment, and the President as its symbolic head, were daily accused of crimes ranging from pollution of the water to murdering babies in Vietnam. While the previous administration's political base had been somewhat more diverse and had forced it to be relatively less aggressive in responding to the opposition, President Nixon's political base placed no such restrictions on him.

The Moral Organization of the Drug Crisis

The beginning of the antiheroin movement shows no signs of having been oriented toward the moral conflicts in the society. Although "drug arrests" which the FBI compiled every year had been rising for a number of years, the relatively articulate spokesmen for marijuana users had been able to use this as further evidence that the Establishment was trying to repress them and as another chance to publicize the irrational repression of American society (e.g., Glennby, 1968). The law enforcement personnel who made the arrests and did the prosecuting were not nearly as effective as the expressive passivists in presenting their definition of the situation to the media.

The first major shot fired in the drug war was probably the establishment by the National Institute of Mental Health of six experimental drug treatment programs in various cities around the country. In so doing, the National Institute of Mental Health apparently intended to extend its community mental health center programs into one more social problem area. There was no particular evidence of a sense of crisis about heroin use at this point, although concern about marijuana and LSD was already widespread. The sense of crisis was to come later.[12] How that sense of crisis was generated we will discuss below. However, it is important to note at this point what sorts of advantages accrued to the instrumental activists by making a major issue out of "the rising tide of drug addiction." This will require looking directly at the societal moral schema of drug use, as we noted earlier, and the organization of the conflict around the moral schema.

First of all, "drug problem" was accomplished in a particularly interesting way. The schema was organized in what can be called an Aristotelian manner; it was defined by its final or end state. Since drug use of any sort "led to" heroin addiction, it followed that it was reasonable to speak of all sorts of drug use as though heroin addiction were the end state. While this proposition had been shown many times to be dubious (Goode, 1969), it had certain rhetorical advantages for those seeking to further support against drugs, the people who used them, and their moral claims. To begin with, an important element of the moral schema was the "fact" that heroin addicts committed crimes. They were forced to do it by their addiction and their need for money to buy the heroin. Thus it was possible to tie in drug use with the chronic political issue of crime in the streets. Perhaps equally important was the symbolism of liberation and enslavement involved in the moral schema of addiction. While the expressive passivists had been relatively effective in claiming that they were the "free" individuals in this society and thus heir to the great romantic tradition of the cowboy and the rebel, this issue seemed to put the shoe on the other foot. Instead of being free from the chains of convention, the counter culture was shown to be enslaved by drug addiction.

Another important aspect of the moral schema of drug use was the groups who were allegedly involved, namely blacks and hippies. The empirical evidence that millions of nonblack, nonhip Americans, from truckers to bored housewives, used illegal drugs was ignored in this rhetoric. It was the use of heroin and drugs that led to it by the blacks and hippies whom the police arrested that became the public moral example of illegal drug use. While the federal government did make a mild effort to educate the public as to the danger of overuse of amphetamines and barbiturates by middle-aged and middle-class America, the repression never approached the magnitude of the repression of marijuana and heroin use by the hippies and blacks.[13]

The concept of addiction as part of the moral schema of drug use was also useful for its medical origins. It allowed drug use to be defined as a medical, and thus a psychiatric, problem. This made it possible to both discredit the drug user as incompetent and sick and at the same time present those who were sponsoring the treatment as trying to "help" the user (Crane, 1972). The "incompetency" question was particularly important, since, if the user (and by association, all blacks and youths) were incompetent, his (and their) political and social views could justifiably be discounted. Those who opposed the government's policies on income distribution and the Vietnam War could thus be shown to do so only because of their moral corruption.

The moral schema of drugs was also useful vis-à-vis what sorts of groups could be mobilized to support an effort to abolish drug use. While most of the other issues which had been used to try to condemn the blacks and the counter culture had the disadvantage of alienating other important groups in the society, one major asset of drugs as an issue was that it garnered the support of mental health professionals of various sorts and the liberals who wanted to improve society. While drug treatment was at the beginning and has remained to this day a relatively low-status subprofession in psychiatry, as the administration began to cut back on mental health funds for other programs and increase money for treatment of drug addiction, it found numerous mental health professionals who were pleased to take the job. Some mental health professionals found the job attractive because it involved "helping" blacks and other minority groups to whom many mental health professionals had developed ideological commitments as part of the development of community psychiatry. Another latent function of the involvement of mental-health professionals in this field was that, as practitioners of community psychiatry, they were very experienced in the process of focusing moral concern among community groups and in the media about issues which they defined as threats to the mental health of the community. The prestige of the medical profession was very useful in this regard.

The second interesting group of people whom the drug issue allied with the government were some black activists. Some more conservative blacks found the use of drugs among young blacks to be an uncomfortable reminder of their own previously repressed status and an aspect of black culture which hindered assimilation into the larger society. The more radical activists saw drugs as, literally, the "opiate of the people." In both cases, they ignored the symbolic meaning of the repression of drugs in the hope of pragmatic gains.

More conservative groups—particularly the business and labor communities—found the Drug Crisis attractive, since it symbolically condemned those who did not honor the work ethic which was so important to their legitimation. Middle-class parents who found themselves uncomfortably confronted with hostile children (who may or may not have been motivated by something to do with expressive passivism) now had an effective argument against their children's claim that there was something morally wrong with them.

The law enforcement authorities, although they were to be largely outflanked by the mental health professionals, supported the attack on drug addiction. They were easily mobilized, since they saw drugs as causing crime. They were also able to effectively use the Drug Crisis to increase their budgets. The news media, sensing a popular and interesting story, also buried their differences with the Nixon administration on this particular subject.

Theoretically, the most interesting group to get involved in mobilizing the Drug Crisis was the users themselves. Although they organized the moral facts of drug use quite differently than the other groups, they agreed to the reality of growing numbers of drug users. When presented with the "established fact" of growing heroin use, they presented accounts of it which implicitly involved acceptance of the "fact." Believing that perception of the growing crisis would eventually force the Establishment to legalize marijuana and make some concession on other issues, the drug users could generally be counted on to provide the news media with vivid and usually exaggerated accounts of how many people around them were using drugs (e.g., Lemar, 1969). Furthermore, since drug use was the major membership ritual for the expressive passivist counter culture, claims of growing drug use were predictions of ultimate victory.

In a further effort to produce the sense of crisis which seemed to give them a special importance, they would also occasionally be persuaded to tell horror stories about the effects of drugs. Usually the counter culture moralisms about this being a result of bad parenting, repression, or the war were included in such stories but were drowned out by more conventional moralisms. If regular drug users could not be found to provide such accounts, ex-addicts employed in drug treatment programs could always be counted on to "speak for" the drug users. Their major function in generating news stories seems to have been to provide horror stories from their own lives and to set "shining examples" for the rest of the country to see the effectiveness of treatment.

Finally, drugs as an issue had a major advantage as an effort to repress the expressive passivist movement in that it was an issue that the counter-culture leaders could not duck. As the membership ritual of the expressive passivists, it was too central a theme to be denied. Any leader of that group who sought to deny that drug use was growing would be denying that his support was growing. Denial that his group believed marijuana use to be a "good thing" would have been a betrayal of the movement. To claim that drug use was trivial would be to claim that membership in the movement was trivial.

The interesting point here is that, in contrast to some labeling theory accounts of similar phenomena, the participation of the deviant in the creation of the crisis is critical. Had the counter-culture leaders objected that there was no Drug Crisis, the evidence would have had to have been examined much more closely. But they did not. Indeed, the expressive passivists were the first group in the society to claim that drug use was increasing at an epidemic pace. It was also part of their effort to do a moral crisis. Although the moral schemas on which their crisis was based were quite different from the one which eventually succeeded, they also needed a Drug Crisis as an indicator of their success.

We have discussed at some length the political and moral struggles that made drugs an important issue and who supported the crisis. We must now turn to the question of how the crisis was produced. We must move from the use of moral schema to their production.

Moral Crisis Production

Howard Becker's (1963) concept of moral entrepreneurs is the major conceptual contribution of sociology to his area of study. "Rules are the products of someone's initiative and we can think of the people who exhibit such enterprise as moral entrepreneurs" (Becker, 1963: 145). Crisis entrepreneurs must also exhibit such zeal although the production of moral crises that we are talking about involves both more than and less than a rule change.

But the existence of a moral crisis entrepreneur does not, by itself, create a moral crisis. Specifically, five more elements are necessary to produce a moral crisis.[14] First, there must be available a behavior or condition which can be focused on, made visible, highlighted, denounced, and moralized about. A vague apprehension that there are great evils in the world will not suffice to produce this type of crisis. The evil must have a specific focus such that action can be taken against it. This behavior or condition may be the object of the group's apprehension and anxiety or it may only symbolize and make visible a less tangible or less easily denounced threat. We can call this behavior or condition "the activity." In the case of the Drug Crisis, the activity was "drug use."

The second component of a moral crisis is a group of persons who can be alleged to be responsible for or involved with as proponents of the activity. These are the individuals whom the moral entrepreneur denounces. We will call them the "deviants." The moral entrepreneur usually directs appeals to them to reform and join him in trying to stop the activity. However, the content of these appeals is often such that the appeal is clearly meant less for the deviants than for another audience. In the Drug Crisis, the deviants were blacks and hippies.

Any moral crisis needs an audience of members of the relevant community to whom the moral entrepreneurs can appeal.

The members of the audience are treated and are expected to act as moral judges upholding the relevant moral schemas of the community to which all participants belong. It is not, strictly speaking, necessary that the members of the audience believe in the schemas which they are expected to hold, just that they will act as though they do. For example, Matza (1964) argues the juvenile delinquents do not generally believe in the delinquent code which they, nonetheless, normally can be counted on to uphold in the company of other delinquents. Likewise, in our case, the audience (the American working, middle, and upper classes) clearly has considerable ambivalence about the many elements of the expressive passivist moral schema the crisis entrepreneurs denounced as present in drug users. However, as a matter of public statement, the audience could be counted on to uphold instrumental activist values.

The next requirement for a moral crisis is a means of communication between the moral entrepreneur and his audience. In small communities of a few hundred people, the traditional mechanisms of gossip and public deviance validation serve this purpose perfectly adequately. In a modern mass society of 200 million people, the mass communications media of television, radio, magazines, and newspapers perform the same function. While the news media are certainly a major component of this communications network, the fictional portrayals of aspects of the crisis are at least as important. While the news media portrayed increases in crime, drug overdoses, and addictions and other statistical pictures of a crisis, the fictional portrayals turned the crisis into personal tragedies. The heroic policeman fighting the Mafia heroin connection in the movies, the T.V. doctor saving the junkie from certain death and reuniting him with his desperately concerned family, and the comic book superhero who fights the monstrous conspiracy to destroy the country by putting drugs in the drinking water all make personal and direct the tragedy of drug use. The moral communications through fictional media seem to result from secondary elaborations of the news media, but they are just as important.

How and why such thematic material appears in fictional media is a matter that needs more investigation.[15]

Finally, the crisis requires a series of moral schemas which the deviant can be shown to be violating and desecrating. These moral schemas, which compose what Durkheim called the "collective conscience of the society," may be only partially shared by members of the society. Indeed, their meaning is partially, perhaps even primarily, created in the denunciation of the deviants and their activity. We have noted that there was always considerable ambivalence in the United States about instrumental activism. But without at least a general willingness to provisionally agree that some vague moral schemas are important to "what we are and believe," there can be no moral crisis.

In order to create a moral crisis, the moral entrepreneur must accomplish several things. First, he must transform the activity from a mundane ordinary activity engaged in by ordinary people into an extraordinary activity engaged in by people who are of special note (e.g., Anslinger and Tompkins, 1953). The people involved can no longer be allowed to be "just like you and me." This is one of the reasons that civil liberties issues are so often involved in moral crises. The basis of such rights is that they are accorded to all ordinary citizens. They are justified on the basis that each of us would want such rights for ourselves. A successfully produced moral crisis, however, breaks this bond of identification between the "ordinary citizen" in the audience and the deviant.

In the Drug Crisis, the moral entrepreneurs seeking to set off drug users as exceptional people and the use of drugs as exceptional activities had very important help from the drug users themselves. They had long argued, as we noted earlier, that the use of drugs created special people of a basically different and better nature than ordinary individuals.

Obviously, then, in order to create a moral crisis, the moral entrepreneur must do more than just show that the deviants are extraordinary. He must also show that they are a basic threat to various moral schemas that the audience can be counted on to uphold. The activity or one of its byproducts must be made to look like a basic threat to the social order. The W.C.T.U., for example, contended that drinking undermined the foundations of the American family and the productivity of American workers (Gusfield, 1963). The denouncers of drug use added to those two the sanctity of private property. Indeed, to a large extent, the moral entrepreneurs had the cooperation of the drug users in persuading the audience that they were a danger to the values that the audience held dear. The drug user's public spokespeople repeatedly informed the audience that "the times they are a'changing" and that the audience's values would have to change as well (e.g., Monroe, 1968).

This, of course, is somewhat troublesome, since it seems paradoxical that deviants would do anything that would aid in their own repression. However, it is important to realize that in doing so, the spokespeople for the expressive passivists were only doing what they had been doing for several years, which had won many converts. If an expressive passivist movement were to take control of the culture, it would be very helpful if it appeared to be something extraordinary, something which would provide its leaders and followers with the prestige and importance of being part of a historic movement, not just an unimportant pattern of activity (e.g., Kupferberg, 1968).

Another aspect of the denunciation of drug use and its transformation into a moral crisis was the need to depict it as not self-regulating. The moral crisis entrepreneur, if he is to successfully mobilize the audience, must show that the crisis will not abate unless the audience takes action. This view of events is deeply ingrained in the Judeo-Christian cosmology which depicts the world as a continuing struggle between the forces of good and the forces of evil and insists that each person must take a stand. This contrasts with, for example, the Buddhist belief that the moral universe regulates itself.

It was not easy to demonstrate that drug use would not abate by itself. Because the condemnation of the irrationality of the use of drugs was so broad, it was hard to show how any reasonable person could choose to use drugs, much less how they could become a threat to the viability of the society. It was thus necessary to introduce elements into the moral schemas to account for why a normal person would try drugs, why such a person might continue, and how drug use spreads. Concepts of curiosity and misinformation were used to partially solve these problems. Drug users started on drugs because they thought they might be fun and because they thought they didn't know any better.[16] The spread of drug use was largely accounted for by "peer-group pressure." This is a process whereby an innocent group of children can be turned into evil drug addicts simply by being together. An equally important way to account for the spread of drug use was the concept of the "pusher." The pusher was the most totally evil force in the drug scene. For material gain, he corrupted the young and introduced them to the joys and horrors of addiction. Thus the concept of the innocence of youth could be preserved and the source of the corruption focused on the pusher. Finally, the persistence of drug use in face of the manifestly evil experiences involved was accounted for by addiction and/or more peer-group pressure. Addiction was a particularly useful concept for the medical community because it meant that the individual could use the drug without being himself evil and thus deserving to be punished.

Clearly, one of the major tasks of the moral entrepreneur is to formulate the motives of the deviants in the appropriate way. This is a complex task in some instances. One requirement is that the deviant and the deviant activity must be degraded to a status level far below that of the audience. In this way, the crisis entrepreneur elevates the status of the audience and ties it to the highest symbols of the society. Either the motives of the deviants must be shown to be evil in and of themselves or the behavior of the deviants must be shown to be out of their control and the result of some other evil force.

The motives of the deviants in the Drug Crisis were depicted in various ways, depending on what type of remedy the crisis entrepreneur was trying to promote. We have already noted that medical-psychiatric entrepreneurs promoted the notion of addiction both because it was a medical concept and because a person who is addicted does not choose his behavior and thus merits sympathetic treatment, not punishment. Law-enforcement personnel liked the pusher theory because it allowed them to exercise their power over someone in a relatively unequivocal manner. Pushers deserve punishment, and since roughly a third of the serious addicts dealt heroin to their associates (Hughes et al., 1974), this argument left the law-enforcement system with clear-cut control over a large section of the addict population. Education specialists, on the other hand, liked any theory that stressed group interactions, including pusher theories, but peer-group influence was clearly their favorite, for only they ever had contact with large numbers of potential addicts grouped together in their natural setting. Adequate preventive education could, in theory, isolate the addict from his nonaddict peers and prevent epidemics of drug use. Finally, political activists, poverty programs, and black radicals liked social causes of addiction because this provided them with a mandate to change the social structure.[17]

It must be emphasized that although they disagreed about the causes of and solutions to the Drug Crisis, all of these experts agreed on the existence of a Drug Crisis. A casual observer of the dialogue among experts would probably pick up that two things are uncontrovertible truths: that a Drug Crisis exists and that drug use and drug users are a problem.

Having listed the major different types of crisis entrepreneurs above, we want to note that in spite of their differing views, their presentations of self share several important aspects. First, all effective crisis entrepreneurs must effectively present themselves as, in Parsons's phrase, "collectivity oriented." They must show that they are only concerned about the crisis as public citizens. They have nothing personal to gain from alerting the audience to the crisis. A university appointment is a nice platform for helping create this image, since university professors are widely believed to get paid for teaching, not for crisis entrepreneurship.[18] An employee of a "nonprofit" or a government agency is almost equally well placed.

The crisis entrepreneur must also show that he has no personal or political hostility to the deviant group. Once again, university professors and employees of service agencies were excellently placed to be moral crisis entrepreneurs, whereas conservative politicians and police officials with their "well-known" hostilities to blacks and hippies were very poorly placed. This requirement was also rather well met by black activists and liberal-radical organizers of all sorts. Since they were known to be allied with blacks and hippies, any claims that they made about the seriousness of the transgressions that drug users made were strong confirmation of the objective seriousness of the crisis. Obviously this is equally true for "ex-addicts" who, if they were warning against the activities of their friends, must be taken seriously.

Finally, the crisis entrepreneur must present himself as a credible expert on the problem of the crisis—in this case, drug abuse. Obviously a businessman, an ordinary clergyman, or a surgeon, despite generally high prestige in the society, cannot function as a drug crisis entrepreneur. These people lack credentials as specialized experts who can claim to know in detail about the crisis. However, if the surgeon identifies himself as a doctor working in a drug clinic, the clergyman has been running a program for teenage drug abusers of his faith, and the businessman is chairman of an organization called "Businessmen Against Drugs (BAD)," all of them can claim such expertise. In general, the society has several roles which allow one to claim to be an expert on almost any social problem. These include psychiatrists, psychologists, sociologists, and social workers. In the Drug Crisis, a new specialized role developed, that of the "ex-addict." This role could not be played by anyone who had once used drugs. He or she had to be certified by a drug-abuse practitioner as genuine. However, once certified in a particular situation, the ex-addict's word was very influential. He or she had direct experience with drugs and thus knew better than anyone else. The weakness in this position is that one could not get a certificate stating that one was an ex-addict. One needed a basis of support to show the genuineness of the prefix. This required depending on a clinician or having one's own drug program.

Conclusion

This chapter has sought to describe doing morality of a specific type, the doing of a moral crisis. We have tried to show what did and did not go into the creation of the heroin crisis of the late sixties and early seventies. Several things seem reasonably clear. First, it seems that there was not "really" an epidemic increase in heroin use, although there was an enormous increase in public concern and social control efforts. Second, a moral crisis of this nature could have generated statistics of the sort that crisis entrepreneurs used to demonstrate the existence of such an increase without the increase "really" having occurred. Most of those statistics seem to have resulted from increased police activity.

On the other hand, the Drug Crisis was not an enormous fuss over nothing. It was a response to a growing threat to the dominant moral schemas of the society which focused around instrumental activist values. The crisis seems to have involved a creatively organized (although nonconspiratorial) attack by diverse groups on the counter culture with its expressive passivist moral schemas and on black radicals. The structure of the specific moral schemas about "drugs" which allowed symbolic attacks on both marijuana and heroin at the same time greatly facilitated the generation of the crisis. The generation of the crisis involved the cooperative effort of many groups in the society, each of which found a place for itself in the moral order that the crisis generated. Particularly interesting among these groups were the "expressive passivists" and black activists themselves. Although the crisis did serious and perhaps irreparable moral damage to both groups, both found reasons to participate in the claim that "drug use" was increasing. Their

efforts to present alternative schemas to interpret it were not
very successful.

NOTES

1. Including refusal to answer questions, lying, and dropping out of the population being studied.

2. Efforts by the National Commission on Marijuana and Drug Abuse (1973) to
produce reliable data on use by compiling nonidentical data from different areas
strike us as dubious for many reasons.

3. Rates for drugs other than heroin were, of course, much higher.

4. For similar articles, see *Time* 86: 16-17, Dec. 24, 1965; *Newsweek* 69: 48,
Mar. 13, 1967; *Time* 92: 44-45, Aug. 30, 1969.

5. This pattern begins to appear more prominently as the crisis heated up. For
example, *U.S. News & World Report* 65: 43-45, Sept. 2, 1968, captioned its lead
drawing "Alienated Youths Sometimes Move Up from 'Pot' to 'Big H'–Heroin."

6. There are some serious problems with how Durkheim actually did his analysis
which have plagued sociology ever since. In spite of his argument, Durkheim proceeds
to treat the societal rates as aggregates of individual behaviors and then tries to
establish the motives of individuals in certain social situations based on this statistic.
Recently, Garfinkel (1967) and Douglas (1967) have shown that there is reason to
treat the social decision of whether or not a death was a suicide as an independent
process. Presumably these processes, as well as heroin statistics, might be affected–at
least over the long run–by the perception of the likelihood of suicide.

7. In describing these schemas, we have tried to keep in mind the dictum of
Edmund Husserl that the description should not be clearer than the phenomenon
itself.

8. Interestingly, in 1965, when a group of policy-oriented scholars decided to
form a major new journal for policy debate, they named it *The Public Interest*.

9. This was very visible in the press during that period. See, for example, *U.S.
News & World Report* 67: 74-78, Nov. 17, 1969.

10. Also note that the Black Panther Party's "Ten Point Program" specifically
enjoined party members from using narcotics.

11. For an interesting analysis of Nixon's position at that point, see *New
Republic*, "Nixon's Choice" 159, 20: 5-6.

12. Reviewing the major news magazines leaves us with the impression that it was
not until late 1969 that the crisis about heroin entered these magazines.

13. See Inciardi (1974) for an interesting discussion of the prominence of
mythical thought in the American perception of drugs.

14. In the analysis that follows, we have borrowed heavily from Harold Garfinkel's paper on degradation ceremonies (Garfinkel, 1956).

15. A conspiracy theory of this process was encouraged by a report in the *New
York Times* in August of 1970 to the effect that President Nixon and Attorney
General Mitchell had met with 35 top broadcast executives, and this meeting

"accounted for much of the emphasis on drug abuse in fall T.V. schedules." Furthermore, it was reported that Nixon and Mitchell had emphasized using entertainment programs as the media for the message (New York Times, August 26;26:4). However, extensive communication with the source of the report that the *Times* cites does not support the view that the networks were pushed or even prodded into the action. Rather it seems that the meeting was largely devoted to "informational presentations" about drug abuse by various government authorities. The direct roles of Nixon and Mitchell seem to have been largely introductory. The tone of the meeting seems to have been general agreement that the media could help solve a major social problem.

16. Defense lawyers found these motives very useful when defending first offenders. How could one punish for misinformation or curiosity?

17. We were privileged to have an opportunity to observe this process in the training of drug abuse specialists at a federally funded training center in Riverdale. Several examples of each type of expert were paraded in front of students and allowed to give their denunciation of drug abuse.

18. Since many university appointments for drug specialists were contingent on so-called "soft" money and the position would have disappeared had the soft money disappeared, this was not an entirely accurate assumption.

Chapter 3

IDEOLOGIES AND ACCOMMODATIVE SCHEMAS

In the previous chapter, we described the process of doing the morality of "drugs" at the societal level and particularly the creation of a crisis around "drug use." Yet such work is not the totality of what is necessary for the doing of societal morality about drugs. Those processes are not completely castles in the air. They are built on "real" events. The portrayals of police, addicts, addicts' families, psychiatrists, etc., which the media so actively developed and around which such conflicts developed, would not have been nearly as interesting or invoked nearly the passions if they were not represented as real.

In a particularly intriguing parenthetical comment in *Wayward Puritans*, Erikson observes that the ritual of public hangings disappeared soon after the invention of the general circulation newspaper. The clarifying of societal moral schemas which was the function of public punishments could be done just as well or better in the newspapers. The further development of mass media has taken this process one step further and eliminated the need for the elaborate moral work involved in deviance validation rituals. The criminal court trial, the paradigmatic case of deviance designation, has been reduced from a public elaboration and confirmation of the criminal's sins to a negotiated agreement that the defendant fits a moral typification (Sudnow, 1965). Television's fictionalized versions of the nature of the deviant and his sins is both more dramatic and freer to develop a "good" story, since it is unencumbered by the facts of any particular case.

Television versions of addicts, addiction treatment, prosecution, etc., have not, however, completely abolished the role of "real life" in the doing of drug morality. It has just reduced "real life's" role to the generation of evidence that the world is essentially like television. This largely involves the generation of statistics (based on demonstrably accurate procedures) to show that television adequately reflects the nature and distribution of good and evil,[1] i.e., that the decisions made about the moral nature of cases are substantively just.

The chapters that follow concern the "real-life" doing of morality in the context of the Drug Crisis. However, our focus will not be on describing the doing of the morality itself, but on the use of the type of moral schemas which we call ideologies in the process of doing the morality of drugs. Ideologies are important because, even aside from the moral crisis, deviance and control activities are not done in a moral vacuum. They occur in the context of moral schemas that function primarily to make sense out of such activities. In order to make the real life events become satisfactory dramas which will exemplify the moral schemas, the psychiatric clinician doing treatment must, in public, behave the way psychiatric clinicians do in the society's moral schemas about heroin. This is facilitated by societal moral schemas about what psychiatric treatment is like. These schemas are intimately related to what we call the treatment ideology, which, in turn, is deeply imbedded in the history of the psychiatric profession. In this chapter, we describe three such ideologies which are used by various groups in the drug scene as moral justification and to orient their activities in deviance-validation activities. What we will call the punishment ideology mandates the activities of law enforcement personnel, the treatment ideology mandates the clinicians who treat drug addiction, and the outlaw ideology mandates the heroin users. It is perhaps worth reminding the reader here that we explicitly mean ideologies to correspond, in their structural location, to Durkheim's concept of occupational moralities. Like occupational moralities, those ideologies are the "collective conscience" of the groups that they mandate and are specifications of more general societal moral schemas.

These ideologies and their effects on the day-to-day activities involved in producing verified deviants will be our topic for the next four chapters. In this chapter, we will try to spell out the relevant ideologies and try to show in a general way why none of the groups could implement its own ideology. Then we will try to show how each type of interactive situation generated its own compromise definition of the situation which we call an accommodative schema. In each of the following three chapters, we will explore different aspects of accommodation between conflicting ideologies. Although it will require a complex analysis, we believe that the type of analysis we will outline in these four chapters will provide a much fuller understanding of the moral structure of deviance validation and its relationship to societal moral schemas.

The Concept of Ideology

The discussion of ideologies of deviant groups is not new to sociology. The study of juvenile delinquency which thrived in the fifties and early sixties continually dealt with this issue under the rubric of "subculture." The relations between subcultures and juvenile delinquency produced various positions. Walter Miller (1958) argued that delinquency is simply a reflection of the lower-class culture. Albert Cohen (1955) argued that delinquents had their own subculture which was a reaction formation to the dominant American value system. David Matza's (1964) argument holds that delinquents' concepts of justice and proper behavior are only slight extensions and modifications of societal concepts of justice and proper behavior as seen in the legal system—which itself modifies the societal concepts for its own practical purposes.

At a more general level, it is probably a fair summary of most research to say that some deviants more or less accept societal moralisms about their behavior and identity and others do not. As Howard Becker puts it (1963: 3):

> The traffic violator usually subscribes to the very rules he has broken. Alcoholics are often ambivalent, sometimes feeling that those who judge them do not understand them and at other times agreeing that compulsive drinking is a bad thing. At the extreme, some deviants (homosexuals and drug addicts are good examples) develop full-blown ideologies explaining why they are right and why those who disapprove of and punish them are wrong.

While we find more ambivalence in drug addicts than Becker indicates, we will propose a model of the behavior of drug addicts that depends in part on an ideology that the addict has a special relationship to. The outlaw ideology is, in part, a very general formulation of the moral schemas of the addict as well as certain other types of deviants in American society. However, we are in a somewhat different position than previous theorists because we are trying to analyze the activities of both the deviant and the control agents that he deals with. As deviance studies have shown, many deviant groups seem to "have" their own moral schemas which are at least somewhat different from the institutionalized societal moralities. However, control agents also have their own ideologies. Although the ideologies of the control agents seem to have the force of law and the prestige of academic writings to legitimate them, they are not unchallenged in the society as a whole. Even if they do not conflict with the general societal morality, they are at least specifications of that normative structure and not identical to it. Other specifications of the societal morality are possible. Indeed, we will suggest below, following Matza's lead, that the outlaw ideology is also grounded in the general societal morality. Both the control agents and addicts derive justifications of their roles and their behaviors from quite generally accepted societal moral elements. Likewise, both addicts and control agents, be they psychiatrists or law enforcement agents, can be attacked on the basis of generally held moral schemas.

In the three chapters that follow this, we will try to describe the patterns of relationships that evolve in the triangular relationship between addicts, law enforcement personnel, and drug-treatment clinicians. In doing so, we will refer continually to the ideologies that mandate the various groups. Before we go any further, however, we must discuss the concept of ideology as a special type of moral schema.

While the concept of "ideology" has been widely used in psychology, sociology, and political science, the concept remains vague. Although our use of the term does not conform to his definition, Shils's explication of the term in the *International Encyclopedia of the Social Sciences* is an interesting reference point (1969: 66-67).

> Ideology is one among the variety of comprehensive patterns of beliefs . . . [including] outlooks and creeds ("suboutlooks"), movement of thought, and programs, as well as ideologies.
>
> These comprehensive patterns differ from each other in their degree of (a) explicitness and authoritativeness of formulation, (b) internal systemic integration, (c) acknowledged affinity with other contemporaneous patterns, (d) closure, (e) imperativeness of manifestation in conduct, (f) accompanying affect, (g) consensus demanded of exponents, and (h) association with a corporate collective form deliberately intended to realize the pattern of explicitness of formulation over a very wide range of the objects with which they deal; for their adherents there is an authoritative and explicit promulgation. They are relatively highly systematized or integrated around one or a few pre-eminent values (e.g., salvation, equality, or ethnic purity). They are more insistent on their distinctiveness from and unconnectedness with other outlooks or ideologies in their own society; they are more resistant against innovations in their beliefs and deny the existence or the significance of those which do occur. Their

acceptance and promulgation have highly affective overtones. Complete subservience to the ideology is demanded of those who accept it, and it is regarded as essential and imperative that their conduct should be completely permeated by it. All adherents of the ideology are urgently expected to be in complete agreement with each other; corporate collective form is regarded as the appropriate mode of organization of adherents to maintain discipline over those already committed and to win over or dominate those not already committed to it.

The three ideologies which we wish to outline fit this ideal type to varying degrees. The treatment ideology is probably the closest to Shils's ideal type, and the outlaw ideology is certainly the furthest from the model. Indeed, our "ideologies" are probably as close to "outlooks" in Shils's sense as to his concept of ideologies. We do not mean to use Shils's formulation as a definition, but we believe he has noted many of the relevant dimensions which we must consider. Let us now consider how these ideologies do and do not fit Shils's definition. It should be noted, however, that although originally the concept of ideology was intimately tied to the idea of distortion and unproven assumptions, this pejorative implication is not intended here. All belief systems "distort" in some manner or another, and all involve assumptions that are ultimately unprovable. (Whitehead, 1933; Geertz, 1973).

The most important, for our purposes, of Shils's properties of ideologies is that they are associated with "a corporate collective form deliberately intended to realize the patterns of belief." To this we must add that they may be associated with a lifestyle, certain activities, and roles as well as with collectivities. *Ideologies function to ennoble certain types of roles, groups, and activities, raising them from the level of mundane and ordinary to the level of special and privileged.* Correspondingly, these ideologies ennoble the individuals who play the roles, belong to the groups, and perform the activities. The police version of punishment ideology, for instance, transforms police work from the mundane ordinary task of keeping society's least reputable members from injuring each other and the property of others to the almost sacred task of maintaining public order and safeguarding the citizenry against danger to their lives and families. The addict's version of the outlaw ideology transforms a dirty, disreputable, and often unpleasant lifestyle into the last refuge of the truly free and independent individual who has not succumbed to the oppressive society. The drug clinicians' version of the treatment ideology reformulates the mundane job of trying to cajole, blackmail, and persuade addicts to play dependent low-status conventional roles into a noble effort to better the lot of a poor and unfortunate group of afflicted people. We do not mean to imply that the mundane formulation is somehow more real than the ideological one, only that it is an alternate description which suggests itself to the various role incumbents when the ideological definitions become neutralized.

These ideologies are, of course, self-serving. But in being so, they make possible the persistence of the interactions we are concerned with. A policeman who loses his belief in police work as a noble enterprise has little to defend himself with against the rampant cynicism and corruption that are routine parts of his working environment. The addict who gives up the ideological image of his enterprise will eventually find heroin use unappealing, and the clinician bereft of his ideology will find little to justify the long hours away from friends and family trying to reform disagreeable characters. Without these ideological supports, none of the role relationships that we will discuss would maintain the form they have today.

While Shils notes that these ideologies are "consistent in their distinctiveness from and unconnectedness with other" ideologies, his formulation misses the degree to which ideologies are formulated in *opposition* to other ideologies. Each of our ideologies predicates the role of its adherents as in conflict with some other group. It ennobles its own enterprise in part by labeling the enterprise of some other group ignoble. Indeed, all three ideologies define the enterprise of the groups that they support as in opposition to the other two groups. Punishment ideology defines its enterprise in opposition to that of the treatment personnel and the addicts. The people mandated by it are shown to be, at a minimum, engaged in a more worthwhile and important enterprise than the others. Likewise, treatment ideology looks down on the law enforcement personnel and punishment as a primitive technique of control. Even though treatment is explicitly formulated as an effort to help addicts, that hardly involves a respect for the addict's enterprise.

Our major departure from Shils's formulation concerns his first four elements: explicitness and authoritativeness of formulation, internal systemic integration, acknowledged affinity with other contemporaneous patterns, and closure. That is to say that these moral schemas do not have the level of formality to them that schemas like Stalinism or Nazism had. Even the treatment ideology, which most closely approximates Shils's model, is relatively loosely organized. There is no one authoritative statement, but rather many loosely accepted statements. The logical coherence, closure, and distinctness from other moral schemas are less clear. Nonetheless, the subjects of this study, almost without exception, believed strongly in the ideologies that mandated their roles. Although some took "heretical" stands on particular issues, the core of the ideologies that we will describe below received general support when stated as general positions in the language of their particular group. But few of the people we studied were dogmatic orthodox ideologues. The propositions of their ideologies were general truths, but truths that admitted of exceptions. They are propositions that are true except where they are not.[2]

Furthermore, as we will make abundantly clear in the rest of this volume, these are ideologies which are primarily emphasized in what Matza (1964) calls the "situation of company." They are primarily talked about with colleagues who are mandated by the same ideology and are presumed to hold the same views.

Finally, we must realize that these ideologies are not studied in the way an academic studies his field. Although an occasional lawyer or psychiatrist has done systematic thinking about his mandating ideology, few social workers, nurses, addicts, policemen, etc. have. Because a Roman Catholic goes to Mass twice a week and expects salvation is no reason to expect that he understands the intricacies of Augustine. Thus the actors we studied were often able to generate practical positions they believed to be ideologically acceptable which would not necessarily be so to the theorist.[3]

This has very basic advantages for the actor. Indeed, if actors were required to be consistent in a narrowly formal way to a limited set of propositions and values, they would be severely hindered in their practical activities. The looseness of the use of the ideologies allows the actor a much greater degree of freedom in his actions than would otherwise be the case.

Punishment and Treatment Ideologies

It is now time to consider the specific moral schemas that we have been calling ideologies in some detail. Because the punishment and treatment ideologies have developed largely in opposition to one another, we will discuss these two first and postpone the discussion of the outlaw ideology until after the other two have been dealt with.

Although this is by no means a historical study, the nature of both of these schemas will be clarified if we discuss briefly their historical origins. Although we now take for granted that treatment and punishment are different and partially conflicting ideologies of the control of deviance, the treatment ideology is a comparatively recent invention which, in turn, has forced modification of the punishment ideology.

The origins of a concept of punishment for deviants' acts may well be as old as the social organization of man. Such, at least, is the assumption of such theorists as Durkheim (1933) and Maine (1863). Durkheim believed that punishment was an integral part of mechanical solidarity. Pollack and Maitland's history of English law traces the notion of punishment back to state sanctioning of personal revenge against the criminal and the expulsion of the outlaw from social protection and finds that, as far back as King Alfred, *punishment came only as a response to an act* (Pollack and Maitland, 1968: 450-451).

We believe that this reflects the central property of the punishment ideology. *A punishment is a response to a deviant act.* As such, it is tied to codes which prohibit certain acts and prescribe punishments for them. The treatment ideology, on the other hand, prescribes that *treatment should come as a response to a deviant character structure.*

The notion of the sanction responding to the character of the individual seems to have its modern origins in a very nonpsychiatric source, Protestant theology. As Weber (1958) pointed out, the Protestant Reformation (and especially Calvinism) created a new image of man and his salvation. Although in Catholic theology salvation depended on God's grace, it was attained through the sacraments of the Church and thus depended on one's overt acts. For Calvin, and to a lesser extent Luther and Zwingli, salvation was predestined. One's activities had nothing to do with *determining* one's salvation. However, one's acts did *reflect* the state of one's soul. Saved individuals would act as if they were saved, although ultimately whether one was saved or damned was unknowable. Membership in the church was reserved for those presumed to be among the elect, which in practice was close to saying that it was reserved for those whose righteous behavior reflected their election.

In Calvinist communities, church membership was the sine qua non for membership in the community. The nonmember was, in many ways, the analogue of what we call a deviant. Beliefs about the nature of immorality were identical with theories of salvation. Deviance was not so much a quality of an action, but rather of a soul. A deviant action was not deviant in and of itself; it was deviant as a reflection of the damned soul.

The Calvinist doctrine of action as reflective of—but not affecting—the soul provided a new basis for moral orientation in a society that was becoming increasingly differentiated and in which proper *behavior* became increasingly difficult to specify in detail as criminal law had traditionally done.[4] In America, the Protestant church functioned as the instrument of social control, supplementing—and to some degree overlapping—the law until the beginning of the nineteenth century. At that point, increasingly secular concepts of man, the increasing separation of church and state as institutionalized in the First Amendment, and the growth of large cities which made control by one or a series of churches difficult rapidly broke down this pattern. Rothman's (1971: Ch. 2) data shows quite clearly that psychiatry's initial development in America corresponded with the breakdown of tight religious control (see also Lipset, 1963: Ch. 4).

It is hardly surprising that psychiatry and social work would borrow these basic moral structures for thinking about the inner being of man. The medical model of disorders of the body, particularly in psychiatry, also led to a similar pattern. By treating acts as "symptoms" and mind as parallel to the organism, the same pattern could be achieved.[5] Although many of the clinicians we observed thought that a medical model of addiction as a disease was silly and would have shuddered at the formulation that addiction was a sign of nonelection, the basic structure remained throughout all of their formulations. Although, as we will see, compromises were made with the addicts, clinical accounts for colleagues and for professional audiences continued to treat addiction as a sign of something wrong in the addict rather than as the cause of the problem as the addicts believed.

In marked contrast, the moral schemas institutionalized in the criminal law have increasingly come to hold that deviant internal states of the individual are not justifiably punishable. Thus, in Robinson v. California, the U.S. Supreme Court insisted that while one could be imprisoned for the possession of narcotics, one could not be imprisoned for being an addict. Similar rulings about other status crimes such as "being a vagrant" and "being an alcoholic"[6] have also been made. The Court has not forbidden punishment for being drunk in public (the act), but the status (of being an alcoholic or a vagrant), however much it requires an illegal act, cannot be punished.

Thus we see that the core distinction between the moral schemas of treatment and punishment is what invokes the control. The treatment ideology responds to internal states as reflected in behavior, and the punishment ideology mandates response only to behavior. In practice, these often produce sanctioning responses to similar behaviors, since criminal acts are often seen as signs of deviant internal states. However, the distinction can be seen in that what is treated as trivial in one schema is important in another. Thus a psychiatrist treating a patient might treat a criminal act as a trivial manifestation of a temporary phase in the cure but take the response to a Rorschach test—a behavior that is morally trivial to the society at large—as indicating very serious pathology.

A vague jurisdictional boundary line has developed. The criminal law mandated by the punishment ideology has taken jurisdiction over behavior that is commonsensically formulated as being rationally motivated in the pursuit of pleasure, profit, or other acceptable values but which violates societal norms. The control agencies mandated by the treatment ideology have gained jurisdiction where rationality is not presumed in the deviant's actions. Unfortunately, in several cases, including the uses of illegitimate drugs, plausible cases can be made both ways. Heroin may be thought to be so pleasurable that all the disadvantages of use are rationally justifiable to the addict. In this view, stiffer punishments are needed to prevent further use. Treatment ideologues, on the other hand, have argued that the pains and disadvantages of heroin use were so great that no rational person would use it. The conflicts between these two moral schemas of deviance validation occur mostly at these vague boundaries, of which heroin use and control is only one.[7]

Although the focus of control on act or agent is the key point of differentiation between the two ideologies, it is not the only one. The issue of man's freedom or nonfreedom to determine his own behavior has been much debated in both ideological contexts. In practice, however, it is difficult to justify punishment unless one assumes that the deviant chooses his activities. Treatment ideologies are often formulated in the hard determinist rhetoric that human behavior is determined by environment and his heredity, but in practice the treatment position is more ambiguous and reveals the Christian and medical background of the ideology. For Calvin, the only thing that is determined outside of the individual is election or nonelection (read deviant identity or nondeviant identity). In medicine, the only thing that is out of the patient's control is his disease (deviance). The deviant (qua patient) is expected to cooperate with treatment. He is expected to try to get well (Parsons, 1951: Ch. 10).[8] But this view is nonetheless quite different from the view of the punishment ideology which explicitly holds the deviant (qua defendant) responsible for his deviant act.

The punishment ideology views man as free to choose between good and evil. Order in the society is therefore maintained by societal efforts to structure the options available to individuals so that they will choose to behave in an orderly manner and by mobilizing the individual's conscience to do the right things. The law reflects this ideology. The law provides sanctions which encourage the rational actor to make the "right" choice in his own best interest. At the same time, by making the law just and in the best interests of the society and by organizing the law so as to support collective values and sacred symbols, the law appeals to the conscience of the actor.

Treatment ideology in its extreme forms sees such efforts as essentially a waste of time. A healthy personality will behave in socially desirable ways because socialization experiences have trained him or her to do so. This person's personality structure is such that he or she will obey the law as well as the informal norms by which society regulates behavior. If the individual fails to obey the rules, punishment is essentially a waste of time—as well as unjust—because the person is unable to behave otherwise. The society must work toward changing the deviant individual and doing away with the pathological aspects of his personality. This process, whatever the specific method, is called treatment.

A variant type of this ideology is what we may refer to as social treatment ideology. It sees an individual as a product of the environmental conditions under which she or he grows up and lives as an adult. According to this theory, deviance and crime indicate that something is wrong in the structure of the society, and social reform is the proper cure. Since the group of clinicians whom we observed held mixed views on whether addiction was a social or psychological pathology, this variant should not be forgotten.[9]

For the punishment ideologue, social control is evoked by the deviant act. There is no specific need to be concerned with what the individual believes or with the structure of the individual's personality. What the individual *is* is irrelevant. What is important is what the person *does*. Indeed, with such concepts as "justice is blind," and "equality before the law," the American legal system explicitly forbids concern with what the individual is.[10]

For the treatment theorist, such ideas are silly. They place arbitrary limits on the availability of data with which the treatment personnel make diagnoses. What the individual is will, sooner or later, be reflected in what he does. What one does shows what one is. While the law limits social control to responding to what the offender has done, treatment concerns itself with the history and current functioning of the individual. If the personality structure is in need of treatment, waiting until the individual commits a crime in order to treat him is foolish and irresponsible.

This brings up the issue of limits on the social control mechanisms. The criminal law, reflecting punishment ideology, provides the individual with substantive and procedural rights designed to guarantee that his understanding of, and his evidence on, the possible crime will be heard and that only fair punishments will be given out. This reflects the punishment ideology's focus on the act. The major problematic issue is the nature of the act which the individual committed. Treatment theorists find it strange that procedural matters should be given such weight. What sort of "right" is it, they ask, that prevents the individual from receiving help when it is needed? That the individual may not want the help that is in his own interest may only be another symptom of his disorder. The limits on social control mechanisms in the treatment ideology are the individual's needs. The professional dedication of the treatment agent is to help the individual to a healthier personality structure. This professionalism prevents abuses that might arise if the power were given to someone who did not have the individual's best interests at heart. In this sense, the treatment ideologues clearly have a much more optimistic image of what men typically do with power than the punishment ideologues.

Treatment and punishment also have different views of the relation of the deviant to the control agent. For the punishment ideologue, the individual chooses what to do and thus is expected to resent suggestions that what she or he did was wrong. The deviant is expected to resist social control. One may come to see the error of one's ways and repent, but the most likely means of reform is through learning that crime does not pay (Bentham, 1961). The legal procedure thus provides for an adversarial process which allows the individual to express a view of his or her own act.

The treatment ideology, following a medical model of sickness, assumes that anyone who is ill will usually seek a cure for the illness, since illness usually involves some sort of suffering. Deviants are assumed to suffer from their deviance and to want help.[11]

The distinctions between these two ideologies are summarized in Table 4.

The Outlaw Ideology

To this point we have not discussed the outlaw ideology because it has several special qualities which require our attention before we can compare it to the other two. Perhaps most obviously, the outlaw ideology mandates the activities of deviants rather than control agents. While there are major differences between the punishment ideology model and the treatment ideology, at least they both agree that a good and orderly society is a major goal. The outlaw ideology is not explicitly hostile to the maintenance of social order, but it sees that goal as definitely subsidiary to the development of the free and even

TABLE 4   Three Ideologies of Deviance and Control

Subject/Ideology	Punishment	Treatment	Outlaw
1. Relevant ennobled group	Law enforcement and court-related personnel	Psychiatrist and psychiatrically oriented therapists	Addicts
2. General mandating value	Justice	Health	Freedom
3. Institutional supports	Law	Psychiatry and the social sciences	Rock music and popular stories
4. Focus of social control	Behavior	Condition or status	Political needs
5. Limits on social control	Individual rights	Individual needs and professional responsibility	The power of the oppressed
6. Deviants relation to society	Adversarial	Submissive-needs help	Adversarial
7. Reasons for deviance	Hedonism	Sickness	Honor and self-expression

heroic individual. Historically, the outlaw ideology draws sustenance from the traditional argument about the conflict between personal liberty and social order. Sociologists have often taken substantive positions on one side or the other of this conflict. We, however, are not concerned here with whether our society needs more liberty or more order, but with uses of the ideological positions by the addicts and the control agents.

The history of the argument between personal liberty and social order begins at least with Plato's writings on the trial of Socrates. Although there are roots of this conflict in Greek and Christian philosophy, the modern argument begins with Hobbes. In response to the increasingly individualistic view of moral obligations which was spawned by Reformation theology, Hobbes asked his famous question: What is to prevent the war of all against all? His answer was to depend on the absolute power of the sovereign. Rousseau's image of the Noble Savage in the State of Nature provided an image which the outlaw ideology drew from. The American Constitution, deeply influenced by the natural-rights philosophies, institutionalized in the United States the concept of power as a danger to that liberty which was essential to liberate the inherent good in each of us.

The French Revolution provided further impetus to this development. The revolutionaries, as spokespersons for the emerging bourgeoisie, were eager to do away with all of the feudal regulations which they believed interfered with the freedom of humankind in general and the bourgeois economic individual in particular. The state suppressed the true freedoms of man which were necessary to make everyone happy.

In some ways, this trend of thinking was enhanced by the response of the English liberals to what they saw as the excesses of the French Revolution. The French radicals did not see any opposition between the individual and their new state. Since the people made up the state, how was it possible that the state should oppress the people? (Kirk, 1955) John S. Mill, in his *On Liberty,* reemphasized the idea of the state's opposition to the individual even when the state belonged to the people as a whole. The only justification for the state's intervention in the affairs of an individual was the protection of another citizen.

However, nowhere was the belief in personal liberty so all encompassing as in America. The founding document of the Revolution claimed that the purposes of government are to encourage "life, liberty, and the pursuit of happiness." It has even been suggested that these beliefs constitute part of an American "civil religion." (Bellah, 1967). American culture has spawned a mythology of a perfectly free individual, the outlaw, whose activities inevitably lead to conflict with the state. The American value of *individualism* is an important component of this mythology. The myth of the outlaw and its associated ideology stands in radical contrast to both the punishment and the treatment ideologies. For both of those latter ideologies, the suppression of deviance is an inherent goal. For the outlaw ideology, deviance is often an expression of human freedom, and its suppression is itself evil.

Another important difference between the outlaw ideology and the other two is the nature of contemporary acceptance of the outlaw ideology. Although the concept of personal freedom has enormous support throughout the modern West, and particularly in the United States, ideological support for the concept of an outlaw is another matter. When most Americans speak of personal freedom, they do not mean freedom to be an outlaw. The prototypical referents in academic and conventional writing on individualism have usually been people like Andrew Carnegie, Henry David Thoreau, and beatnik poets, not outlaws. Robert Bellah (1975) puts it well, noting that the original notion of liberty in the American colonies was that one should have the liberty to do right.

The outlaw ideology lacks any formal authoritative integrated statement at all. It is true that some of Nietzsche and certain writings in the sociological theory of deviance can be read as supportive of the outlaw's moral schemas.[12] But if these writers support the outlaws, those who practice the outlaw lifestyle do not draw their ideology from these writers. Although many addicts do read somewhat and some have even been to college, their reading matter rarely is so intellectual. Even those who might have read Nietzsche or Becker did not relate to their works in the way that clinicians did to Freud or Dole and Nyswander and the lawyers did to legal theorists or Supreme Court rulings. In the case of addicts, if they came upon someone who had written something that expressed their views on the matter, they might comment on it, but their views did not derive from it. For clinicians and lawyers, reading the views of one theorist or another was often an important turning point in their lives.

The outlaw ideology has drawn its general societal support as an expression of personal freedom and American individualism from popular stories in the form of detective and western novels and movies. (Nelson, 1976: Ch. 3). Perhaps its most sophisticated renditions are in the lyrics of the rock music of the 1960s, particularly the works of Bob Dylan and the Rolling Stones, and the country music of the 1970s, particularly the songs of Willie Nelson and Waylon Jennings. These stories ennoble the outlaw. He is the heroic figure wronged by the "powers that be." One of the purest renditions of this moral schema that we have been able to find is Woody Guthrie's song "Pretty Boy Floyd."

It tells the story of Pretty Boy Floyd, who becomes an outlaw by protecting his wife's honor against a deputy sheriff. In a fight with the deputy, he kills him. There follow a number of stories about Pretty Boy Floyd's generosity to farmers threatened by foreclosure and the poor on "relief." The conclusion of the song is that while you can be robbed with a pistol or a fountain pen, outlaws don't drive families from their homes.

The common theme of the outlaw moral schema is heroic struggle against impossible odds. The outlaw typically begins a criminal career as an effort to right a wrong caused by a person with political power. This almost invariable ends up as a hopeless effort. The system is stacked against the person, and he or she ends up being labeled an outlaw and expelled from conventional society. To remain an outlaw and live by illegal means in order to survive is therefore the only option (Cleckner, 1977: 158). The outlaw, however, maintains a personal war against power and privilege and for the persecuted. These efforts are appreciated by the poor and resented by the rich and the powerful, who must spend substantial proportions of their time, energy, and resources hunting the outlaw or paying others to hunt him or her.

A slight variant of the story is the outlaw who is outlawed because of personal nature. Outlaws are too full of life or enjoy themselves too much. Once again, however, their real crime is crossing the rich and the powerful. He seduces the rich man's daughter; she fails to cower in front of the politically powerful.

The myth of the outlaw is at least as old as Robin Hood, but nowhere has it thrived as much as in the United States. Movies such as "Butch Cassidy and the Sundance Kid," "One Eyed Jacks," "One Flew Over the Cuckoo's Nest," "Steelyard Blues," and "Electric Horseman" all draw on this theme. All of these stories demonstrate that the outlaw is a personification of personal freedom and individualism.

The outlaw ideology is not only grounded and learned differently, it has a different structure. Outlaw ideology is probably better described as a mythological system than as an ideology. It takes the form of a theme of a series of stories rather than a series of direct propositional statements about the world. Lévi-Strauss (1967, 1969) has described the ways in which primitive mythological systems can be used as quasi-scientific theories which generate expectations about how the world will respond if certain procedures are performed. In a similar manner, we are proposing that this myth is used as a moral schema in doing the moral work of deviance validation.

The story of the outlaw functions as a basis for a moral schema which serves as an orientation point for the addicts in much the same manner that the other two ideologies function as moral points of orientation for their respective mandated groups. It provides answers to the same questions as the other two ideologies, but it operates by analogy rather than by deduction.

While the punishment and treatment ideologies debate the abstract question of the responsibility of individuals for their actions, the outlaw ideology treats it as an individualized question. In the outlaw ideology, the issue of responsibility is moot for most people. The average citizen never expresses her or himself, but simply conforms to conventional expectations. One who does not "really" act cannot be responsible for his or her acts. The outlaw freely chooses to fight the system. If he or she does not willingly become an outlaw, at least the act of rebellion is by personal choice and the realization of the risks involved. Yet in the end, the outlaw's life and fate are determined by factors much larger than her or himself. An outlaw is doomed in spite of resourcefulness and righteousness. The only question is how long it will take. The outlaw is responsible for his or her actions, but not for his or her fate.[13]

Nowhere does the outlaw ideology differ as radically from our other two ideologies as in its images of the agents of social control. For the other two ideologies, the rectitude and good intentions of the agents of social control are never in serious question. The outlaw ideology sees only political convenience in the actions of the social-control agents. While the outlaw shares the legal concept of the opposition between her or himself and the agents of control, the two ideologies differ radically in regard to the moving force behind the confrontation. The outlaw sees the social-control agents as persecuting him or her for political convenience, whereas the punishment and treatment ideologies believe that the control agents are forced to act by the behavior of the outlaw and their obligations to Law or the patient's welfare.

Furthermore, the outlaw does not see any basic differences between the punishment and treatment methods of control. They are both means of limiting freedom. Whether one or the other is more effective at it is not a relevant distinction (Walker, 1972).

Finally, the outlaw ideology differs from the other two ideologies on the basic motivations for deviance. While the outlaw ideology does not deny hedonism as a motivating force in an outlaw's actions, the basic motives are much grander. The prominent ones are honor and self-expression. The idea of sickness, prominent in the treatment ideology, does not enter into the outlaw's formulations of his motives at all. If anything is sick, it is the society.

Before we leave the discussion of the outlaw ideology, two points should be clarified which might help the reader understand our enterprise. First, the reader may find it peculiar that outlaw ideology shares so little with the expressive passivist moral schema outlined in the previous chapter. The answer is, however, not particularly obscure. The moral crisis involved focusing attention on "drug use" and thus glossing the distinction between groups which shared very little in common. It is precisely our point in the previous chapter that the attack on heroin users was an attack on a group which was essentially uninvolved in the moral conflicts between instrumental activism and expressive passivism. The addicts served only as a societal symbol for expressive passivists.

A second peculiarity of this model is that it treats the ideologies of deviant groups and control groups as parallel. Moreover, the chapters that follow will analyze the interactions between deviants and types of control agents in analytically parallel ways. The notion that the relationship between a cop and an addict should be analyzed in the same way as the relationship between the prosecutor and the treatment specialist is certainly unusual. However, it must be remembered that we are not searching for the cause of deviance, but trying to describe the use of ideological moral schemas in deviance validation and the effect of the deviance validation process on societal moral schemas about drug use and users. *The deviance validation process is one into which all three groups have input.* No group is either privileged in its importance to the process or analytically uninteresting. This is not to say that there are no differences in these relationships, only that we want to know the same thing about each of them.

Accommodative Moral Schemas and the Limits of Ideologies

Ideologies play an extremely important role in the system of interactions that we will analyze in the next three chapters. They provide the actors with a sense of meaning for the roles they play. To a large extent, they also provide moral orientation for the actors involved. This aspect of ideology, as we noted above, has been discussed many times in the literature of delinquent subcultures.

There are, however, many reasons to believe that simply describing these conflicting ideologies will not suffice as a means of describing the actions between these groups. First, as Matza (1964) has noted, this will overpredict the amount of conflict between the groups. To cite only a few of the anomalies that cannot be explained: (1) addicts would sometimes volunteer for treatment, and even when coerced into treatment they would sometimes voluntarily follow the clinicians's directives; (2) policemen would sometimes pass up viable arrests of known addicts without receiving any information in return; (3) the clinic would occasionally press the police to make more arrests; (4) prosecutors in Riverdale rarely demanded punishments for addicts, but encouraged them to get treatment.

In spite of the fact that the three ideologies define the three groups as in conflict with each other, clinicians, addicts, and law enforcement personnel often found it necessary to cooperate with each other in one enterprise or another. In order to perform their daily tasks, they could not be in a constant state of conflict. Even their conflicting goals often required a minimal degree of cooperation. This would not be possible if all of the expressive symbolism that they used in their encounters were drawn from their ideologies.

At this point, it might be objected that we are overstating the matter. While it is true that the punishment and outlaw ideologies mandate conflict with each other, the treatment ideology does not do so. It expresses a serious concern for the well-being of the addict and mandates an effort to improve his life. What is more, it does not express any particular hostility for the agents mandated by the punishment ideology, only the belief that their efforts are misguided.

Yet this barely mitigates the conflicts between the treatment agents and the law-enforcement agents and the addicts. Both the addicts and the law-enforcement personnel believed in the essential importance of their enterprises. The addict could not, consistent with his ideology, accept a role as the passive recipient of the benevolent doctor's treatment of the addict's failings.

So despite the fact that the three ideologies proclaim that oppositional or at least competitive relationships between the three groups are a moral necessity, they had to interact peacefully and even cooperatively at times. Indeed, precisely *because* they are opponents or competitors they had to cooperate. Like two football teams playing a game, some cooperation was a necessary prelude and aftermath to the conflict.

In order for any two groups whose ideologies mandate conflict to cooperate, they require some sort of shared moral schema about their interaction which facilitates cooperation with the opposition even if it does not require it. We will call this type of moral schema an "accommodative schema." Accommodative schemas must perform at least two functions. They must provide one or many reference points which allow and facilitate cooperative action. They must also provide the actors with ways of neutralizing the binds of their mandating ideologies so that they are released from the moral obligations inherent in those ideologies. This applied equally to addicts, prosecutors, drug counselors, and all the other ideologically mandated role occupants whom we studied.

What we are proposing by the notion of accommodative schemas is to take symbolic interactionism as an explanation of deviance and control more seriously than labeling theory typically does. Almost without exception, labeling theorists have tried to account for the deviant behavior of the deviant actor as a result of the label imposed on the deviant by the society in the person of the social control agent. The behavior of the social control agent, on the other hand, is accounted for in terms of societal demands, its bureaucratic structure, the personality structure of the social control agents, historical patterns, law, professional ethics, or some other factor external to the interactive system composed of the deviant and the social control agent.[14] We have no doubt that these factors are very important in explaining the control agent's behavior, and our model recognizes some of those in the form of ideologies. But it is hard to understand why the behavior of deviants and control agents should be explained by such radically different factors.

Sociological literature is not entirely devoid of truly interactionist studies of deviance and control. Gresham Sykes's (1958) brilliant study of prisons shows beautifully the nature of the accommodation between prisoners and guards. Werthman and Piliavin (1967) come close to recognizing the reciprocity between police and street gangs. Lemert's (1962) study of paranoia, while heavily emphasizing the persecution of the "paranoid," does show some concerns for the "paranoid's" input into the "conspiracy" against him. There are several less-known studies of police work that are truly interactionist

(Jackson, 1967; Lidz, 1974; Walsh, 1975). Danet (1971) does study the interaction between nondeviant clients and bureaucrats in roughly the manner we are proposing. But these are isolated fragments, not a coherent body of truly interactionist studies of deviance and control in the society.

Part of the reason for this asymmetry in the study of the deviance validation process is the belief that the social-control agents have more coercive ability to affect the behavior of the control agent. This, as we will show, is no more necessarily true about police and addicts or clinicians and addicts than it was about Sykes's guards and prisoners. As Sir James Frazier noted, the king is every bit as constrained in the presence of the peasant as the peasant is in the presence of the king.[15] Addicts were perfectly capable of causing both police and clinicians to give up their ideologically prescribed rhetoric, and to behave in ways that would not be ideologically acceptable.

This point can be clarified somewhat by reference to Figure 7, complex as it is. Much of the model shown in this figure involves the ideologies and the roles that they mandate which we have discussed in this chapter. Ideologies A and B can be any of the three we have discussed, but for the moment let us use them to stand for the punishment ideology and the outlaw ideology respectively. These ideologies, as we have noted, have both historical and current relationships with the societal moral schemas. Analyses of interaction have often been done by treating societal moral prescriptions of roles as though they were the primary orientation points for actors functioning in a particular situation. Parsons's (1951) analysis of the doctor-patient relationship is a classic in this tradition. Durkheim's notions of the "non-contractual elements of contract" also implies this model. Whatever virtues such an analysis may have for analyzing interaction between two actors where the moral nature of one actor or his activities is not an issue, we will see in Chapter IV that this is not totally adequate here.

Labeling theory can be described in terms of Figure 7 as believing that ideology A (the social control agent's ideology) is the critical variable. Becker (1963) particularly treats ideology

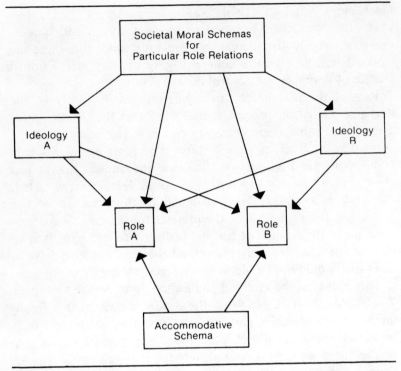

Figure 7

A and the societal moral schemas as largely identical. His analysis of deviant behavior is that the deviant role (role B) is largely a result of ideology A, the social-control agent's ideology. The "label" is ideology A's prescription of role B. Although Becker recognizes ideology B and its formulation of roles A and B when he speaks of the deviants seeing the society as outsiders (Becker, 1963: 2), this ideology seems to be largely impotent in Becker's view in that it does not have much to do with the behavior of either party in the deviance validation process. Most sociologists of deviance seem to assume that the social control agents' role (A) is not seriously affected by ideology B.

We find that labeling model too simple. It ignores the fact that there are societal moral schemas that serve as reference points for interaction between role incumbents A and B which are quite different from the role prescriptions contained in ideology A. For example, in recent years the law has moved substantially away from the policeman's ideology in specifying the role relationships between police and suspects. Although the effect of the law on this role relationship has not been very great (Yale Law Journal, 1967; Lidz, 1974b; Williams, 1975), neither can it be entirely ignored. The same can be said of the recent developments in informed consent law and malpractice for the relationship between doctor and patient (Meisel, 1977).

However, from our point of view, the most critical failure of both labeling theory and more traditional arguments that depend on the societal moral schemas is that they do not take account of the fact that there is often an emergent and ongoing *accommodation* between the role incumbents who are mandated by the two different ideologies. If our interest is in explaining the patterns of interaction between deviants and control agents and between different types of control agents in the deviance validation process, these emergent accommodations cannot be ignored. The three chapters that follow try to spell out, in three analytically different contexts, the development of and the nature of these accommodations.

The specific accommodative models that we will be describing and their relations to the three ideologies are shown in Figure 8. The "welfare schema" regulated the interactions between clinicians and the addicts. The schema which we call "therapeutic control" regulated relationships between the clinic and the law-enforcement community. Finally, an accommodation schema focused on the concept of "fairness" regulated interaction between those mandated by the punishment ideology and those mandated by the outlaw ideology. This last involves two concrete relationships: the police addict interactions and the interactions between prosecutors and what we call the outlaw-lawyers.

In the next three chapters, we intend to give the notion of accommodation models some concrete meaning by explaining these concrete examples. Each chapter will focus not only on a different accommodation, but on a different aspect of the

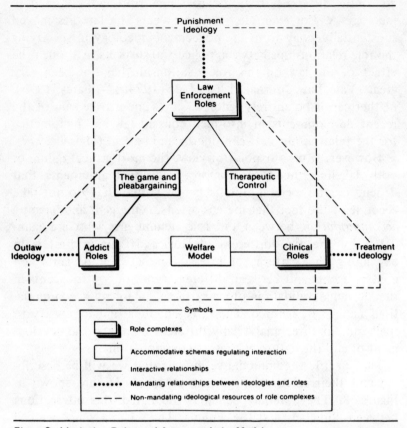

Figure 8: Ideologies, Roles, and Accommodative Models

accommodation process. Therapeutic control will be discussed with special reference to the relationship between court and clinic as organized systems, and interactional particulars will be mentioned only when necessary. The fairness chapter will concentrate on the nature of the interactions themselves in much more detail. The welfare schema will be considered particularly with reference to the way in which such an accommodation can be built into the structure of an organization, namely, the N.A.U. The decision to focus only on aspects of each accommodation was dictated by a number of factors. While in principle the three accommodations could all have been described identically, it would have required a great deal more space and would not have added to our theoretical understanding of the accommodation process.

NOTES

1. In the nineteenth century, the study of the statistics of crime, insanity, suicide, etc., was called the study of moral statistics. The name was more appropriate than its users may have realized.

2. See Harold Garfinkel's (1967: 76-103) discussion of this phenomenon.

3. One way of summarizing much of this discussion of the looseness of these ideologies is to say that the actors usually used concrete operations rather than formal operations in thinking about their practical problems. (Piaget and Inhelder, 1958; Flavell, 1963; Lidz and Lidz, 1976).

4. Of course, as Weber demonstrated, this doctrine not only provided a new moral orientation for a more complex society, but was critical in producing that society.

5. One interesting thing that Rothman (1971) records is that the early American asylum superintendents had an obsessive concern with the causes of mental disorder rather than treatment or study of the disease process. We believe that this is best understood by seeing that the new secular moral schemas of deviance could accept the whole Calvinist account of deviance except the idea that God willed the deviance. The source of the deviance had to be naturalized.

6. Coates v. Cincinnati and Powell v. Texas.

7. Alcoholism, juvenile crime, homosexuality, child molesting, and child abuse are some other prominent boundary areas.

8. Compare this to Matza (1964: Ch. 1).

9. See Rothman (1971) for a discussion of the American roots of this variant ideology.

10. The distinction here is admittedly quite tricky. The law is, of course, concerned with motives. The absence of intent vitiates most crimes. But the concern is with intent, not with personality state. Whether a murderer is insane or not is irrelevant. What is relevant is, depending on the formal criterion used, whether the murderer appreciated what the consequences of the act would be, whether that person knew right from wrong, or some other measure of intention.

11. Christian theology would, of course, have the deviant suffering after death rather than in this life, but fear of hellfire should yield the same result. Of course, in Calvinist theology Man can do nothing about his own salvation—a position which corresponds to biological schools of deviance (Lombroso, 1918; Ferrie, 1917, Kraeplin, 1902). American thought has always been more comfortable with the Wesleyan and Arminian positions that man participates in his own salvation (Lipset, 1963: Ch. 4) and has generally expected that therapy can be successful.

12. See particularly the various works of Howard Becker. If we properly understand his presidential address to the Society for the Study of Social Problems, "Whose Side Are We On," Becker would like to be seen as expressing the ideological position of the deviant population, although his writings are not quite as generally oppositional as the outlaw ideology we describe here.

13. Here too there are some interesting parallels to the Calvinist notion of nonresponsibility for election or nonelection. Matza (1964) also notes the Latin and Greek origins of the belief in fate.

14. For example, Goffman (1961) explains psychiatrists' behavior largely in terms of the medical model and the patient in terms of his interaction with the hospital. Skolnick (1966) explains police behavior in terms of legal constraint, "working personality," organizational ideology and values, and organizational structure. Even when, for example, Skolnick brings in the behavior of prostitutes, it comes in terms of policemen's beliefs about their behavior. Certainly this last qualification may be warranted, but it is difficult to see why explanations of deviant behavior are not similarly explained in terms of the deviant's perception of the label.

15. Parsons and Bales (1955: 48, n. 18) tried to answer a similar objection from Albert Reiss, who suggested that the child's dependency on the parent confers equal or greater power on the child. Their response was that we must discriminate between two things often called power. They were speaking only of "relative importance in carrying out the functional performance of the system," in this case, carrying out the socialization of the child. The other sense, "ability to cause trouble by threatening to disrupt the system," is the basis of the child's power. While this may be useful for their purposes, it does not help here. We are concerned with the ability to cause the other side to accommodate one's definition of appropriate behavior.

Chapter 4

PUNISHMENT-OUTLAW RELATIONSHIPS

In this chapter, we begin describing the relationships between groups mandated by conflicting ideological schemas and their use of accommodative schemas to allow some types of cooperation. Specifically, in this chapter we want to describe that part of deviance validation which involves those mandated by outlaw and punishment ideologies. Moreover, this chapter will focus particularly on the social psychological details of the interactions around the moral schema both as foci of orientation and as ongoing accomplishments of the actors. The next two chapters will then focus more on the organizational and systemic aspects of ideology and accommodation.

Let us begin, however, with the very structural observation that probably the most important statement that can be made about heroin use in America over the last half century is that it has been illegal.[1] Heroin use is not simply illegal in the pro forma way that adultery is; it is actively suppressed. Thus over that period, relatively stable patterns of interaction have emerged about the legal control of drug use (Lindesmith, 1965; Burroughs, 1953). Those patterns tie together the activities of an extremely heterogeneous collectivity of people: addicts (and para-addicts), police, defense attorneys, prosecuting attorneys, probation officers, judges, and so on. In this chapter, we will analyze these interactions with reference to the Drug Crisis that was discussed in Chapter 1.

In a sense, we are confronted with a matrix of relationships (prosecutor-defense attorney, prosecutor-cop, cop-addict, and so on), each of which could be approached separately. But the analysis can be somewhat simplified by the fact that each of the positions in this network is mandated or ennobled by either the outlaw or the punishment ideology. More specifically, all of the positions we would call agents of the law (police, probation officers, and prosecutors) are ennobled by the punishment ideology, while addicts and some defense attorneys are ennobled by the outlaw ideology. The relationships of primary concern, for our purposes, are those which entail the interaction of two parties ennobled by different ideologies. Interactions of this sort will be termed law-outlaw interactions. The two primary instances of these relationships are interactions between prosecuting and defense attorneys, and between police and addicts.

Given the moral nature of ideologies, each ideology (punishment and outlaw) provides any subscriber with an idealized schema of how law-outlaw interactions should proceed. Since our purpose here is to understand how those interactions *actually* proceeded, our first analytic task is to describe the specific ideological schemas about how *these* interactions should take place. Then we will try to show how and why the actual interactions deviated from the ideologically given models.

Ideological Models of Law-Outlaw Interaction

The addict's ideology portrays an addict as an essentially passive participant in the relationship with the police (Gould et al., 1974: 52-59). The addict has done nothing to the cop, but the cop pursues and harasses the addict anyway. The cop, in the addict's stereotype, is motivated by "political" considerations. A cop needs the "bust" to please the boss and advance in the police hierarchy.

Moreover, the cop is stupid. The outlaw's only real defense is being cleverer than the cop. Addicts also believe that they can count on the cops never to leave them alone because, even should they stop using heroin and "go straight," the cop would not or could not cease the persecution (Gould et al., 1974: 59). "Going straight" is not a real possibility. The trouble is not self-motivation, but rather the unwillingness of the law to leave him alone.

The policeman's professional ideology agrees about the possibility of the addict going straight (Gould et al., 1974: 80). It greets any such claims from an addict (or any other source) with considerable skepticism. The addict cannot reform because of weakness, and must be watched because an addict is bound to continue his criminal ways. For policemen to do otherwise is to renege on their duty.

In the policeman's professional ideology, the policeman's role is to "fight crime" and protect the innocent citizen. The ideology bifurcates society into criminals and citizens. The former "prey on" the latter. The citizenry's only defense against the criminal is the police, although, unfortunately, many citizens do not recognize this (Gould et al., 1974: 70). Addicts provide perhaps the best example of the criminal character.

Both ideologies permit differentiation between types of addicts and types of police. To the vice squad policemen, addicts have varying degrees of degeneracy and troublesomeness. That they are all morally corrupt is not in question, but some are particularly so. The addict also finds all policemen reprehensible and dangerous, but some are smarter and more dangerous than others. "Narcs" and undercover agents are particularly evil and dangerous, and some particular "narcs" more dangerous than others (Gould et al., 1974: 53-57).

Interaction between the confirmed junkie and the narc must involve a confrontation. Ideologically, the committed outlaw "has no truck" with a narc unless forced to do so. The junkie despises the cop as a tool of the Man. The cop equally can find nothing ideologically pleasant about relating to a junkie. In the policeman's professional ideology, any confrontation with a junkie that does not involve arrest, or at least information, can only be seen as a failure. To the junkie, any contact at all with the police is an unfortunate occurrence.[2]

The prosecutor's ideology requires that he or she protect the public and see that the guilty are punished. A prosecutor relies on the police to capture the guilty and marshal the basic elements of the case against the criminal. Knowing that the police are also trying to catch those who are guilty, if they say the person they have arrested is an addict, the prosecutor is obligated to presume this is so. The prosecutor, as the legal specialist of the law enforcement team, tries to see that arrests are made in ways that conform to the technical legalities necessary for a successful prosecution. However, the ideologically-given goal of the prosecutor is to see that the public order is preserved,and that generally means the prosecution and conviction of as many criminals as possible. Because of their intimate involvement with all types of crime, addicts must be considered primary candidates for the most severe sentences.

The prosecutor's relations with defense attorneys are supposed to be those of colleagues, but since many defense attorneys stubbornly insist on blocking the processes of justice at every turn, these relations are often strained. Many defense attorneys must be dealt with as enemies. While prosecutors recognize the necessity of having someone represent the defense, they also feel that the legal tricks that the defense attorney often uses do not serve the interests of the public.

The prosecution focuses its work on the trial, although some defendants see the futility of a trial in their case and plead guilty. The prosecutor may agree to remind the judge of this before sentencing, since it shows some sign of an inclination toward repentance.

The defense attorney who draws a professional identity from the outlaw ideology[3] sees the goal as providing the defendant with the best conceivable defense. This is a defense attorney's constitutional duty. The defendant, although perhaps technically guilty of the charges, is fundamentally innocent, a victim of police harassment and, at a more basic level, of the society in general. The society never provided the defendant a chance to succeed. Furthermore, the police, welfare, and all the other bureaucracies alien to the defendant's culture have continually refused even to leave her or him alone. In the face of this persecution, the defendant needs an advocate, and any legal efforts to keep such a person out of jail are reasonable. The defense attorney's primary effort, of course, goes into good trial work. The trial is the major arena for relieving the pressure on the defendant. Preparation involves careful analysis of the case with reference to both the substantive issues of guilt and the legal and constitutional issues. The latter are particularly important because winning on these grounds helps keep the police under control and is an important exercise of the defendant's constitutional rights.[4] It also strikes a small blow for the remaining minimal degree of freedom left in the society.

The defense attorney's version of the outlaw ideology involves representing the outlaw, and the attorney works in the client's interest. Through the use of constitutionally safeguarded procedures, the defender has a chance of defeating the oppressive machinery of the state, although in the long run, the state is bound to prove stronger. The defense attorney believes the best chance of winning against the prosecution and the police is by cunning, but each battle for the client is at best a Pyrrhic victory. Each successive rearrest makes it harder to keep the client out of jail.

The reader might have noticed by now that all of the above accounts of these various relationships cannot be true in any simple sense of the word.[5] They are blatantly inconsistent accounts. They are not our descriptions of the people and events involved in these relationships, but rather moral schemas that mandate the activities of certain groups. As mandating ideologies, they ennoble the speaker's role in the process. Like the moral crisis, these ideological schemas make the activities

involved significant and important, elevate the moral character
of the speaker, and degrade the moral character and motives of
the "opponent." The cause of the ugliness in the events is the
opponent; the glory and nobility comes from the speaker and
the speaker's associates. This is not to say that this sort of
ideology can be dismissed as pure egotism, for these ideologies
invest the activities we are interested in with their "worthwhile-
ness."

However, in spite of the importance of these ideologies, they
do not exhaust the moral schemas that these actors use. Events
do not always transpire the way ideologies would suggest, even
given the flexibility of these schemas. Prosecutors may find it in
their immediate interest to forsake their adversarial relationship
with defense attorneys, and vice versa. Likewise police and
addicts may find advantages in cooperation. The nature of this
cooperation and the moral schemas that make it possible within
the contest of conflicting ideologies provide the major focus of
this chapter.

The "Game" as an Accommodative Model

Let us now look at the nature of the accommodative schemas
that facilitate law-outlaw interactions.[6] Evidence of these
accommodations was not the sort of thing that a researcher
could pick up in a brief interview with one or another participant. The cooperations between such institutionalized enemies
as cops and junkies and lawyers and prosecutors was something
like a trade secret. Many studies of police, for example, have
been done without seemingly noting the types of cooperation
which we will describe here.[7] As a trade secret, the accommodative schemas were generally not shared in front of strangers,
including social scientists. Nonetheless, if one observes enough
of their day-to-day activities, it becomes almost impossible to
hide these accommodations, since they are integral and functional parts of their routines.

Generally, there were two different major foci to the accommodative schemas which became important in different types of

situations. "Fairness" was the basis for moral rhetoric in inter-active situations involving opponents. Pragmatism was the basis for justifying cooperation to one's associates. Let us start with "fairness."

Fairness and the Cop-Addict Game

Between the addict and the vice-squad detectives, interaction was often spoken of as a "game."[8] This formulation was also an "insider's" way of describing the motives of the opposition. However, its principal use was as a moral schema for talking to the opposition in certain types of situations. The analogy is to a game such as football where only one side can gain at a time. When one side gains, the other side loses.[9] In game theory, this is called a zero-sum game.

In this descriptive context, several potential points of conflict were neutralized. One of these was the moral quality of both sides. There was a kind of live-and-let-live assumption built into the game model. In particular instances of police-addict inter-action, both sides acted as though, whatever general moral dislikes they may have had for each other, they did not apply in the present situation. They spoke as though ideological schemas of opposition were as far from their minds as they would be if they were just two teams playing a game of hockey. Moral evaluations of one another sometimes worked their way into the discussion, but almost exclusively in the practical claim of "unfair" play or "not playing by the rules." As in a football game, some participants played more fairly than others, but the moral quality of the opposition was *achieved* in the game, not *ascribed* to their status. Sometimes, of course, in the context of talking about what is happening between them, the subject of their respective moral statuses as cop and addict came up. In this case, the moral issues were avoided by claiming that, unlike other addicts (cops), the particular addict (cop) that the cop (addict) was talking to had always been fair in his dealings with the speaker. Of course, the context in which this type of rhetoric was used is quite restricted and relations between police and addicts often looked more like two linemen in the midst of a football game than two linemen having beers together after the game. We must emphasize that the accommo- dative schemas we observed, including the police-addict game, were not descriptive of what actually happens, but moral resources which were used in formulating motives by the parti- cipants.

Another potential problem that was neutralized in the game model was whose side the actor is on. Whether an actor is a cop or a junkie was every bit as clear as if he were wearing a jersey. On the surface, this seems like a rather uninteresting observa- tion, except when its ramifications for the role of the police in the legal system are considered. Formally, the law presumes the innocence of the defendant until guilt is der..onstrated "beyond a reasonable doubt." Since, in Riverdale, less than 10% of the narcotics arrests resulted in any sort of formal trial,[10] this legally mandated presumption of innocence was not often struc- turally supported by courtroom procedures. The police pre- sumption that an officer could always "spot" a junkie was rarely contested in court.

Perhaps equally interesting, the game model's assumption of two unequivocal sides was not totally warranted. Undercover agents are good examples of actors who appeared to be on one side and are "really" on the other. Indeed, some undercover agents find that their loyalties are peculiarly ambivalent, and more than one has been known to quit the police force and change sides, especially in the political cases. Informers are another interesting case that we will discuss more later on.

The concept of a game implies rules. It was not unusual for a policeman to say to an addict who had just been arrested, "If you want to play this game, you've got to play by the rules," but we never observed the specification of these "rules" in any detail by either side. While it is true that there were certain actions which regularly seemed to call forth condemnations,[11] they were not very numerous. Indeed, it is reasonable to hypoth- esize that there were few true rules to the game. There was no referee to decide who had broken them and no rule book to refer to. Rather, the moral element around which this typical situation was organized was the value of fairness. Sometimes, when listening to cops and junkies argue about an arrest, one could come to the conclusion that as long as the activities of both sides met the criterion of fairness, they had no personal concern with the outcome. While this was certainly not true, most negotiations about whether or not an addict should cooperate or a policeman make an arrest were formulated in terms of fairness. For example:

> We pushed open the door and entered the apartment. Two women and a man stood there and watched us somewhat dazed. "Hey Bull," the man said. "What do you want. I don't do none of that shit anymore."
>
> "Hell you don't, Harold! What you holding that rag on your arm for." Bull pulled the rag away to reveal a bloody arm. "You just got off."
>
> They searched the apartment, and one of the women followed Bull everywhere, presumably to see that he didn't plant a bag somewhere. All they found was a paper bag with a set of works in it.
>
> Bull finally said, "Well, one of you is gonna have to take the rap for this stuff. Mitzi, are these yours? (Mitzi denied it.) Sandy, are these yours? (she also denied it.) Well then, Harold, I guess I'm gonna have to take you in."
>
> "That ain't fair, they ain't mine."
>
> "Whose are they then? (no response.) Well, they got to be somebody's, they didn't just walk in the door."
>
> "Well, I don't know, but they ain't mine."
>
> "Look, you gotta play fair. Someone is gotta take this bust, and if you can't agree on anyone else, I'm gonna give you a chance to be a gentleman and take this bust for the ladies."
>
> "Thanks Bull, you're all heart."

Or, in the case of a raid on a crap game:

> It was a small game with only five people in or near it. Al got out of the car and told them that he was going to arrest them all. This was

immediately followed by a series of exclamations: "What for?" "I wasn't doing nothing!" "Aww, Al, what you doing that for?" Since only three were in the center of the game, the other two were protesting loudest and two of the center circle players supported one of them. Al said: "Okay, you can go, if Jimmy and Hooch say so, I'll take their word." The others continued to protest but Al just said: "I'm playing fair, now you guys have gotta play fair too." Eventually, only the one remaining "outsider" still objected and was doing so in a quiet, morose tone. While waiting for the police van the rest joked a bit, occasionally objecting. Finally, as the van arrived, one of the gamers said to Al: "Hey, Al, he was just watching, really!" Al turned to another gamer that he apparently knew and said, "I'm gonna take you in anyway, but I'll let him go if you tell me he was just passing through." With some hesitation, everyone agreed he was not in the game.

The concept of fairness was an important part of these interactions in two ways. First, it functioned as a means of expressing conflict in a way that does not call for immediate confrontation. Built into the concept of fairness was an inherent vagueness about just which actions are fair. This allowed an argument about the appropriate evaluation of almost any activity. In a situation that was typically deeply charged with hostility, these arguments functioned as means of expression of the hostilities. They provided a rhetorical basis for the anger that is different from the mandating ideologies of both sides. Since the mandating ideologies of each side were structured so as to degrade the opposition, violent confrontations would be almost impossible to avoid if rhetoric were to stay true to those ideologies. Generally, both sides were happy to avoid fights.

Perhaps more important than the above, the value of fairness also provided a small measure of moral regulation to the interaction between vice-squad detectives and addicts. This came about because the value of fairness provided a moral reference point in the ongoing negotiations between the two groups. Indeed, it was precisely because the claim that something is "unfair" seemed to require a response that negotiations tended to get started. On the other hand, it must be reemphasized that it was never clear what fairness entailed. Thus to say that fairness regulated the interaction must not be understood as saying that certain prescribed procedures were followed and certain predetermined decisions were made when the value was invoked. Fairness only provided an agreed-upon reference point for the negotiations.

However, the very vagueness of the value also enhanced its usefulness as a negotiating tool. What particular resolution actually emerged between the two parties was apparently dependent on many situational factors which directly affected the power balance between them. All cop-addict interactive situations were not treated the same. If, for instance, the detectives found fifty bags of heroin in the addict's pocket after entering his apartment with a valid search warrant, the addict was not likely to try to claim that any arrest would be unfair. An addict in such a situation would consider it a stroke of luck to negotiate the bond down to under $10,000. The detective, on the other hand, would hardly be willing to listen to a lot of "back talk." If, however, the detective had broken down the door without a warrant and found ten people in the middle of a birthday party, then the detective would feel lucky to get out of the apartment without a complaint on his or her record. The vagueness of the concept of fairness provided a flexible context for the "reasonable" interests of each side to be advanced. "Fair" always meant "fair in light of the circumstances." Just which circumstances were relevant to the situation and the obligations of the participants was an artful creation of the speaker.

Accommodative schemas are not highly ideologized, and thus their values tend to be rather situation specific. The schema that facilitated cooperation between the police and addicts had other components besides "fairness." While that value was the focus of the accommodative schema in situations of confrontation between the two sides, a different set of values was necessary in the situation where the actor was alone with his associates. This can be indicated by the concept of pragmatic justification.

Police and Addict Use of Pragmatic Justification

If a cop were to make any compromises with an addict, it was necessary to be prepared to account for them to fellow detectives or face the objection that he or she was too "soft." Dealings with addicts were most often carried out in the company of other cops. Because so much of this talk with other cops was governed by professional police ideology, which had no real room for compromising, the officer had to find a way to justify such actions in a way that did not too obviously violate the obligations of professional ideology.[12] In Riverdale, the police usually did so by casting ideologically questionable behavior as an instrumental activity, as a means to a generally approved end. Thus a vice-squad detective would explain that she or he passed up an arrest because "we couldn't make it stick (couldn't convict in court) and I've got better things to do than useless paperwork" or because there was "no sense in getting into a big hassle for a petty pinch." In short, the detective accounted for this action as a "practical" decision which may have been unfortunate but was "necessary under the circumstances."

The addict had several ways of handling similar problems. To retain the respect of one's peers, one had to maintain the appearance of a proper outlaw. Since the outlaw ideology presumed a fundamentally adversarial relationship with "The Man," cooperation of any sort required some sort of account to the outlaw's peers.

One method of dealing with cooperation was to hide it from other addicts. This was almost a necessity when "setting up" another addict. The vice-squad detectives understood this to a certain degree and were willing to cooperate. Interestingly, the vice-squad detectives and the addicts discussed the need for secrecy in quite different ways. Addicts saw informing as a shameful activity, while the detectives saw it as dangerous (Gould et al., 1974: 76). Once when we were observing the vice squad trying to convince a young addict to inform on the man for whom he was dealing, the addict objected that "if I do, you guys won't respect me."[13] The detective found his comment very funny. Their world view allowed little grounds for respect for any addict, informer or not, but the addict saw informing as shameful and expected the detectives to see it that way as well.

Informing, which involved "setting up" the arrest of another addict, required secrecy, and if discovered it was generally followed by a loss of status on the part of the addict (cf. Gould et al., 1974: 58-59). However, there was another type of cooperation with the police which the addict did not always feel must be hidden from his or her associates. The vice-squad detectives strongly believed that successful operations required not only specific information about who is holding how much heroin at what specific time (so that they could decide who to arrest), but also general street gossip. They believed they needed to know who was hanging out where and with whom, where people were living, who was new on the scene, how heavy each person's habit was, and so on.

Addicts would sometimes reveal (or even brag) that they shared street gossip with the police, and sometimes the giving of the information occurred in front of another street person. One way addicts handled the discontinuities between these actions and the outlaw ideology was similar to the police's ways of accounting for their cooperation with addicts to other policemen. The addict would present this action as pragmatic, emphasizing that he or she personally was not in control of the situation. The cop had the addict in a position where to minimize risks was the only option. This account thus emphasizes the power of the detective over the addict's life and minimizes the addict's concessions. Implicitly or explicitly the addict was saying that she or he did the only reasonable thing, given the circumstances.

A somewhat more aggressive version of this rhetoric was the claim that in acting as he or she did, the addict was demonstrating the outlaw virtue of cunning. The previously discussed neutralization emphasized the degree to which addicts were in a bind and the power which the detective held over them. How-

ever, here the addict emphasized her or his cleverness in getting
out of the situation, having given up so little. For example:

> "So Smith come up and jacks me up against this wall and I figured I
> was gone because I was holding four half-loads. So I started doing a
> song and dance like I was afraid he was gonna beat me up and he fell
> for it like a baby. He shoved me again and tried to make that ugly
> mug of his look tough and says 'What you gonna give me.' I says 'I'll
> sing, I'll sing, just don't hit me. So I told him that Bunny and Bert
> are dealing on the Avenue which he knew because he already tried to
> bust them and some shit about thinking that they had it taped under
> Bunny's sink. That dumb cop walked away grinning from ear to ear.
> I told Bunny that if he had any stuff in his apartment that he'd
> better get it out and he even left some tape under the sink to cover.
> Smith is an ass."

Plea Bargaining as an Accommodative Model

The problem of how to deal with law-outlaw cooperation is
somewhat more complex in court than in the streets. We noted
earlier in this chapter that there were some defense attorneys
who formulated their roles primarily with reference to the
outlaw ideology. However, others did not. These latter attorneys seemed to see themselves as brokers who negotiated
between their clients and the prosecutor. With reference to the
courts, then, we had two different patterns. In one pattern, the
defense attorney conceived of her or himself as representing the
outlaw and outlaw ideology before the court, while in the other
pattern the defense attorney conceived of her or himself as
mediating between the outlaw and the prosecutor. In the analysis to follow, we will focus on the first pattern (the outlaw
lawyers) rather than the second (mediator lawyers) for analytic
reasons. As closely as we could determine, the major dispositional pattern of drug cases in Riverdale was established through
ongoing interactions between prosecutors and outlaw lawyers.
For the most part, the dispositions reached by mediator lawyers
were substantially the same as those that resulted from the
adversarial negotiations between prosecutors and outlaw law-

yers. Since our present interest is in the emergence of these dispositional alternatives, we feel it appropriate to focus our attention on these negotiations.

As in most cities, the pressure for cooperation between the defense and the prosecution was very strong in the Riverdale court system. The response to this pressure, like all other aspects of the interaction between the defense and the prosecution, took form in the context of the court personnel's private definition of the interactive system between defense and prosecution, which is known as plea bargaining.

While plea bargaining is not quite as much of a trade secret as the police-addict "game"—it has been recently discussed in the New York *Times* as well as in the legal and sociological literature—it serves a similar function (Newman, 1956; Blumberg, 1967; Sudnow, 1965). Like the police-addict game, plea bargaining is also introduced to the novice with the implicit or explicit statement that this is what "it's really all about," in contrast to the more formal ideological statements that are often used in political and academic-legal discussion of the court.

The plea-bargaining model in Riverdale postulated certain conditions about the court. The most important was that there were far too many cases for the court to process through trials. The prosecutor was obliged therefore to find less time-consuming ways of settling cases. At the same time, it was assumed that the defendant was almost certainly guilty of what was charged and even more certainly guilty of some criminal activity. The occasional defendant who was not guilty of the specific charge could still make use of a formal trial. For the defendant who was legally guilty but for whom there were important mitigating circumstances, the prosecutor would take appropriate steps. This is not to say that, even when plea bargaining was ongoing, court personnel thought this a desirable arrangement. Plea bargaining was a necessary evil in the minds of the participants because both the form and the results were wrong. However, both prosecution and defense had good practical reasons, easily explainable to colleagues, defendants, relatives, and other inter-

HEROIN, DEVIANCE AND MORALITY

ested parties, for their continued participation in the process. According to their accounts, they did not choose to compromise, but were forced into it by circumstances beyond their control. The defense counsel would emphasize the strength of the prosecutor's case and the tendency for juries to convict, playing down the defender's freedom to manipulate the case.[14]

The prosecutors as well were under certain obligations to explain their cooperation with the defense to the police and members of the public, both of which groups were sometimes displeased with the cooperation they perceived. In doing so, the prosecutors would emphasize the enormous number of cases that they had to deal with, the tendency of juries to acquit defendants, the ability of the defense to slow down the progress of a case by using various procedural technicalities, and so on. They would conclude by pointing out that it was physically impossible to bring all cases to trial and that they must settle for the best deal they could get (Gould et al., 1974: 106-107).

The moral schema that mandated cooperation and allowed the prosecution and the defense to negotiate directly with one another was complex, but it too was built into the plea-bargaining model. Plea bargaining is conceptually interesting from our point of view because it both mandated negotiated compromise as the proper goal and at the same time emphasized that prosecution and defense have fundamentally opposing goals (Gould et al., 1974: 133 ff.). By emphasizing the scarcity of resources available to both prosecution and defense, the plea-bargaining schema assumed the commitment on both sides to their respective goals of freedom and just punishment and, at the same time, suggested that cooperation would be the best means to their attainment.

This emphasis on pragmatic adjustment to the specifics of the situation also provided a normative regulator of the interaction between defense lawyer and prosecutor. The value of "reasonableness" took the form of explicit requests by *both* sides to "be reasonable" and implicit reference to the value in rejecting other proposals because "you know I can't do that." As we will see below, the criterion of "reasonableness" tacitly assumed the concept of "fairness."

It must be emphasized that reasonableness was given substance by reference to typical bargains that are made for typical cases. David Sudnow (1965), in his paper on "normal crimes," has emphasized this part of the court work. He notes that both prosecution and defense share typifications of criminals, criminal acts, criminal interests, etc., which are the bases of their negotiations. There are typical dispositions of typical cases. Being "reasonable" referred to agreeing to a typical disposition for the type of case at hand.

However, if court work were simply a matter of assigning typical dispositions to typical cases, there would have been no need for negotiation or even for a prosecutor or defense attorneys. But, as Sudnow points out, a critical question for any particular case is what type of a case it is. Equally important, although Sudnow largely ignored this, prosecution and defense had to eventually agree on what ways it was different from the ordinary case of its type and what ramifications these differences should have for the outcome of the case. The major role of the defense was to search out the aspects of the case which did not fit the type and to demonstrate that they mitigated the seriousness of the case. This involved reformulating the motives of the defendant, the situation surrounding the crime, or the nature of the act so that its moral meaning changed in a way that was more positive to the defense perspective (Lidz, 1974: Ch. 3). The prosecutor then decided whether the defense's formulation was plausible, although the prosecutor had relatively little specific information about the case, generally only the police report, the defendant's record, and what the defense attorney chose to say. He or she therefore had to depend very heavily on common-sense knowledge of what was plausible and what was not.

Structural Similarities and Differences
Between the Street and the
Court Accommodative Schemas

From what we have said so far, it might seem that the similarities between prosecution and defense interaction and police-addict interaction were not very great, considering that they both had to deal with conflicting ideologies derivative of the same basic conflict between punishment and outlaw ideologies. Although we have shown that the cop-addict game and plea bargaining played similar roles in allowing cooperation between conflicting groups, there seemed to be several important dissimilarities. First, the "fairness" value as a normative regulator and focus of argument in cop-addict interaction appeared to be supplanted by the concept of "reasonableness" in the courtroom. On the other hand, the role of typical cases as a mediator of courtroom decisions seemed to have no parallel in cop-addict interaction. It seems that despite some similarities in the problem that the two groups face, the solutions are quite different.

We wish to argue that these differences are not as great as they might seem at first glance. It is clearly true that vice-squad detectives and heroin addicts did not share typifications of types of arrest situations which called for specified types of routine resolutions.[15] This reflects the relative infrequency with which individual addicts get arrested. To learn even a simple system of typifying arrests requires a more extensive exposure to the arrest situation than most addicts got. Detectives quickly developed their own typifications of arrest, but these were shared only to a minimal degree with addicts. They negotiated the outcome of arrest situations in a much more ad hoc fashion around the addict's demands for fairness. Thus this difference from the plea bargain seems to reflect only the frequency with which the outlaw and the vice-squad cop interacted.

The other difference we noted was the absence of specific references to a value of fairness in the courtroom. This stems from the same disparity between the two situations. Court work was very routinized due to the familiarity of all the participants (except the defendant, whose role is minimal) with similar situations. Police-addict interaction was much less routinized because the individual addict had far less familiarity with the arrest situation. In court, *the sense of fairness was built into the typifications of the cases.* Despite the impression that Sudnow gives, the typification of cases and the components of the cases was not morally random. That the "typical" addict involved in a possession case was young, black, and stole to pay for heroin were not morally neutral observations. This becomes apparent when exceptions to the typical case are considered. A middle-aged white woman arrested for possession of heroin would have required a disposition totally different from the typical defendant just described: probably, according to our informants, private psychiatric treatment, because she would clearly have emotional problems. Or consider the following case:

> Art [the prosecutor] told me about a case he had last week that he said puzzled him. A woman was walking down Blake Street about noon and a guy grabbed her pocketbook and pushed her into the bushes in front of the Mid-City Hotel and started to act like he was trying to rape her. "Now I guess you could prosecute the guy for rape and purse snatching but, when you stop and think about it, what sort of a guy would commit rape in the middle of the day in front of the Mid-City Hotel." He sent the guy to the State Hospital.

or:

> One interesting case today was of a middle-aged white guy who was charged with "theft from person" from a guy who lived in his building. The guy has been in court twice on drunkenness charges while I have been here. The Public Defender said, "I believe him. He says he is not guilty and I believe him." The prosecutor read the police report and said, "Yeah, but they found $10 in his pocket when they got him. I'll tell you what, talk to him and see if you can get him to plead to a breach." Afterwards, the prosecutor said to me, "They probably just had a fight. It's another thing with two

drunks. It isn't a theft from person. I think I could get him for theft
but it certainly isn't a felony. So I guess justice is being served."

The point here is that because of the special circumstances
involved in these cases, the standard disposition was not fair, it
was not morally appropriate. The standard disposition for the
case involved an implicit judgment of what would be a fair
punishment for the typical set of facts in a typical case. These
cases had special properties to them which changed the nature
of what would be a fair disposition. As in the cop-addict
interactions, judgments of fairness were important aspects of
the prosecution-defense negotiations over cases, but because of
the high frequency of these interactions, the judgments were
imbedded in typifications and the governing moral regulator
became "reasonableness" in applying those typifications.

Situational Types

Accommodative models and ideologies were used to define
situations, to explicate the nature of appropriate acts and interpretations at any given time and place. But situations were not
entirely within the short-term control of the actors involved in
them.[16] A concert hall is not the setting for a football game, and
it would be hard to transform a heroin arrest into a beer party.
Much of the human condition involves efforts to make slight
adjustments in already defined situations.[17] This was the
primary use of the accommodative models we have been discussing.

We now want to propose several analytic abstractions which
will allow further description and analysis of interactions
between outlaws and law-enforcement personnel. However, it
must be emphasized that situations do not present themselves
to the participants as examples of the analytic categories that
we are going to outline here. Unlike "the game" and "plea
bargaining," which are terms and situations immediately recog-
nizable to the participants, these situation types are our formulations.

These formulations of the types of situations that occur between actors primarily mandated by the outlaw model and those primarily mandated by variants of the punishment ideology will presuppose the essentially conflictual nature of their interactions and will deal with cooperation in that context.[18] In our view, cooperation developed out of the competitive intentions of the actors. We believe this to be consistent with the moral schemas that both sides used in accounting for their actions. The types of situations that we will discuss here are (1) strategic and tactical planning, (2) confrontation, (3) aftermath, and (4) betrayal.

For our purposes, it is critical that the reader understand that these situations exist inside the contexts of the moral schemas that we have described: the crisis, the ideologies, and the accommodative schemas. The activities in these situations are quite literally meaningless and unsustainable without their moral context.

Strategies and Confrontation in the Streets

Tactical planning took different forms depending on whether the planner needed offensive or defensive tactics. Vice-squad detectives planned as though they were commando groups. They generally saw themselves on the offensive and requiring surprise attacks (Gould et al., 1974: Ch. 4). Both sides saw the "fight," in the short run, as being fought over the eventual possession of the heroin that the addict had and the detective wanted for evidence. Thus information about who had heroin, when, and where was the first requirement of the detective's work (Gould et al., 1974: 72 ff.). The most important aspect of the prestige hierarchy among vice-squad detectives was the quantity and quality of the detective's informants. Enormous amounts of time and effort were put into developing and maintaining informants, and police-science textbooks often spend many pages discussing the subject (Hughes et al., 1974: 137). We will return to the subject later when we discuss betrayal.

The model of commando raids was almost always present in the detectives' minds. They dressed in dark clothes, since most operations were at night. They used the phrase "a raid" to refer to the entry into the house. White detectives would occasionally comment jokingly that they are at a disadvantage vis-à-vis the black detectives, both because they are easier for a suspect to see at night and because they were much more conspicuous in the black neighborhoods.

Specific tactics were generally developed at the scene. They would consider all of the possible escape routes that the addicts could use and try to station at least one detective at each one. When raiding a first floor apartment or a house, a detective would usually be assigned to cover each side of the house in case someone jumped from the windows, as well as at front and back doors. Furthermore, efforts were always made to gain entry in as rapid a manner as possible. Usually deception was tried. In a hotel, they would identify themselves as bellboys; at a house, as friends of the suspect. If the door was not immediately opened and the sounds from inside the apartment indicated either movement in any other direction or panic, the door was kicked in. This was done because they anticipated the addicts' strategy of immediately disposing of the dope, generally down the toilet.

Vice-squad work was not especially strong on strategic planning. Detectives rarely discussed the theoretically best modes of "cleaning up" heroin in Riverdale among themselves. If the topic came up, it would typically be answered with a simple repetition of the standard refrain that one arrests users to try to get information on dealers and dealers in order to get information on the "big boys", the suppliers. The theory was that if one could arrest enough suppliers, one could cut off the supply and end heroin use.

An alternative but less favored strategy was that if enough pressure were placed on the user, he or she would be forced to quit.

Addicts had both long-term and short-term tactics for managing the police. The short-term tactics of escape and destruction were, of course, risky operations, since cops have guns and have been known to use them on fleeing suspects, and the addict's ideology certainly did not downplay this aspect of the police's actions. Getting rid of the evidence was usually done by swallowing it, flushing it down a toilet, or when outside, throwing it as far as possible and hoping that it would not be found.

Most often during a raid, addicts would not do anything at all. Sometimes this reflected the hope that the heroin was well enough hidden to foil the detectives' search. Other times, there simply was not any on the premises. In this case, experienced addicts in Riverdale would try to protect themselves from a "plant" by following the detective whom they trusted the least all over the apartment to make sure that a bag of heroin did not fall out of the detective's pocket.

However, the addict's strongest defenses against the police, and the ones relied on the most heavily, were long-term strategies. We can identify several of these. None of them were related in any way to the proper use of the legal channels. At best, a lawyer was a temporary expedient used when the addict had lost a battle and did not want to lose the war.

Unlike some legal theorists, the junkie believed that her or his battle was not with an abstract concept like the legal system, but with a specific policeman. This was the cornerstone of the junkie's defense. We can isolate four strategies of defense; they were not mutually exclusive, but generally the addict relied primarily on one or another. They are: avoidance, anonymity, protection, and cooperation. All of these techniques were built around that element of the outlaw ideology which holds that police and the criminal justice system are operated by people and that personal relationships (or the lack thereof) are the key to a defense in one way or another.

The most basic strategy was *avoidance* (Agar, 1973). Getting caught was not considered a question of breaking the law and having it found out. Both the game model and the outlaw ideology emphasize the personal nature of the competition between the addict and the cop. As long as you can avoid your personal antagonist, you have little trouble. Thus, every time things got too hot, one simply shifted out of the range of one's personal antagonists. This system of defense was based on the knowledge that police work at this level was primarily local.[19] A detective's jurisdiction stops at the city line, and while he or she may know the detectives in the next town, ten or fifteen miles away, the addict is essentially out of reach. True, the addict might soon pick up a new antagonist in the new city, but as a defense against the immediate news that there is a warrant out for his or her arrest, avoidance was an effective tactic. It was not without its price, however. Each time the addict moved, new connections had to be made and old friends were lost.

A related tactic was *anonymity*. Avoidance depended on the fact that it would take the new local police some time to learn one's identity (Gould et al., 1974: 57). How much time, though, depended on the intensity of the "heat" and the addict's effort at keeping hidden. However, some addicts made a special effort at keeping themselves anonymous as far as the police were concerned. This had many substrategies, but essentially it involved making oneself appear to be an ordinary respectable citizen. This certainly involved holding a regular job and not "hanging out on the Avenue" with other addicts. The extreme cases were called "woodwork addicts" because they seemed to disappear into the woodwork. Not only were they unknown to the police, but also to other addicts—except for a single supplier. They thus protected themselves against informers and undercover agents. It is, of course, impossible to estimate how many woodwork addicts there were in Riverdale, but they are only the most extreme example of a frequently used technique of defense.

A prominent defense technique among older addicts from certain ethnic groups was *protection*, which was essentially dependent on the old fashioned "fix." The addict worked for an "organization," selling heroin, boosting, running numbers, or whatever. It was expected that as part of the payment for this job the addict would be protected from arrest or, if not from arrest, at least from spending any time in jail. In practice, this technique seemed to be worthless in Riverdale, but in at least one of the suburbs there existed a dealing organization strong enough to provide bail for its customers and employes. There is reason to believe, however, that in other places and times this technique was more viable (Sutherland, 1934). Numbers runners in Riverdale could count on bail service from their organization but were apparently unable to fix court cases. Instead, the organization paid the fines. As far as we could ascertain, there was no systematic fix in the Riverdale courts, although in one suburban court there was some reason to believe that in special instances a case could be fixed.

Finally, when all else failed, the addict could try *cooperation.* Cooperation implied giving up the outlaw image and going along with the police. At the very least, this involved smiling and trying not to antagonize the cops. At the extreme, it involved daily informing for the police. Almost all addicts used this technique to some degree when the other techniques failed. Almost all addicts also found it a shameful activity to engage in, and they certainly didn't brag about it. Unfortunately, it was not a very effective technique for dealing with the police. Because the vice-squad detectives' need for information was almost as insatiable as an addict's need for heroin, they pressed their informers very hard. This usually involved having other members of the squad arrest the informer for various crimes so that the "patron" could then secure the informer's release in return for more information.[20] (Gould et al., 1974: 58-59). Often the detective would threaten to arrest the addict personally if the addict would not provide more information.

Strategies and Confrontation in the Courtroom

Offensive and defensive planning was exactly reversed in the courtroom. There, the prosecutor (agent of the law) had to protect the charge from the defense attorney's (agent of the outlaw) efforts to destroy it. This may seem peculiar, given the legal presumption of innocence until proven guilty, but in practice it worked out that the "defense" had to go on the offense. This came about for several reasons, but mainly

because the simple "factual" aspects of the case—did he do it or
didn't he—were generally a question of the addict's word against
the detective's (Gould et al., 1979: 132-133). While even the
prosecutor and the judge were sometimes skeptical of the detective's story, they felt bound to uphold the assumption that
policemen tell the truth under oath.

Thus it was the defense which was compelled to make the
offensive moves. If the defense lawyer simply let the case drag
on, his client would end up in prison. The prosecutor also played
an active role, but the purpose was different. The prosecutor's
goal was not simply to defend prosecution cases against "the
defense," but to "dispose" of the case in a fashion that would
minimize the overcrowding of the docket (the aggregation of
cases before the court on any particular day).

In discussing the prosecutors' and defense attorneys' strategic
planning, we will have to discuss the question of how they
handled the next stage, "confrontation." This is inevitable
because, unlike the police-outlaw confrontation, the prosecutor
and the defense attorney dealt with a case in many stages, with
each stage usually separated by at least a week. Thus the
outcome of one stage almost always led to the modification or
even total abandonment of the previously made plans. So in
court work, planning and confrontation were alternating phases.

Court work had two main foci, the case and the docket. Most
work was done around the process of constituting and disposing
of the individual case. This work consisted in part of a series of
short-term moves and plays which sought to dispose of the case
in the manner most favorable to one's own side. Managing the
docket, however, involved the consideration of how the cases
should be handled as a group. This created entirely different
strategic problems which, however, directly affected the outcome of each individual case.

Managing the docket was each prosecutor's main administrative problem. Somehow the prosecutor had to deal with all of
the cases that were on the docket for the day. There were three
ways of dealing with cases on a day-to-day basis. First, the
prosecutor would simply delay the case for some period of time

(usually for two weeks). This was an efficient way of dealing with the day's problems, but only made some future docket worse. Often the prosecutor had no choice about postponing a case, but generally it was not thought to be a good option.[21] Another option was to go through the formal legal procedure appropriate to that particular stage of the case. Unfortunately, this usually involved considerable time. When one has between 100 and 150 cases on the day's docket as the Riverdale District Court prosecutor usually did, there is not enough time to do that for the entire docket. The final possibility was to negotiate with the defense attorney a way in which the defendant waives the "right" to the legal procedure in return for a concession of one sort or another from the prosecution. The most effective negotiation from this point of view was a bargain whereby the defendant would plead guilty in return for a favorable disposition, because this would preclude all of the legal procedures except entering a plea and sentencing. However, many "small" deals such as waiving the right to a hearing on the bind-over to Superior Court in return for dropping one of several charges were sought and made routinely.

The defense attorney's strategic planning was based on the knowledge that on the one hand it was necessary to actively take charge of the case to win it, and on the other hand that the prosecutor was heavily burdened by a large docket. Typical defense strategy was thus to delay and obstruct as much as possible until he could get a good disposition for the case. He would often choose to forego a delay or an obstruction in order to improve his case, but not without receiving a consideration.

Generally, defense attorneys in Riverdale managed their cases within the presumption of the accommodative schema that there would eventually be a negotiated disposition. Occasionally they found cases where there were good reasons to plan for a trial, but these were rare, usually cases where one side or the other was under political pressure to have a trial. A murder, a dramatic rape, a large seizure of heroin, or an arrest of political militants—these were the types of cases which routinely went to trial in Riverdale. These, however, were statistically very rare, as

was the occasional defendant who insisted on his or her innocence and demanded a trial.

It was the defense attorney's responsibility to present an
initial formulation of the case to the prosecutor. He or she
would gather together all of the evidence[22] believed to be
relevant and which was either favorable to the defense attorney's cause or bound to come to the prosecutor's attention
anyway. This formulation was by no means unbiased. The
defense would try to make a plausible case that, in spite of what
the police report said, the defendant was innocent (or if not
innocent, at least less culpable than the police believed). Doing
these formulations was intensely moral. It involved producing
an account of commonly known evidence which mitigated the
"badness" of the defendant and the defendant's act. This process is very similar, on a much smaller scale, to the process of
producing a moral crisis (cf. Garfinkel, 1956). Sometimes this
presentation was effective enough that the prosecutor would
nolle the case.[23] This solved the problem for both sides, since
the defense attorney had won the case and the prosecution had
helped clear the docket. Obviously, though, the prosecutor
cannot afford to do this too often without being accused of
"giving away the court" by the other prosecutors, the police,
and other interested members of the community.

Even when the case was not nolled outright, many cases
could be settled with a little tactical maneuvering. But this
maneuvering required a mutually acceptable deemphasis on the
ideologically mandated conflicts between the prosecution and
the defense. Unless both sides were willing to forego their
rights, disposition could only be reached through the time-consuming mechanisms of the formal courtroom. In Riverdale, the
District Court public defender almost always proceeded in this
manner. However, we are more interested here in the tactics of
the outlaw lawyer.

Outlaw lawyers held an advantage over mediating lawyers like
the public defender in some circumstances for precisely the
same reason that they were at a disadvantage in others. Their
advantage vis-à-vis the mediating lawyers was that the prose-

cutor had every expectation that the outlaw lawyers would do everything in their power to obstruct easy but unfavorable dispositions. Not only would they not waive any of the standard procedures, but they would file motions which were meant only to obstruct, which had no chance of winning (Gould et al., 1974: 113-114). The concomitant disadvantage, of course, was that prosecutors felt they must not give outlaw lawyers any unnecessary breaks for fear that other lawyers would adopt the same strategy.

Outlaw lawyers had both a long-term strategy and a short-term strategy. The long-term strategy concerned all of their cases and their role in the court. They wanted to "bottle up" the court as much as possible because their cases would presumably be given the best break when the prosecutor was under substantial pressure. This, of course, was really a collective strategy for *all* outlaw defense attorneys, and even the mediating lawyers were known to appreciate the outlaw defense attorneys for it. The exhortation from one defense attorney to another not to waive some privilege was a frequent part of the talk in the hallways and lunchrooms of the Riverdale courts.

On the other hand, most defense lawyers generally agreed that it was a disadvantage to have a reputation as noncooperative. While they all wanted it known that if the prosecutor was "unreasonable" they would push the case as hard as possible, none wanted the reputation of deliberately trying to block up the courts. They felt this won them only the ire of the prosecutor.

A further structural peculiarity influenced the defense attorney's case-management tactics. While several different prosecutors would handle each case, only one defense attorney did. Consequently, the defense attorney could often work on each stage of the case separately, formulating moral accounts of the essential elements of the case differently depending on the practical purpose at the time, with only minimal concern for consistency between accounts. For example, we noted in one case all of the arguments that the lawyer made for an addicted client over several different appearances. At the first appearance the issue was bail. The lawyer emphasized that his client had lived in Riverdale since childhood, that he came from a respectable working-class family, and that he had always appeared when he had other cases before the court. The next time the case came up, the defense attorney argued vigorously before both the prosecutor and later in open court that his client was the victim of an illegal arrest made without a warrant. In this account, the defendant was depicted as an innocent victim of police harassment, and his long history of previous arrests was ignored. This tactic failed, and two weeks later the same defense attorney was back arguing how much his client was interested in getting treatment. This argument foundered when the prosecutor asked whether he was a member of a program, and if so, for how long, and it became apparent that the defendant had applied only the day before. Two weeks later, at sentencing, the defense lawyer did not object when the prosecutor explained their agreed recommendations for inpatient treatment as keeping a dangerous person off the streets. In all of these diverse moral accounts of the nature of the case and the defendant, the defense attorney never actually lied. He simply differentially emphasized and reinterpreted various aspects of the case. Lying was not an unknown tactic, but it entailed serious risks, since the eventual disposition depended heavily on the prosecutor's acceptance of the defense attorney's depictions of the case (Gould et al., 1974: 101).

The defense often gained advantage from, and based its strategy over a period of time on, the shifting of the case from one assistant prosecutor to another. Defense attorneys always tried to deal with the "right" prosecutor. Some prosecutors were known as "reasonable" about bail and "unreasonable" about dispositions. Others could be counted on to favor treatment for addicts, and still others to see the "reasonableness" of technical legal arguments about cases. Judges were "shopped for" in the same way, especially when it came to sentencing (Gould et al., 1974: 107). Frequently a defense attorney would agree to plead guilty if he were allowed to have his client sentenced in front of the judge who was hearing motor-vehicle cases or who was taking jury trials rather than the one who was currently hearing criminal cases. That "judge shopping" was a procedure familiar even to the judges is shown in the following instance:

> About noontime, Cleary (the prosecutor) began to worry about ever getting through the day's cases and sent someone to find out if any cases could be handled in either of the other two courtrooms. Apparently the jury trial for the day had been cancelled and Rosenberg (another prosecutor) agreed to take some cases upstairs. Cleary decided that he would simply give him all the P.D.'s cases. However, when Cleary announced that, Moore (the P.D.) objected; he naturally didn't want his cases heard before Hindesmith because he is very tough, and DiSimone, who has the downstairs court, is an easy sentencer as well as a good legal thinker. DiSimone, with a slight grin, asked Moore why he objected to the transfer and Moore sputtered and finally said something about the inappropriateness of special treatment for his clients. DiSimone grinned and added, "Besides, it would spoil your research on the judge." The whole court laughed.

The prosecutors' strategic thinking focused primarily not on the case, but on issues of managing the aggregation of cases that make up the docket. They had to find ways of disposing of cases without violating the ideological commitments to stiff sentences for wrongdoers and "giving away the court." Their ongoing enterprise was to make deals with the defense so that they could dispose of cases without having to go through with all of the legal formalities and without undercutting the general pattern of dispositions that had evolved in court. Although, for instance, the prosecutor wanted very much to agree to a sentence of one year's administrative probation for six college students arrested for LSD, each of whom had a private attorney who could file endless motions, the prosecutor was reluctant to do so because that would set a precedent. While it might be possible to let these six off easily without having to let everyone off that way, one could not do so too often. For this reason, prosecutors were all eager to find exceptional cases which allowed them to give better deals in specific instances without undercutting the general pattern of dispositions. The bank robber who did it to pay his mother's private psychiatric hospital bills and the prostitute caught before any money actually changed hands were both eligible to be seen as special cases, either morally or legally, for which prosecutors could agree to a sentence lighter than usual. This allowed them to meet their essential requirements of maintaining the pattern of dispositions without having to fight the case out and waste precious time.

On the other hand, prosecutors had ideological problems with giving out sentences which were lighter than could be justified by the case. They had to be wary of defense attorneys who lied or deliberately hid information from them. One way to do this was to try to gather as much knowledge about the case at hand as possible. The file would usually contain enough information about the incident, in the form of the police report, for the prosecutor to arrive at some rough typification of the crime itself. In addition, the file would also usually contain the defendant's arrest record, which could be counted on as accurate, at least for arrests in Riverdale. However, the case was not entirely made up of the criminal act and the defendant's record. It also involved factors such as the defendant's intent, status, personality, and so on (Sudnow, 1965), which the defense attorney was most likely to distort because none of that information would be in the file until the final stages of disposition.

Prosecutors had several techniques for managing this problem, the most prominent of which is the use of memory. A very large number of the cases that a prosecutor saw every day involved defendants the prosecutor had tried previously, or if not the defendant, the defendant's father or mother, sister or brother. In other cases, the prosecutor might have known the codefendant from some prior trial. If the prosecutor did not know any of the people involved, practical knowledge of types of peoples, places, and crimes might help him or her decide whether or not the defense attorney were telling the truth. The prosecutor generally knew the part of town the defendant lived in and who hung out at the bar where the crime took place, as well as the defendant's race, ethnicity, age, and sex. All of this information, both general and specific, helped determine the plausibility of the defense attorney's representations. As a supplement to all this information, prosecutors spent endless hours swapping stories about cases and people over lunch and after work, as well as plying other court personnel (including the police and defense attorneys) for whatever information they could get.

In doing their job, the prosecutors made a distinction between petty and serious cases. Petty cases, such as public drunkenness, breach of the peace, shoplifting, marijuana possession, and fights between husbands and wives, were not considered worth the time they took. The best thing to do was to get them over with as quickly as possible. Serious cases, however, required serious attention and took up the major part of the prosecutors' time in Riverdale. Paradoxically though, the only real managerial gains that prosecutors could make was by finding ways of shortcutting serious cases. Petty cases were already cut back as far as possible. This was one reason Riverdale prosecutors were so willing to accept the peculiar series of bargains that led to the therapeutic control system for drugs that will be discussed in Chapter 5.

Here it is only necessary to note that heroin possession and sales cases were serious ones for the District Court prosecutors. Furthermore, as the number of cases began to mount in the late 1960s and early 1970s, it seemed to many court personnel that drug cases would become the straw that broke the back of the court system. Thus a system which would essentially allow for quick and easy bargains on serious cases was accepted much more readily than might have been expected on the basis of the punishment ideology which mandates the prosecutor's work.

Victory and Defeat

Precisely because they were formulated by the members as a game (a competition or a war), the interactions that we have been discussing could end in a victory for one side and a loss for the other. Like all confrontation encounters between outlaws and law enforcers, both cooperative and conflictual elements of the relationship were expressed in this type of encounter.

To the vice squad, victory generally meant an arrest, although every arrest was not a victory. Sometimes arrests were made as a way of neutralizing a loss. A "good" arrest generally entailed finding the addict in possession of all the dope that they had been told that he had, and a good arrest was a victory. However, occasionally arrests were made to cover defeats. This occurred when the vice-squad detectives had become heavily committed to a course of action which was highly public or in which their reputations seemed to be on the line. Thus any confrontation which drew a crowd or which occurred in front of witnesses who would be likely to report the event to other addicts was particularly likely to produce this sort of reaction from the detectives. On the other hand, a search of an empty apartment which had yielded no results was likely to be merely written off as a waste of time and forgotten. One simple technique for making an arrest to cover a defeat in the making was a "plant"— dropping one or more bags of heroin on the suspect or in his dwelling which could then be found a few minutes later. When addicts discovered they had been "beaten by a plant," they tended to object strenuously, both because they then would have to spend time and perhaps money in court and face jail or treatment, and because they were being "beaten" unfairly. However, as a technique for winning an otherwise lost confrontation, planting was relatively safe and effective. Generally an addict could not be certain that he had not lost a bag or two behind the dresser a few weeks previously. Likewise, he might have had a bag or two in his pocket that he had forgotten about. The pace of events during these encounters was certainly not such that he could leisurely reflect about what happened to his heroin the last two or three times he wore that pair of pants.

There were other techniques for trying to turn defeat into at least a stalemate. Sometimes addicts were arrested for minor violations such as breach of the peace or assaulting a police officer. More frequently, the police would try to convert the situation into something that was not really a confrontation in the first place. Such comments as: "Just thought we'd remind you that we're here"; and "That was just for fun, next time it will be for real"; would partially transfer a defeat into a non-confrontation (Hughes et al., 1974: 137).

Victory elicited two types of responses from police. On one hand, it was an occasion for rejoicing, and it brought out statements grounded in their mandating ideology which emphasized their moral worth and put down the addict's. This type of talk drew very heavily on the competitiveness that was a cornerstone of the "game" formulation of the interaction. Comments like: "You lousy son of a bitch, we got you this time. You guys better learn not to fuck with us"; "Three half loads. Boy are you gonna go away for a long, long time."; "You better get yourself a fancy lawyer because I'm gonna see that they lock you up and throw away the fucking key"; were common in this situation.

However, not all victories lead to that sort of response. While arrests were sometimes ends in themselves, more often they were simply part of a longer fight. Strategic consideration for the next arrest would enter at this point. The suspect would be worth even more to the detective if he could be convinced to inform on his dealer. Following an arrest, then, the detective would often try to play down the sense in which he and the suspect were on sides in fundamental opposition to each other. Like the previously mentioned type of response, this response relied heavily on the concept of the game, but rather than emphasizing the victory it emphasized the "it's only a game" and the "that's the way the game goes—you win some, you lose some" aspects of the concept. We will discuss this further when we discuss betrayal.

The addicts' victory celebrations were generally carried on in the company of their peers and not in front of the detectives. An occasional smile or grin was about the extent of celebration expressed in the presence of detectives. They simply could not afford to be more open about triumphs because of the nature of the power balance. The detectives of the Riverdale Vice Squad were notoriously poor losers, and their ability to turn defeat into "victory" made it extremely unwise for the addict to "rub it in."

In the company of addicts and other sympathizers, however, addicts freely gloated over their victories. By their own accounts, addicts were almost never beaten fairly. The police would plant dope, break down their doors, and use deceptive practices to entrap them. Their own victories were due entirely to their own cleverness. The police won through brutality and ruthlessness, whereas outlaws won with their wits. For addicts, as well as their opposition, victory is a time to express their ideology.

Victory and defeat in the courtroom, unlike on the streets, would occur half a dozen times a day for the defense attorneys and many more times for the prosecution. For the prosecutor especially, there was never time to celebrate any but the most important victories or be upset by any but the most colossal defeats. Perhaps for this reason, prosecutors tended to see their job as an endless holding action against the defense attorneys. Only rarely did they win anything. Most of the cases ended with dispositions that were outrageously soft. To the prosecutors, their job involved almost continuous defeat due to circumstances far beyond their control. This explanation of their status and a sort of mournful attitude toward their work was built into their accounts of plea bargaining.

Yet prosecution was not without its moments of triumph. It was not unusual for a prosecutor to turn to one of our researchers after a bargain had been struck and explain with a grin how and why he had gotten the best of an outlaw defense attorney. This never happened with the public defender. Indeed, the prosecutor would frequently recommend to the public defender which procedure he ought to pursue. There was very little sense of competition in this relationship.[24] However, prosecutors' sense of triumph against the outlaw lawyers was rarely publicly acknowledged because the victory was not complete until it had been finalized in open court, well after the actual negotiated victory was achieved. Furthermore, as we noted above, much of the smooth functioning of the court depended on the ability of the prosecutor and the defense attorney to count on the other's truthfulness. Since many of the victories depended on a failure of one side or another to disclose faithfully all of the "relevant" facts, a proclamation of victory would have been very disruptive of efforts by the winner to achieve further victories. The prosecutors also had an interest in encouraging defense attorneys to believe that they were too busy dealing with the multitude of cases to be able to accomplish anything very subtle on any particular case. As long as a defense attorney did not know that he or she had been defeated, there was no reason to worry about it happening again.

Betrayal

One of the things that we have seen consistently in this volume is the flexibility and ambiguity in moral definitions of the social world; actors make use of varying and diverse moral schemas with which to constitute the "real" nature of the activities in which they were engaged. There was, however, a consistent aspect to the fluctuating definitions of the law-outlaw interaction. Invariably the parties were all seen as "belonging to" opposing sides. Conflict was the invariant assumption of the various ways in which this interaction was understood by its participants.

Built into this definition of the situation was the possibility of betrayal, that is, an actor who is formally assigned to one side acting in a way that deliberately helps the other side. Few moral acts are as interesting, as complexly motivated, and likely to produce such feelings of anger and hatred as is the act of betrayal.

In the context of outlaw-law officer interaction, the primary instance of betrayal was an addict turning informer. The entire police antinarcotic effort in Riverdale for many years depended for its effectiveness almost exclusively on addicts betraying other addicts[25] (Hughes et al., 1973: 137). In the process of coming to depend on betrayal, the detectives became extremely proficient at persuading addicts to begin and to continue informing.

A critical aspect of persuading the addict to "cooperate" was some sort of threat or inducement to inform. While addicts and much of the public seemed convinced that financial and/or the direct giving of heroin were major inducements for informants, our observation was that neither money nor heroin was a major factor in Riverdale. Occasionally some money would be paid out, but rarely was important information gained in that manner. Much more important was the promise by the police to grant a low bail or to intercede with the prosecutor either in Riverdale or some nearby jurisdiction. The low bail release became an increasingly important tactic as addicts began to learn that they could escape jail by entering treatment programs. Low bail was particularly important to addicts because if they could not make bail they would have to undergo withdrawal in jail with only the unreliable medicinal aids provided by the jail doctor. Thus the beginning of any effort by the vice-squad detectives to "turn on" a potential informant was always the threat that "we're gonna slap a $10,000 bail on you and you can rot in jail." This would then be followed by the subtle suggestion from another detective that perhaps this fate could be avoided through cooperation.[26]

It is worth reiterating here that the "game" conceptualization of cop-addict interaction was an important resource for the detectives trying to "turn on" a potential informant. To some degree, it neutralized the addict's view of himself as the noble outlaw. By being able to contend that "it's only a game," the detectives could try to direct the addict's attention to his own immediate situation and their contention that informing would be pragmatically justified. Their pitch to the arrested addict relied heavily on pure pragmatism. A typical argument would go: "Listen, Charlie, you're in big trouble. You're gonna sweat out your time in jail until your trial and then you'll get five on top of that, so maybe you'd better think about what you can give us."

Other arguments were used as well. Reminiscent of Sykes and Matza's (1957) observations of delinquents who "condemn the condemners," the detectives would try to persuade the potential informant that he or she owed nothing to the person they wanted him to inform on. In response to the objection that the addict could not "rat on" the man whose dope he had been dealing because "he's my friend," a detective responded: "Your friend, hell! That dude is using you. What do you get out of him? A dozen bags a week. Hell, that ain't shit. He's pulling in a grand a week easy. All he's doing for you is getting you strung out on his dope."

Keeping an informant "on the line" was generally a matter of trying to keep the pressure on. This involved having other detectives arrest her or him as often as possible and where that was impossible the detective would arrest the informer or threaten to do so himself. Then the "patron" would alleviate that pressure in return for more information. Being an informant was not a particularly enjoyable status, and many addicts got tired of the constant hassle after a relatively short time and simply accepted the jail time.

The courtroom also had its forms of betrayal. Defense lawyers who found it easier to accept the prosecutor's viewpoint on the case rather than their client's, prosecutors who had become too familiar with the defense attorneys and accepted their understanding of the case rather than the one mandated by their own ideology, and policemen who become too chummy with the addicts all can be seen as betraying their own cause. All of them shared the problem of becoming more involved in cooperation with their "opponents" than their colleagues found acceptable.

While it would be difficult to prove or document, it seems to us that all of the groups we observed needed a certain amount of betrayal. Consistent with Durkheim (1964) and Erikson's (1966) proposition that deviance helps to define group boundaries, we believe that defining an ally as having betrayed you can be seen as defining the limits of acceptable cooperation with the enemy. All of the groups we have discussed in this chapter had one or more members about whom the other members were suspicious because they cooperated too much and whose every action was carefully examined for signs of betraying the mandating ideology.

The Practical Uses of the Treatment Ideology

Neither outlaws nor law enforcement officials drew their formal mandates from the treatment ideology that we outlined in Chapter 3. Thus it would seem that we can at least save ourselves the trouble of having to worry about its effects on the interaction between outlaws and legal control agents. It is certainly true that few encounters between the two groups were so structured that the treatment ideology is a very important part of the activity.

Nonetheless, it is important to realize that such concepts as "sickness," "helping," "determinism," and "needs" are part of the general culture and as such were available to both law enforcement personnel and outlaws. Even though the most frequent and comprehensive uses that are made of the ideology of treatment are not activities that glorify either of these two groups, in specific instances parts of the rhetoric of treatment were useful to both. Although the use of treatment rhetoric by the wrong policeman at the wrong time might lead to the suggestion from a colleague that the policeman ought to be a social worker, very rarely was a shift from one ideology to another noted by other participants. The fact that most people associate a "helping" orientation with medicine and social work and not with prosecutors did not stop an individual prosecutor from claiming that he had decided to resolve a case in a certain way in order to help the defendant. Likewise, the fact that the law does not recognize the idea that an addict is not responsible for a burglary because of his addiction did not prevent an addict or his attorney from using such an argument successfully in some circumstances.

Let us look at several typical uses of treatment moralism in the interaction between law enforcement agents and outlaws, beginning with street conflicts between cops and addicts.

Both cops and addicts used the rhetoric of treatment ideology against each other when it suited their needs, primarily in the negotiations following the arrest. For the detectives, it, like the game model, was used to "cool out" the addict's objections to what was about to happen to him (or occasionally what had happened to him in the past). Cops used it to undercut the diffuse definition of their interests as in conflict with addicts. This facilitated the effort to get the addict booked peacefully or to inform on friends. An addict who objected to an arrest for a bag of heroin found in the back seat of his car might hear, "Don't give me any of the 'innocent' crap. I don't care if it's your bag or not. You've got a big habit, and if we don't get you locked up soon you'll be dead of an overdose". We heard many other variations on the theme that going to jail would be good for the addict. Such an account was also used to explain a past jailing to addicts or ex-addicts.

> Wilson arrested three people even though there was only one bag and it probably belonged to Smitty. El took the two women aside and said that they shouldn't worry, that he would talk to Wilson later. That is part of El's style, he doesn't like to be hated. The conversation flowed easily with the friendly gossip that El and Wilson like in order to keep them abreast of current happenings on the street. One of the women started into a mild denunciation of El for arresting her without a warrant a year ago. El just said, "Yeah, but look how much good it did you, you were strung out and thin as a waif a year ago. Now you're all cleaned up and looking fine." She admitted it was true and went back to other gossip. El later told me that she is strung out now.

In this case, the detective ended a potentially difficult conflict by using a "it's for your own good" line and got the addict to accept that in return for a tacit acceptance of her statement that she was not addicted.

Another way in which detectives used treatment-oriented theories of addiction was in polemics about addicts to non-addicts. Here they tended to characterize addicts as lacking independent reason and acting solely because of their cravings.[27] The treatment-oriented conception of the actor as lacking a free will was used rhetorically in degrading addicts in general or one addict in particular.

Addicts used the treatment ideology at least as often as the detectives. David Matza (1964) has argued persuasively that delinquents use treatment ideology to make excuses which neutralize their obligations to the law and conventional morality. While we cannot go into the detail here that Matza did, we observed similar theorizing on the part of addicts. However, while Matza characterized his delinquents as generally insincere in accounting for their delinquency as instances of mental illness, the addicts we observed seemed to be episodically sincere in believing that their addiction determined their actions and that they were not totally free to do as they chose.

More important than the addicts' use of this ideology was their lawyers' use of it, both in open court and in bargaining behind the scenes with the prosecutors. The lawyers, both those who seemed to take their mandate from the outlaw ideology and the more conventional ones, used this ideology to undercut the prosecution's justification for punishing the addict by imprisoning her or him. With some success, they argued both that the addict could not be held totally responsible for his or her addiction and thus it would not be fair to punish the addict, and also that punishment would not be an effective social policy against addiction, since only treatment could get "to the problem."

However, there was another side to that same argument. Prosecutors could argue that if it is true that punishment is not a meaningful social response to addiction and that addiction, rather than the acts of the addict, is the appropriate focus of the court's attention, then due process and guilt determination are less important issues than the substantive question of whether or not the individual is an addict. Prosecutors rarely used this argument in open court, but it became an increasing part of the understanding that existed in the back-room bargaining sessions. In those sessions, prosecutors were generally unwilling to listen to defense attorneys' arguments that the defendant was innocent or that his rights had been violated. They felt that if the addict needed treatment he should get it. Since the defense attorney's best chance to get a client off completely was always persuading the prosecutor to nolle the case, the prosecutor's ability to use this moral schema created an important change in the conditions under which an addict's case was disposed of. As we will see in Chapter 5, the permeation of the court by the treatment ideology was an important part of the development of the accommodative schema we call therapeutic control.

The Crisis and Accommodation Between Outlaws and the Law

One final topic must be considered before we leave our discussion of the interactions between outlaws and their opponents in the legal system. In the beginning of this volume, we discussed the structures and effects of the Drug Crisis at the societal and community levels. While in many ways the moral order that governed law-outlaw interaction was independent of and had emerged historically before the onset of the Drug Crisis (Burroughs, 1953), the crisis could not help but affect those people whose day-to-day lives were involved with drugs. Just how important the changes in the routine practices in court were will be discussed in Chapter 5, but here we must discuss the relationship between cops and addicts and how the crisis affected it.

We have suggested that addicts and cops reached a very tenuous peace which was based on a sense that they were both playing an endless game. Since the practical value of this accommodative schema is that it facilitated stability, the continued viability of that model was drastically affected by the Drug Crisis. From the police perspective, the beginning of the Drug Crisis entailed a feeling that the use of drugs was growing, or "getting out of hand." Their worry was that perhaps the endless game could actually be won by the junkies. They entertained the possibility that a day would come when there would be so many addicts on the street of Riverdale that the detectives would no longer be able to "control" them, to keep them from "overrunning" the city. What that would mean never seemed clear, except that it would be apocalyptic. As media attention was drawn to the Drug Crisis, they began to receive comments from friends, relatives, and other policemen which they interpreted as demands for more action. At the high point of the crisis, the detectives frequently used metaphors like "flood" or "tidal wave" to describe what they were dealing with.

At the same time, within the ranks of drug users there was a general expectation that soon everyone in America would be using drugs and that "they" would be forced to legalize marijuana and provide some sort of legalized access to other drugs. This led to a rather generalized attitude on the street of relative intolerance toward legal intervention. While this was much less prevalent among addicts than among "heads," some of this belief seeped into their subculture.

Thus, for both the police and the addicts, there was a strong tendency to feel that the police had their backs up against the wall and that very soon the whole game might be over. The police began to feel that they had to do something desperate. The upper levels of the police bureaucracy responded to this crisis by creating the Riverdale Regional Crime Squad. With the aid of federal money, this program took young policemen and put them into other towns where they were unknown to do full-time undercover work.

At the day-to-day level of vice-squad work, the immediacy of the crisis meant increased emphasis on effectiveness. Proper legal procedure, never a major concern among the detectives, became even more peripheral to their primary concerns. More important, we have some reason to believe that there was an increase in what could be called cheating. While it is almost impossible to tell with any certitude when something as vague as unfairness between police and addicts increases, several observers on both sides of the game reported to us that between 1968 and 1971 police tactics got steadily more aggressive, and such practices as planting heroin on suspects became more frequent. This culminated in a false-arrest scandal and a total reorganization of the vice squad in 1972.

Both undercover agents and the increasingly aggressive tactics of the vice squad undercut the minimal degree of trust that was necessary to maintain the game model. Although we are not in a position to prove it in any way, we believe that this led to greater hostilities between police and addicts and accompanying problems of violence and "cheating."

NOTES

1. For a fine review of the role of opiates in American history, see Musto (1973), Lindesmith (1965), and Schur (1962).

2. For more academic versions of the police world views, see many of the police science textbooks. Howard Becker's *The Outsiders* is an explicit attempt to depict the world through the eyes of the outlaw and his camp followers. However, motion pictures and television police shows are the best portrayals.

3. Many defense attorneys reject this ideology almost completely, preferring to see themselves as "officers of the court." Their role will be discussed briefly later in this chapter.

4. For an academic exposition of the "due process" model of criminal process which is an important part of this viewpoint, see Packer (1968).

5. At least if the reader assumes, like most people, that reality is simply one way or another. It is, however, equally reasonable to assume that despite the blatant discontinuities of these accounts, they are all what "really" happens, but only some of the time and from only one perspective.

6. We are speaking here of the structure of the cultural subsystem of these action systems, to use Parsonian terminology.

7. Jerome Skolnick, in what is otherwise one of the finest studies of day-to-day police work, *Justice Without Trial,* formulates police motives almost entirely on the basis of the police ideology. See, however, Walsh (1975).

8. Cleckner (1977) argues that "the game" (in a more generalized sense) is a pervasive cultural model in American ghetto subculture.

9. This concept has been described in more detail in Lidz (1974b). Also James Walsh (1975) and Jackson (1967).

10. This figure is roughly comparable to disposition rates in most metropolitan areas.

11. See Lidz (1974b).

12. That is to say that those obligations had to be "neutralized" in the terms of Sykes and Matza (1957).

13. It is interesting to note the similarities between this occasion and the classic situation in which this phrase is used—the negotiating prelude to premarital sex. Our thanks to Victor Lidz for pointing this out.

14. Indeed, defense attorneys who formulated their role as mediator between addict and prosecutor found this to be one of their major activities. They had to "convince" clients who wanted a trial and/or insisted on their innocence that, given the circumstances, it was best to plead guilty.

15. Typifications of types of arrests were shared to a limited extent—i.e., "sales bust" versus "possession bust," "good bust" versus "bad bust"—but conceptions of what qualifies for each of these categories and what actions should be taken were not shared at all.

16. For a striking argument along this line, see Goffman (1974, Ch. 1).

17. However much the social world may be actively constituted by the actor, most of the time we treat the world as a given fact not to be modified except by hard work (see Bittner, 1973).

18. The problem of choosing an "essence" for these interactions is a difficult one with no simple solution and parallels similar problems in sociological theories of society. The question of whether X is the essence of something and other things are superstructure including Y, or Y is the essence and all other things including X should be seen as growing out of Y is essentially a metaphysical question with no empirical solution. In this case, we have made conflict the grounding essence, and this has profound consequences for the description. However, we believe that any description that seeks to extend itself beyond the most basic phenomenology must eventually essentialize. We chose conflict because we believe that without some presumption of divergent intentions, the interactive patterns become virtually senseless to the observer.

19. Hughes et al. (1974: 237) reported that in Chicago, police officers are aware that their tactics "just force addicts from one street corner or police district to another" (see also Agar, 1973).

20. In this case, the cooperation technique looks very much like the classic "protection racket," except that the protector is a policeman.

21. Obviously, constitutional guarantees to a speedy trial are involved here. Paradoxically, it was usually the prosecution that pushed for a speedy disposition of the case.

22. For the most part, the strict formal rules governing the admissibility of evidence in court were disregarded in these sessions. Hearsay, previous arrests, other pending charges, and third party opinions were important resources for both sides.

23. The phrase "nolle" is short for the Latin "nolle prosequi" which is a formal declaration from the prosecutor, in full court, that he does not intend to pursue the case. It has the effect of dismissing the case.

24. This role for the P.D. was partly the style of the particular P.D. we observed. The previous P.D. apparently often operated as an outlaw should and did not have this relationship with the prosecutors.

25. Recently, with the development of undercover agents, a different type of betrayal was added to the police effort.

26. Sometimes by design and sometimes not, the detectives frequently used the ancient technique of one of them "playing" the tough guy and the other taking the point of view of the suspect and arguing that something might be worked out. See Rubinstein (1973), Gould et al. (1974: 58-59).

27. Taylor et al. (1973) would call this neoclassism, because drug addiction is a frequent exception to the classical free-will theories.

Chapter 5

THE CLINIC

In the previous chapter, we described in some detail the relations between outlaw-mandated and punishment-mandated actors. We now begin the description of the organization of relationships between clinic personnel and addicts during the crisis. Once again the central question we will consider is: Did these relationships proceed along the lines dictated by any of the moral ideologies we have identified, or by the accommodative schema called the welfare model?

Fortunately (for our analysis), interaction between medical personnel and addicts in Riverdale occurred virtually exclusively in the context of an organization known as the Narcotics Addiction Unit (N.A.U.) of the Riverdale Mental Health Center. If it had been the empirical case that medical personnel were interacting with addicts in a variety of contexts (e.g., emergency rooms, "outreach" work on the streets, private physician-patient relationships, and so on), our analytic task would have been much more difficult. But in Riverdale, the N.A.U. exercised a virtual monopoly over these interactions, so an analysis of the structural characteristics at the N.A.U. will suffice for our purposes.[1] It should be remembered, though, that the N.A.U. is a *social* organization, not a *physical* location. Its physical facilities were not concentrated in one geographical spot, but were rather dispersed throughout several downtown locations.

In order to understand the social patterns that emerged at the N.A.U., one must realize that the exact nature of the N.A.U. was problematic from its inception for three reasons. First, as an "experimental" program it was explicitly requested by the National Institute of Mental Health to explore new methods of treatment and to experiment. In the first year of the N.A.U.'s existence, that spirit was pervasive. There was a sense among both staff and patients of sailing into uncharted waters. Second, the nature of the N.A.U. was problematic in the way in which any organization is problematic. As Schutz (1967) and his followers have pointed out, every object in the social world is constantly constituted by those who must live with it. Blau (1955) has noted that organizations generally cannot be adequately described by their organization plans. They are constantly evolving to meet both internal and external situational exigencies.

However, the N.A.U. was problematic in a third way which is much more critical to the theme of this volume. The N.A.U. was the meeting place of two differing moral schemas, or ideologies, about the people who were to work there, their "clients," and the enterprise in which they were engaged. This is, of course, not a new theme in the organizational literature. The literature in the sociology of organizations is filled with studies of client satisfaction with various organizational arrangements. However, these studies have usually accepted the assumption that the organization itself is primarily the property of the staff. Goffman notes of mental hospitals that "the institutional plant and name come to be identified by both staff and inmates as somehow belonging to the staff, so that when either group refers to the views or interests of 'the institution,' by implication they are referring to the views and concerns of the staff" (Goffman, 1961: 9). This belief is important for the ethnographer to note, but if he accepts it as an analytic device, it will interfere with his apprehending the extent to which the characteristics of the N.A.U. emerged as responses to the conflict of the ideologies that met in the clinic, the relative capacity of the two groups to implement these positions, and the emergent properties of the organization that resulted.

In this case, at least, the clients and the staff of the organization came into contact with each other preferring radically different moral interpretations of their relationship. Eventually a tacit working accommodation, which we will describe in this chapter, was worked out. However, throughout the four years of our study, the two disparate ideological definitions of the N.A.U. persisted. Before we describe the accommodation, which we call the welfare schema, it will be fruitful to present two descriptions of the N.A.U. as seen through the staff's and patients' ideologies respectively.

The Infirmary

The drug epidemic of the late sixties and early seventies took a high toll in human misery, especially among the young and disadvantaged. The government and the medical profession realized the social and psychological damage that was resulting from the epidemic and set up a number of clinics wherein those individuals who had become addicted to drugs could be treated. This treatment served the dual function of caring for the population that had already become addicted, and protecting the rest of the society by neutralizing the carriers of the disease. The N.A.U. was one of these treatment centers.

As a treatment center (albeit experimental), the N.A.U. was staffed by a number of clinicians who were interested in the treatment of drug abuse and experienced in working with youth and minority-group patients. They were supported by a number of rehabilitated local ex-addicts who personally knew most of the patients and who served as useful role models for the *patients. Since no single therapeutic regime was right for all addicts, the N.A.U. organized three different clinical programs to deal with different types of drug abuses: the methadone clinic for the hard-core addicts, Zeta House for drug abusers who needed a total therapeutic environment, and outpatient treatment which provided counseling and outpatient therapy for younger drug abusers who could still benefit from more traditional outpatient services.*

The clinic always emphasized helping addicts play a productive role in society. To that end, all N.A.U. programs involved both a psychological rehabilitation and an effort to encourage the resumption of social rights and obligations.

Psychological rehabilitation was encouraged through mandatory patient participation in appropriate chemotherapy regimes and individual or group psychotherapy. At the same time, the N.A.U. actively helped the patient solve accumulated real-world social problems, and facilitated the playing of more positive roles in the community. The patient was given extensive assistance in overcoming the chronic legal, marital, and educational problems that addicts routinely accumulate. It was the clinical experience that unless the patient could solve the various real-world problems that accrue to addicts, all the psychological rehabilitation in the world would not help.

This is not to say that the clinic had no problems. Psychiatry has long known that addicts are an extremely difficult group to treat, because of both the nature of addiction, and the lifestyle that most addicts adopt. Indeed, the N.A.U. was always thought of as an experimental unit precisely because of the clear necessity to develop new treatment forms for this type of patient.

The clinical staff members learned very quickly that they could not really help an addict who did not want to "kick" his or her addiction. Thus one of the primary functions of the pretreatment evaluation was to screen out those applicants who were not sincerely motivated to forego their drug dependence. Applicants were required to prove, in clinically acceptable fashion, their commitment to rehabilitation before they were actu-

ally admitted to any of the clinical programs. Many applicants never made it through this screening process.

Even among those who were admitted to the programs, temporary lapses of motivation were not unusual. They were acted out in various ways: continuing (or resuming) the use of illicit drugs while under treatment, attempting to manipulate staff in countertherapeutic ways, selling medication on the black market, and so on. Problems of this sort seem to be endemic to any addiction treatment program.

The N.A.U.'s approach to these problems was essentially two-pronged: increased monitoring of patient behavior, and the development of quasi-judicial structures to deal with counterproductive patient behavior. Formally, increased monitoring was accomplished through a scientific schedule of urine testing which showed the presence of metabolates of illicit drugs in the patients' urine. Informally, increased monitoring was facilitated by encouraging "confrontations" in therapy groups between poorly motivated patients and other patients who had first-hand knowledge of counter-productive behavior. Confrontations of this sort had the dual benefits of increasing the patients' sense of responsibility, while at the same time alerting staff to the problems that individual patients were having in maintaining their commitment to rehabilitation.

Since these problems were endemic, it was necessary to develop ongoing procedures for handling them, which led to the creation of codes of patients' rights and responsibilities, and procedures for discouraging infractions. Each of the clinical programs eventually developed its own disciplinary body and procedures. While there was always a certain amount of patient dissatisfaction with these monitoring and disciplining functions, most patients and staff felt that they were a necessity.

On the whole, the N.A.U. was an extremely successful drug-abuse treatment clinic. At a time when the drug epidemic and public pressure was at its peak, the N.A.U. was able to respond to the needs of a large and diverse group of drug abusers. Many patients appeared as hard-core addicts and left several years later, living completely drug-free lives. Others made the transi-

*tion from heroin addiction to methadone maintenance success-
fully and have been able to stay away from heroin. Still others,
who were not able to finally sever their dependence on illegal
drugs at the time of their treatment, received invaluable and in
some cases life-saving assistance at the clinics.*

The foregoing account could stand as a roughly accurate,
albeit brief, description of the N.A.U. On the basis of it, we
might now begin to analyze the various relationships characteristic of the N.A.U. as a typical drug treatment center of the
early 1970s. Before doing so, let us consider another description
of the N.A.U.

The Sanctuary

*By the late sixties, drugs provided the focus for an unprece-
dented polarization in American society. An increasing number
of the supposed beneficiaries of "the system" were turning their
backs on it and taking up drugs instead. The Establishment
responded with a paramilitary "war on drugs," complete with
border patrols, rent-a-narcs, technologically sophisticated gad-
getry, and propaganda campaigns. Troops of detectives, agents,
and secret agents took to the streets to ferret out the drug users,
but they could not stop the wave of defections from the
straight life.*

*One aspect of the war on drugs was a proliferation of treat-
ment programs. In the big cities, there might be fifteen or
twenty of these programs; in the smaller cities, one or two. The
N.A.U. was one of these programs.*

*In a sense, the Establishment's violent reaction to the tremen-
dous surge in drug use can be seen as having two sides: the
coercive attempts by the police and other law enforcement
types; and the more seductive efforts of doctors, social workers,
and other "do-gooder" types. Needless to say, most drug users
avoided both of these intrusions into their lives, but sometimes
that was impossible. Once a user's involvement with drugs was
discovered, he was subject to furious harassment. The young
were harassed by their parents and school authorities; those*

who were living independently were harassed by the police. Life was made very difficult for those who opted out of the straight world. By and large, drug users accepted this harassment as an inevitable part of their lives. Many users, however, were snared by police (or other authorities), and some kind of active coping with the juggernaut became necessary. There were, of course, various ways of coping—running, going underground, making deals, and so on. One way that many people tried was by signing up for treatment programs.

Thus many drug users were hounded into applying to the N.A.U. Of those who applied, many never joined because of humiliating demands made by the clinic on applicants. Those who did join often had friends already on the program who told them what to expect and how to circumvent the screening process. Others joined the program because participation had been made a condition of probation after being busted.

Applicants to the N.A.U. quickly learned that the unit was not a program, but rather three separate programs. This immediately caused problems, because most drug users wanted methadone maintenance, which made some practical sense. However, less than half of those admitted were lucky enough to be assigned to the methadone program. Essentially, though, the various programs were more similar than they appeared to be. The upper echelon staff members were white doctors, psychologists, or social workers, and the lower level staff (comparable to prison trustees) was made up of ex-addicts who had maneuvered their way onto the staff. As long as the program member was in good standing, he or she was relatively secure from harassment from family, the police, courts, probation officers, or any other agents in the war on drugs. Thus membership in the N.A.U. was a fairly good vantage point from which to cope with the pressures put on drug users. For the users who had been having a rough time on the streets, the N.A.U. provided welcomed relief from the usual persecutions and harassments.

This is not to say, of course, that the N.A.U. was without its problems. The problem basic to all programs of this sort was that the people running them were not content with making life *a little easier for drug users, but insisted on trying to convert them to a more "socially acceptable" lifestyle. Put simply, programs for drug users were run by meddlers.*

This problem can be seen in the program member's need to stay in good standing with the clinic. Abstinence from heroin was a valid criterion for maintaining standing, since (after all) stopping heroin use is what the program was all about. A program member might continue using heroin after entrance, but knew that he or she would lose standing if he got caught, and regarded this as reasonable, albeit inconvenient. But clinicians also expected the member to participate in therapy groups, hold down a straight job, straighten out his or her family life, and generally convert to a more or less docile, straight lifestyle. Of course, it was not beyond the abilities of most drug users to fake these things, but there was a principle involved—the right and responsibilities of the individual to choose his own lifestyle. The doctors, psychologists, and social workers were always trying to convert the program members into adherence to the white, middle-class system which is precisely the system which had rejected, and had been rejected by, the members.

Consequently, there was always a degree of tension between staff and members concerning the scope of clinical intervention which manifested itself in various ways throughout the N.A.U.'s history. As a result, many members adopted the pose of the repentant and reformed ex-addict, complete with stories of successful employment, improved family life, and rehabilitated attitudes. The staff, of course, devoted a considerable amount of energy to testing the validity of members' expressed images, and became (with the help of ex-addict junior staff) reasonably adept at doing so.

The role of ex-addict counselors was always a point of conflict. The professional staff always used the counselors as guards and translators, since the professionals generally recognized that they did not speak the same language as the members. Most counselors, however, had been program members, and tended to retain the drug user's commitment to alternative lifestyles. While these counselors usually felt compelled to be "good soldiers," they were also susceptible to pressure from the members to modify or check the meddling of their superiors.

When the staff, responding to political pressure from the government, several times curtailed member privileges unreasonably, the clinic reached the point of open rebellion. However, members were always either able to exert sufficient pressure on the staff to rescind the restrictions, or (more often) simply left in sufficient numbers to make their point. The departed members frequently reapplied for membership several months later, if their personal positions had deteriorated and conditions on the program improved in the interval.

The existence of these problems was not crippling to the program. As long as the clinicians protected program members from harassment, members tried to keep things functioning smoothly under the umbrella. They generally picked up their medication on schedule, attended their therapy groups, submitted to urine-test schedules, did not peddle drugs on the premises, and tried to stay in good standing. After all, it was a lot better than prison.

This description of the N.A.U. is just about as accurate as the first. The first description approximates the honest account that one of the professionals on the staff might offer to a sympathetic listener who was interested in knowing "what goes on at the N.A.U." The second is a parallel description which a drug user who had been on a program might give to an equally sympathetic listener who had evinced exactly the same interest.

Both of these accounts are "correct" in the sense that they are not prevarications and they meet the logical requirements of the hypothetical situation. However, neither of these ideological versions of what the N.A.U. was about suffices as an adequate description for sociological purposes. Both accounts misconstrue the motives of the other side and gloss over the amount of and reason for deviations for moral typifications on the part of the teller's associates.

Even more important for present purposes, these accounts (and the moral schemas they presuppose) are not satisfactory bases for regularized interactions between the two parties. If the symbolic interactionist school of sociology has shown anything, it is certainly that regularized interaction requires some degree of consensus on a definition of the situation (Mead, 1934; Schutz, 1967; Thomas, 1923). Neither of the above definitions of the N.A.U. could be shared by the opposing side without accepting an extremely degraded status. These ideological definitions of the N.A.U. imply activities by the mandated side which would, sooner or later, destroy the feasibility of the other side's ideological definition of the N.A.U.

This raises the general question of how participants can maintain regularized patterns of interaction in the face of such conflicting, ideologically-generated definitions of the situation. Sociology has generally provided two ans·.ers to these questions. Although we are oversimplifying both positions, generally followers of Emile Durkheim (Durkheim, 1933; Parsons, 1951) have evoked the importance of shared general societal normative standards, and followers of Karl Marx have evoked the concepts of power and coercion. (Mills, 1956, 1959; Horowitz, 1964). Each of these is extremely important in explaining what went on at the N.A.U., but ultimately neither of these is an adequate explanation, either separately or together, for the ordered patterns of interaction at the N.A.U. We will discuss first the sanctioning resources of each side and then the societal normative standards which are involved in the doctor-patient role relationship and show that, while both are critically important, a type of working accommodation specific to the interaction of clinicians and addicts was necessary.

Sanctioning Resources in
Clinician-Addict Interactions

One possible way in which the conflict between differing ideological conceptions of the clinician-addict relationship might be settled is that whichever group has the power (negative sanctions) to coerce compliance, or the resources (positive sanctions) to induce compliance, will be able to institutionalize *its* particular conception of how the relationship *should* be structured. So, for instance, while it is extremely unlikely that the slaves and white overseers on a plantation shared the same conception of their ideal relationship, the white overseers had legitimate recourse to sufficient force to institutionalize *their* conception of how a plantation should operate. Whatever dissent was present in the system could usually be overcome through the use of force, and the system operated smoothly, if unhappily and probably inefficiently. Prisons, mental hospitals, and military camps are other examples of systems whose operation seems to depend less upon consensus than upon monopolization of coercive force.[2]

Like coercion, inducement also mitigates the necessity for consensus. In this case, actors are rationally motivated to cooperate by the expectation of some reward for that activity. Most of our present economic enterprises rely heavily on forms of inducement to elicit appropriate behavior. Employees do not have to understand the nature of the overall corporate enterprise, nor do they have to all agree on the worth of that enterprise. It suffices that they are sufficiently induced to perform the appropriate tasks by the scheduled remuneration. In fact, employees may have vastly different and contradictory conceptions of the nature of the collective enterprise (Etzioni, 1964: 5-7), but as long as their tasks are sufficiently well defined and the remuneration is sufficient to induce performance, the system should be able to function adequately (Parsons, 1964).

In each of these hypothetical situations, conflicting conceptions of the nature of the system and nonreciprocating expectations can to some degree be "outflanked" by the flow of sanctions, inducement and coercion. Appropriate behavior is generated not only by the actor's desire to act appropriately, but also by the actor's desire to avoid the unpleasant or to achieve the pleasant. But the successful use of sanctions rests upon disparate access to resources; in order to be able to effectively coerce or reward, the superordinate group must be in a position to make creditable threats or promises, and those threats or promises must be sufficient to elicit the appropriate response from the subordinate group. Where neither group monopolizes sufficient resources (as is generally the case), the everyday moral typifications used by the participants will differ significantly from the moral typifications of their respective ideologies[3] (Jette and Montanino, 1978: 70 ff.). Such was the situation at the N.A.U., but in order to understand that, we must first inventory the resources each group could command to sanction the other.

The rewards the clinical staff could offer were twofold. First, they offered the possibility of "curing" the addicts' affliction, which is the classic inducement offered by the medical profession. Second, they offered the addict legitimate and legitimizing assistance in dealing with legal, school, familial, or other problems that addicts were likely to face (Ray, 1975; Ruiz et al., 1977). While this inducement is not medical per se, it can be seen as the "social work" overlay commonly present in health care delivery systems today. The negative sanctions available to the clinicians were the reverse of the inducements. They could eject the patient from the program, thus stopping treatment—a serious threat to the patient who was addicted to methadone—and forcing the patient to deal with familial and legal troubles alone. Since most of their patients were under pressure from the police or already on probation, these threats could be both credible and effective. At a lesser level, the N.A.U. programs all set up a series of statuses through which the patient progressed or regressed according to her or his known activities (Gould et al., 1974: 195-198). As the patient progressed, he or she was subject to less clinical control. For example, in the methadone program such minor rights as the right to take home a vacation's supply of methadone or get weekend privileges and take two bottles home were distributed this way. In Zeta House, the internal sanctions were much greater, ranging from holding the highest offices in the program to cleaning up after an untrained dog (Gould et al., 1974: 218-219). However, since Zeta House was run by ex-addicts and the line between clinician and patient was not so clear, much of our description in this chapter is not applicable.[4]

We can see, then, that the clinicians had access to consider-able resources for sanctioning their patients. Indeed, they had far more resources for controlling their patients than clinicians in most traditional medical facilities. However, the patients could mobilize some effective sanctions of their own. Patients had something their clinicians needed very badly—information. This information can be broken down into two categories: information about the nature of addiction and information about what was going on "out in the streets."

In order to appreciate the importance of the first category of information—about addiction itself—it is necessary to know that most of the original senior clinical staff of the N.A.U. had had little or no experience with addiction treatment prior to em-ployment at the N.A.U.[5] Most were skilled psychiatrists, psychologists, psychiatric nurses, or social workers who were interested in drug abuse but not particularly knowledgeable about it. Needless to say, one of their initial problems was to learn about the phenomenon they were supposed to be treating. There was some literature on the subject of addiction, but most of it was years—if not decades—out of date. In addition, the N.A.U. (like all other treatment programs) was considered to be an experimental program and the clinicians were expected to develop innovative approaches, which meant that they had to develop their own expertise on drug-related matters (Gould et al., 1974: 203). So the clinicians had to turn to the addicts for information about addiction and drug abuse in general. But this fundamentally and perhaps permanently affected clinician-patient interaction at the N.A.U., because the patients learned that they knew more about their "disease" than their healers did. An information "inversion" of this sort had two ramifica-tions. First, patients were not likely to pass along information to the clinicians which would unduly increase the rigors of patienthood, and second, patients could systematically with-hold information from clinicians whom they did not respect. Under these circumstances, then, the clinicians who were in-clined to support the patients were rewarded with information and were consequently best prepared to argue their case with other clinicians.

The second information inversion resulted from the particular demands of therapy as practiced at the N.A.U. One of the underlying premises of therapy at the N.A.U. was that the lifestyle advocated by clinicians is more advantageous and satisfying than the lifestyle of the street addict. In order to be able to make this argument, though, the clinicians required rather detailed substantive knowledge of the prevailing conditions "on the streets." Since most of the clinicians (with the exception of the ex-addict counselors) did not gain this information from firsthand experience on the streets, it had to come from the patients or the counselors. Of course, one of the attributes of the skilled clinician at the N.A.U. was the ability to extract such information during the course of therapy, but since information is a valuable resource on the streets, many street addicts were aware that they were being "pumped" at the N.A.U., and gave up information only when it was in their interest to do so or they received something in return.

Furthermore, since clinicians believed that a major therapeutic goal was to aid the patient's adjustment to society, and since that largely involved discouraging "inappropriate" behavior, the clinicians needed continuous information about what specific patients were doing. As with the police and the prosecutors, clinicians' effectiveness depended on getting reliable information from the outlaws, and like the police and the prosecution, they had to "pay" for it (see Chapter 4).

It must be emphasized, though, that patients were not well enough organized to be able to completely control the flow of information from themselves (as a body) to the clinicians. Individual clinicians who might be very objectionable to one group of patients were able to establish close relations with another group, from whom they could extract the necessary information. Still, no clinician could afford to completely alienate his patients, since that would result in a total lack of the information necessary to maintain even the pretense of effective therapy. While there were no cases of such a complete breakdown of communication at the clinic, several senior clinicians who hoped to establish more "traditional" doctor-patient relations left after less than a year.

The patients had another negative sanction which, although it was never used at the N.A.U., was frequently used as a threat. This was the threat of "going public" with complaints. Usually this threat was related to "Black Power" and the threat to use black community support against the clinic (Gould et al., 1974: 162-163). In this particular case, the threat was made particularly credible by the poor relations that Riverdale University in general and the Riverdale Mental Health Center in particular had with the black community. The problem, however, was more general than that. As we discussed in Chapter 2, treatment was part of a political symbolic attack on two groups—blacks and hippies—whose moral worth was being questioned. Treatment was particularly valuable because it symbolically demonstrated that the "Establishment" had the "best interests" of these troublesome people in mind. A demonstration against the clinic would undercut that claim, and thus much of the legitimacy of the clinic. The threat of such a demonstration, especially against the Methadone Clinic, was credibly made on several occasions.

The threat of "Black Power" demonstrations is an interesting form of sanction, since it had more salience to the sanctionee (the clinicians) than to the sanctioner (the patients). Most of the black patients at the N.A.U. considered themselves to be outcasts from their own community, and felt unable to mobilize value commitments from that community. Patients did object to certain practices and policies of the N.A.U. as racist, but they never made any effort to solicit organized support from any of the various militant black groups in Riverdale. Such charges, though, were apt to be taken quite seriously by clinicians, partly because they were perceived as credible threats of demonstrations and partly because equality was a value which most of the clinicians responded to. In a sense, then, patients (or at least black patients) had more power to determine clinic policies than most ever realized.

The final resource available to patients was their presence or absence at the clinic. The withdrawal or entrance of one patient was a minor matter to the N.A.U., but "the numbers problem" was a serious one. Although not run on a fee-for-service basis as the traditional doctor-patient relationship is, and thus not immediately economically effected by the withdrawal of a patient, the N.A.U., like most welfare service organizations, justified its funding largely on the basis of number of patients served. Furthermore, in the midst of the Drug Crisis, clinicians (at the N.A.U. and elsewhere) were under considerable pressure to "*do* something" about drug abuse. The simplest measure of how much the clinic was *doing* was the number of drug abusers "in treatment" and previously "cured" at the facility.[6] Thus every individual addict's decision to enter into and continue treatment was not only a clinical success but also a "public relations" victory for the clinic, since it increased the clinic's "treatment rolls" and thus enhanced the clinic's ability to "prove" it was working. Similarly, the decision to withdraw from treatment was seen as not only a clinical failure, but also a potential public relations liability, since it demonstrated that the clinic was less than wholly successful. In order to satisfy "public demands," clinicians were forced to play what they referred to as "the numbers game": the greater the number of patients that the clinic could legitimately claim, the greater its success in the "public eye" (Gould et al., 1974: 204-207). Clinicians were painfully aware of the numbers game, since program expansion was discussed at most senior staff meetings, and junior staff members were explicitly expected to recruit new patients whenever possible. Programs whose enrollments were falling or not meeting expectations were reviewed in detail at senior staff meetings with the goal to correct "imperfections," and the leaders of programs with high enrollments felt free to give advice to their colleagues who were "having numbers problems."

Patients, however, were much less aware of the numbers game at the N.A.U. Some of the patients realized that the clinic could not survive without patients, but very few were able to see withdrawal from the clinic as an effective sanction (Gould et al., 1974: 188). To be sure, many—in fact most—patients withdrew at least once, and often several times, but never *in order* to effect some sort of change in clinic practices. Their departures, if in sufficient number, often resulted in significant restructuring, but that was a largely unanticipated consequence of their decisions. Thus withdrawal was often an effective, but never an intentional, sanction.

If for purely analytical purposes we view the patients and clinicians as sharing an adversarial relationship, it becomes clear that both "sides" have some resources available. Clinicians have the inherent authority, ties with the legal machinery, and the ability to grant or withhold treatment of a troubling problem. Patients, on the other hand, may divulge or withhold needed information, enhance or inflame community relations, and affirm or deny the clinic's claim that it is "doing something" about the Drug Crisis. While we have no way of quantifying the sanctioning powers of each side, it is clear that each side has substantial resources at its command. The nature of the balance of sanctions between the two groups did not allow either side to simply impose its ideological definition of the situation on the other side.

Sanctioning Normative Regulation of
Clinician-Addict Relationships

Let us now consider what might be called the Durkheimian answer to the question of what organizes role relationship, namely, the role of societally prescribed institutionalized normative expectations. This is the level of organization that corresponds to Durkheim's famous noncontractual elements of contract. In this case, we must deal with the institutionalized role relationship of doctor and patient. Talcott Parsons's writings on the "sick role" are particularly relevant[7] (Parsons, 1951: Ch. 10; Parsons and Fox, 1952).

Parsons lists four aspects of the institutionalized expectation of the sick role:

(1) Exemption from normal social responsibilities which "requires legitimation by and to various alters and the physician often serves as the court of appeal." Parsons also notes that the physician is obliged to provide the society with "protection against 'malingering.' "

(2) The patient "cannot be expected by 'pulling himself together' to get well by an act of decision or will."

(3) The state of being ill is in itself seen as undesirable, and there is thus an obligation on the part of the patient to try to get well.

(4) The patient is therefore under an obligation to "seek technically competent help" (Parsons, 1951: 436-437).

On the surface, it might seem that the sick role is simply a general reflection of the treatment ideology. Thus it might be argued that the societal prescription that the addict play the sick role amounts to nothing more than a societal endorsement of the clinicians' moral typifications. A close look, however, belies that belief.

It must be remembered that our initial analysis in Chapter 3 of the conflict between the outlaw ideology and the treatment ideology focused on the moral issue of personal liberty versus social control. In Western civilization, medicine had traditionally served as a social control mechanism only for the physiological and psychosomatic aspects of the patient's behavior. Freudian psychiatry extended medicine's boundaries into what are commonsensically defined as nonvoluntary psychic phenomena, e.g., hysteria, phobias, compulsions, etc. With the growth of social and community psychiatry, however, the extension of medicine into the behaviors which are normally thought of as *voluntary* requires a modification of the traditional boundaries of medical social control. It is here that the outlaw ideology begins to conflict with the societal injunction to cooperate with the process of cure. As we noted above, the outlaw ideological typification of the clinic did not object to restrictions on the use of heroin. The objection was to the "meddling" of the staff in the patients' personal affairs. Moreover, it did not object to the idea that patients may be removed from the program for using heroin, since treatment of heroin addiction was a legitimate goal, and use of heroin by the patient was unwarranted. Thus, to a certain degree, the outlaw's objection to the N.A.U. can be seen as objections to innovations on the part of the staff in traditional concepts of the limits of the doctor-patient relationship.[8] If this seems like an ad hoc rationalization of the

addict's perspective, it should be remembered th\
second decade of the twentieth century, most or\
cine and the society at large also recognized these .
doctor's role in treating addiction (Lindesmith, 1\ ﹃ᴗ,
1973).

However, the addicts did not stick more scrupulously to the
traditional sick role than did the staff. They wanted to have
their cake and eat it too. While they sought to exclude their
personal lives from the control of the staff, they eagerly
demanded the exemptions from those normal social responsibilities (e.g., not stealing, supporting children, etc.) that a
broader conception of their illness would allow them. Furthermore, when the staff's involvement was perceived by the addict
as involving help rather than interference, the addict was
pleased to receive it. Indeed, many addicts objected to the
staff's failure to provide *enough* help with employment problems and educational problems (Gould et al., 1974: 192). The
patients, however, wanted the right to define these matters in or
out of the clinic's control as they saw fit. Staff members
believed that diagnosis and prescription were their responsibility.

Several other situational problems loosened the bind of the
societally institutionalized expectations of the doctor-patient
relationship. We have already noted that the staff did not,
initially, know much about the "illness" that they were treating
and were thus dependent on their patients for training. In
radical contradiction to the traditional doctor-patient relationship, the patient trained the doctor as an expert in this field.
Thus the doctors and their staff had difficulty delivering
"authoritative" opinions which the patient would be bound to
accept because of a lack of technical competence (cf. Weiner,
1975: 385). Only in the specific areas of drug treatment—the
prescription of methadone and antagonists such as naloxone
hydrochloride—did the staff have that sort of independent
expertise.

Kessebaum and Baumann (1965) have noted that some modification of the traditional doctor-patient role relationship is

necessary, even in traditional medicine, when the disease is chronic. The expectation that the patient will cooperate in his care and "get better" is modified. With heroin addiction, particularly in the methadone program, the issue of chronic versus acute disease was not settled for several years at the N.A.U. After several addicts were successfully detoxified from methadone, the traditional Dole and Nyswander contention that opiate addiction was a chronic incurable disease was rejected at the N.A.U. Prior to that, though, the chronicity issue also loosened the tie to the societally institutionalized role expectations.

Given all of these difficulties with the ideologically mandated role expectations, the staff and patients at the N.A.U. innovated and generated the accommodative moral schema we call the welfare model. As will become obvious, this model bore some similarity to the traditional doctor-patient relationship, but we feel justified in treating it as an independent model.

In addition to departing from the societally institutionalized sick role, the welfare model also departed significantly from the moral typifications of both the treatment and outlaw ideologies. As we saw above, the N.A.U. could be described by participants as either an "infirmary" or a "sanctuary," but neither ideological scheme was programmatically adequate, since one schema's heroes were the other schema's villains or fools. And since neither patients nor clinicians controlled sufficient sanctions to be able to impose their favored model on the other group, some sort of *practically useful* and *mutually acceptable* moral accommodation had to be "worked out." By practically useful we mean that whatever accommodation emerged had to be programmatically sufficient to provide all of the participants with enough practical direction to generate activity that was both personally and interpersonally meaningful. And by mutually acceptable we mean that the moral typifications implicit in the accommodation had to permit sufficient self-respect on the part of all the participants to maintain their membership.[9] This is *not* to say that the accommodation that emerged was completely acceptable to all the participants at the N.A.U. all of the time. To the contrary, at some time or another most participants felt there were severe moral shortcomings to the emerging accommodation, and many members of both sides were chronically alienated. The point is that the culturally given, ideological models and the institutionalized expectations of what the N.A.U. "should" be like were irremediably inadequate. This inadequacy was immediately apparent to clinicians when they discovered that large numbers of their patients were withdrawing from treatment as soon as their legal difficulties were resolved, and equally apparent to patients who discovered that clinicians expected them to forsake not only their drug use but their life style as well. If the N.A.U. was to survive, accommodation was necessary from the very beginning.

Negotiation

Before we can describe that accommodative model, we must first pause to consider the negotiation process which produced and maintained it. This requires a conceptual clarification of "negotiations," since the accommodative schema included, among other things, the moral typifications on the basis of which negotiations about particular decisions are made.

Our use of the term "negotiations" is somewhat broader than a traditional "labor negotiation" model would imply. That traditional model of negotiation implies a process whereby representatives of adversary groups interact ostensibly and specifically *for the purpose* of identifying and then resolving in a mutually acceptable fashion the issues which impede more satisfactory relations between the parties. That is, negotiation is a *part* of overall relations between the parties, isolated from the rest of the interaction either spatially or temporally, in which the parties attempt to reach a consensus on "how this operation should be run." The negotiation "phase" of the interaction is a differentiated, self-conscious consensus enhancement period, in the sense that it is ostensibly engaged in specifically in order to produce agreement.

In applying the term "negotiation" to the emergence of an accommodative moral schema at the N.A.U., we mean to imply only a process whereby the possibility of defining and redefining the constituent features of the situation in order to produce greater consensus is discussed either explicitly or implicitly between parties (McHugh, 1968: 21-45). In this wider sense, negotiation need be neither self-conscious nor spatially or temporally differentiated from the regularized interaction between parties. The labor-bargaining case is just one type of negotiation in our sense of the word.

The process of negotiation changed radically over the period of our research at the N.A.U. This is hardly surprising, since during that period the N.A.U. went from nothing more than a gleam in the eye of the psychiatrist who was to become its director to a moderate-sized organization which employed scores of clinicians and served several hundred addicts at any given time. In brief, the process of negotiation developed in a manner rather similar to Durkheim's (1933) description of the evolution of solidarity. We will elaborate this point further below, but first let us describe the developments more concretely.

The earliest form of negotiation to manifest itself at the N.A.U. was an "advise and consent" status accorded the first patients. At its inception, the unit's clinical staff consisted of a psychiatrist, a nurse, a community psychiatry-oriented psychologist, and a similarly oriented psychiatric social worker. Only the psychiatrist had had any experience treating drug abuse, and that was a two-year residency at Lexington (the old and quite unsuccessful federal addiction treatment center). They all agreed that their job was to set up a methadone maintenance program and a more psychiatrically oriented outpatient facility, but beyond this their plans were vague and there was little agreement. Experimentation and the development of clinical expertise were tacitly accepted as short-range goals. Their first exposure to patients would be crucial, and those first patients were somewhat unusual. The first two dozen patients to be seen at the N.A.U. were relatively mature, predominantly black, relatively successful on the streets, confirmed addicts, articulate, and mostly members of the same clique on the streets (which meant that they tended to support each other).[10] Perhaps most important, they convinced the clinical staff that they were genuinely interested in terminating their addiction with the help of the clinicians. This provided the basis for "good faith" negotiations between the clinicians and members of this group. At the same time, the staff of the program, particularly (but not exclusively) the director, established very strong clinical relationships with this group of addicts. They persuaded the addicts that they were genuinely interested in their welfare and could be trusted to listen to all reasonable requests. This basic bond became the basis for a genuine solidarity between patients and staff that persisted throughout the years of our study. No analysis of the behavior of either side which did not recognize that bond could account for the ability of the N.A.U. to maintain solidarity in the face of conflicting political and ideological interests.

By calling this phase of the negotiation structure "advise and consent" we mean that the staff encouraged this group of patients to participate actively in structuring their own treatments. For example, most of the clinicians favored a period of inpatient treatment at the beginning of methadone maintenance in order to watch for adverse reactions, to decrease the patient's ability to interfere with treatment by taking drugs illicitly, and generally to reinforce the patient's conception of himself as occupying a sick role. Patients, though, were very skeptical about "hospitalization," which they considered unnecessary and excessively disruptive of their personal lives. Discussion produced a mutually acceptable compromise: patients would be hospitalized, but only during the workday (since few of them had regular jobs anyway), and only for two weeks. This agreement was not reached through formal negotiations between recognized ideologically mandated adversaries, but rather by a practical discussion by reasonable people with a common bond involving a concern that the program should achieve its goals. With minor modifications, every patient entering the methadone maintenance program (for the duration of our study) began by spending every workday for two weeks in a special ward of the Riverdale Mental Health Center.

Many of the formal structures and background understandings of the N.A.U., especially of the methadone maintenance program, emerged in this fashion. Treatment plans had to be generated, and in the course of planning a number of pragmatically justified accommodations were made. Entrance criteria, screening categories, medication levels, therapy schedules, and the scope of clinical intervention are just some of the constituent features of the N.A.U. which took form with the advice and consent of the patients.

In historical terms, advise and consent was the most important and prevalent negotiation pattern in the earliest stages of the N.A.U.'s development. However, as the N.A.U. developed, this form of negotiation changed into other forms. The charismatic feelings embodied in this process were routinized into other more stable and differentiated structures. Analytically, though, *from its inception, the working structure of clinic activities was not derived directly from either the treatment or outlaw ideologies, but was generated by the accommodative interaction between members who felt most comfortable operating in the context of one or the other of these ideologies.* Advise and consent was not a self-consciously adversarial proceeding, but rather a cooperative venture with clinicians and patients working together to produce a pragmatic structure.

After the first year, the situation became considerably more complicated, with multiple channels of negotiation existing side by side. As the clinic grew, it became more and more complex and differentiated. In different programs and different "tracks" within the same program, different negotiating procedures were institutionalized. For the present, however, our analytic interest simply lies in an explication of the techniques without reference to their particular location in the overall structure.

Up to this point in our discussion, we have considered "clinicians" as a largely homogeneous group, defined in contrast to the "patients." For nearly all of the participants in the system, however, there were two types of clinicians: professionals and ex-addicts.[11] The differences between these two groups were pervasive and immediately obvious. The professionals were nearly all white, academically trained, and experienced in medical, psychological, social work, or nursing treatment, while the ex-addicts were nearly all black, high-school dropouts, and successful "street hustlers."

During the second year, the "advise and consent" status of the original group of patients became institutionalized in the role of "counselors," filled by seven of the first twenty-five patients. The rest of the initial patients either tried to retain their informal advisory status or withdrew from the clinic. The formal (stated) duties of the counselors were: (1) assist the professionals in diagnosis and treatment planning, (2) assist the professionals in running therapy groups, and (3) maintain order among the patients (cf. Kahn and Nebelkopf, 1979).

Informally, counselors were seen from the very beginning by both professionals and patients as "buffers." From the professionals' point of view, this meant that counselors could "implement" program policy by translating it into a vocabulary (of words *and* actions) which was understandable to the patients, while from the patients' point of view, this meant that counselors were expected to be more sympathetic and understanding of their situational problems than the professionals could be expected to be. Thus one of the more sociologically interesting aspects of the counselors at the N.A.U. was that while they were formally "staff members," usually they were also patients and could claim membership in both the professionals' and patients' subgroup.

While it is conceivable that the counselors could have merely served as buffers between the other groups, given our analysis of the pressures toward negotiation at the clinic, it is hardly surprising that the counselors rapidly became the major structural channel for the negotiation process. Both professionals and patients felt that they could express their desires to the counselors and have those desires transmitted to the opposing party. This "mediator" function could be observed in a variety of situations. At program staff meetings, counselors were often called upon to report on patient attitudes and "gripes"; and proposed program alterations were explained to the counselors with the tacit assumption that these changes would be transmitted to the patients and the counselors would return to the next meeting with "soundings" of patient reaction. At the same time, patients with complaints, dissatisfactions, or threats almost inevitably communicated these to the counselors rather than to the professionals, trusting to the counselors to "translate" them into a language that the professionals would understand and listen to.

In discussing the counselors as "mediators," however, we do not mean to imply that they merely passively transmitted information. On the contrary, they were often called upon (or took it on themselves) to play the devil's advocate in discussions with both the professionals and the patients. They often opposed proposed policy changes on the grounds that "they (either the professionals or the patients) will never go along with *that.*" There was considerable variation in the counselors' willingness to actively participate in the negotiation process, but in general the most successful counselors were those who were very actively engaged in the process.

For a variety of reasons, the counselors could not serve as mediators for all difficulties. First, the counselors, generally having come out of one group on the streets, had enemies within the patient population. Many patients preferred to go over the heads of the counselors directly to the staff, and certain other staff members—specifically, nurses and other low-status professionals—also served to some degree as staff mediators.

However, much of the negotiation regarding day-to-day expectations went on without mediation directly between staff and patients. The major focus of staff-patient interaction eventually centered in the various therapy groups. All patients were required to attend these groups regularly, and virtually all the clinical staff members participated in one or more. Consequently, although the original patients (or at least those who were still in the clinic) still occupied specialized negotiating roles, negotiations between newer patients and new staff began to be conducted in these groups. The newer patients used this more universalistic channel and were thus freed from dependence on the older patients.

From the clinical staff's point of view, the purposes of these therapy groups were to elicit information from patients about their behavior, "confront" the patients with "inadequacies" in their behavior, and provide support for behavior which was proper. In terms of formal goals, then, therapy groups at the N.A.U. were essentially similar to therapy groups in other clinical systems. However, at the N.A.U., staff demands for better role performance on the part of a patient were frequently met by patient objections to the demands. Discrepancies between clinical demands and patients' behavior, which was the ongoing topic of discussion in therapy groups, could be resolved by either of two legitimate outcomes: the patients could agree that they should modify their behavior to meet the demands, or clinicians could agree to modify the demands to suit patients' desires. An example of the latter course can clearly be seen in the following exchange in a therapy group involving a clinician and several "day patients."

Clinician: Kathy, I don't understand why your attitude is so bad. This morning while everyone else was working hard repainting the workroom, you were just moping around.

Kathy: I just didn't feel like working.

Clinician: What do you mean you didn't feel like it? You know that learning to be able to finish a job is an important part of what we're doing here.

Kathy: Well, to tell you the truth, I can't get behind all this work bullshit. I mean I came in wanting to talk about problems and all I heard was "go paint the workroom and we'll talk about it later." I mean, why can't we just "group" (have a therapy group) first thing in the morning and put off the other bullshit until later?

David: Shit yes, the only thing I got from painting the room was a bunch of paint in my hair.

Clinician: Well, how do the rest of you feel about what Kathy said? (general, if vague, agreement) So you think we

> should do more "grouping" and less work? (general, if
> vague, agreement) Well then, why don't you elect a
> representative to take the proposal to the next staff
> meeting, since I can't make that kind of a decision now.

In this example, as with almost all negotiations at the N.A.U., the negotiations start with a specific problem that a specific person has. Rarely were the issues negotiated in the abstract until they had first been concretized in a specific example.

The negotiation process in this example is nearly self-evident. It begins with the clinician identifying a discrepancy between expectations that patients engage in constructive work and Kathy's lack of satisfactory performance. While the clinician almost certainly brought up this discrepancy in order to effect some sort of change on Kathy's part, Kathy reformulated the matter at hand into a negotiation about the appropriateness of the expectation rather than the propriety of her performance. Since the other participants in the group were willing to tacitly support her challenge, the topic was turned from the adequacy of Kathy to the adequacy of the clinic.

Needless to say, negotiations of this sort did not inevitably lead to structural or procedural modification of the clinic. In fact, the episode which was just described ended in failure for the patients, since the "representative" sent to the staff meeting was not able to persuade the senior staff that the change would be beneficial. The important point is that therapy groups became a principal focus for patient-staff interaction, and that the possibility of redefining some aspect of the reciprocal expectations was never entirely excluded. This is not to say that all therapy groups were always engaged in the process of negotiation with which we have been concerned. A considerable amount of group effort went into changing the behavior of patients, but for our present purposes, attention should be paid to the effort that went into changing the shared model of what the clinic was all about.

Formal Grievance Mechanisms

After the first few years of operation, most of the programs at the N.A.U. institutionalized some sort of formal grievance

procedures to handle staff-patient disagreement. In the methadone program, where the evolutionary development of the
structures of negotiation proceeded further, there arose two
major settings for different types of negotiation. These two
different settings served roughly legislative and judicial functions. The incident described above with "Kathy" resisting
painting the room was a low-level problem which took place in
the less differentiated outpatient program. If a series of such
incidents took place in the methadone program and the director
became persuaded that they were "really the same problem," he
would call a "community meeting" (Gould et al. 1974:
195-202). Community meetings served a legislative function.
They were episodic occurrences in which staff and patients
discussed the "state of the program" with the specific expectation that program modification would result from the discussion.
At these events, the constraints of the therapist-patient relationship were relaxed considerably to enable all of the participants
to interact on a more politically equal basis. This is not to say
that all distinctions between patients and clinicians were tem-
porarily suspended on these occasions. On the contrary, the
bureaucratic distinction between those who are held responsible
for the state of the program and those who are not became even
more salient. But everyday expectations deriving from the therapist-patient relationship were suspended, and replaced by the
obligation to act in a politically "responsible" fashion.

The advantage of this procedure was that it broadened the
political process by opening it to all program members, granting
them roughly equal participatory status, and by more or less
forcing those in authority to make their policies explicit. However, neither the clinicians nor the patients were particularly
comfortable or effective operating in a quasi-parliamentary situation. In actuality, then, these procedures tended to be un-
stable, transforming themselves into either what were called
"shouting matches" or else quasi-therapy groups where the
generation of socioemotional support took primacy over the
need to resolve substantive discord. In any event, the community meeting served as a "safety valve" with regard to the
maintenance of routine patterns by providing a structural mech-

anism for resolving patient-staff conflict (and occasionally patient-patient conflict) outside of the therapy-group situation.

A complementary negotiation procedure involved the Advisory Board, composed of several clinicians and several "senior" patients. Although formally set up as a judiciary system to determine the appropriateness of punishment of patients who violated program rules, the Advisory Board played a big part in negotiating the appropriate demands on patients. As the theorists of legal realist jurisprudence have noted (Frank, 1936; Levi, 1949), the judiciary inevitably redefines the law in applying it. The Advisory Board's decisions on patient behavior redefined patient obligations and, at least inferentially, staff obligations. Since their decisions were formally only advisory to the staff, they tended to function as mediators between the staff and the larger body of patients. While the Advisory Board, a small group which met regularly, was more flexible than the community meetings, its decisions primarily functioned to negotiate less serious modifications of role expectations.

A Reappraisal of Negotiations

Before looking at the negotiation process at the N.A.U., we concluded that clinicians and patients had very different interests in the N.A.U. and that those interests were often in conflict, but that both were interested in maintaining the viability of the clinic. In the discussion of negotiation at the clinic, we have seen in some detail how these differences were dealt with. During the five years we studied the N.A.U., a variety of different negotiation mechanisms evolved. Some, like "advise and consent," the therapy group negotiation, were highly informal and unstructured. Others, such as the grievance machinery and junior-staff mediators, tended to be explicit and very rule-bound.

The development of these negotiation processes in the N.A.U., as we noted earlier, somewhat parallels Durkheim's (1933) discussion of the development of solidarity from mechanical to organic. The "advise and consent" status taken by the early program members, in conjunction with a generalized willingness by both parties to try to develop a viable and useful service organization, bears some resemblance to "primitive" mechanical solidarity. There was minimal differentiation of members and their value commitments. The focus was on general values and rather direct efforts to specify them in the structures of the organization. The negotiation processes themselves were not differentiated from the rest of the clinician-patient interaction.

As the clinic grew, the specialized institution of the counselor grew up. The counselor personified the early commitment to a joint undertaking between staff and patients and served as a vehicle through which implementation of those values could be carried on, that is, a vehicle of negotiation as to what the specifics of the reciprocal obligations of the staff and patients would be. For reasons we have described, this mechanism alone was insufficient to include all of the patients, and increasingly differentiated and universalistically structured negotiation vehicles developed. The therapy groups focused on negotiating the patient and staff obligations on a day-to-day level, and the Advisory Board and community meetings functioned to negotiate specialized aspects of more general program changes.

Throughout this discussion, we have seen that the structure of the N.A.U.—those regularized and pragmatically moral patterns of interaction—emerged *through* these negotiation processes. To be sure, most (if not all) of the participants in the N.A.U. had ideologically generated conceptions of what the N.A.U. should have been like, but all of them found that the practical demands of maintaining the viability of a system to which many of them were deeply committed forced the generation of an accommodative model of what the N.A.U. *is* like which would be acceptable to both clinicians and patients. That accommodative schema is precisely the output of all the negotiation mechanisms. Because of the conflicting ideologies, it was often impossible or counterproductive for either side to explicitly justify its negotiating position through recourse to ideology, so many of the outcomes were justified only in terms of pragmatic considerations: "Unless we do (such and such) we

won't have any more applicants," or "We've got to do this or
else Washington will cut off funds." And under these circumstances, it is hardly surprising that the moral typifications of the
emergent accommodations differed significantly and fundamentally from the ideological models that the participants had
to draw upon.

The Emergent Model

While this chapter has focused on the processes of developing
an accommodative schema rather than its ongoing functioning,
it now seems appropriate to sketch briefly the accommodation
that emerged between the addicts and the clinicians. This model
was the basic grounding for decisions about what the N.A.U.
was to be.

This model can be said to have five elements.

1. The patients and staff believed themselves to share the
common goal of keeping the patient in "treatment." This is not
to say that they shared a common reason for achieving the goal,
but the reasons were, for most purposes, not treated as relevant.
This common goal provided a basis for more specific agreements, and for a commitment to the survival of the program.

2. Both patients and staff agreed that certain outside pressures threatened the existence of the program. Both the patients
and staff "had to" do certain things if the program were to
survive. There were perceived threats to the program both from
the national government and the local community. The national
pressures were largely for the staff to deal with, but they
sometimes required patient cooperation. This rubric justified
such demands on the patients as entertaining site visitors from
Washington with stories of the glories of the N.A.U., cooperat-
ing in filling out records for the purposes of generating statistics, and tolerating some program modifications.

Local pressures such as the police and the news media were
also seen as presenting a threat, although much less so as the
program became more established. However, the patients were
expected to keep out of trouble with police and therefore not

to engage in serious crimes, i.e., selling drugs, burglary, etc., while on the program. Actually, this was not so much an expectation as a warning. It was generally agreed that anyone who got into serious trouble with the law would be thrown out of the program. More impressive was the fact that some program members came to feel that it was their duty to inform the therapy group of any information that they had of others engaged in those practices. The guilty parties would be warned and harassed, but not thrown off the program unless they were arrested or persisted too blatantly in the activity. Both staff and patients did their best to persuade the local news media of the help that the N.A.U. was providing Riverdale.

3. A related aspect of the accommodative model was that the N.A.U. was essentially a government welfare program more or less like all other welfare programs. This meant first that membership in the program was on universalistic criteria. Everyone who had a "serious drug problem" could and should be admitted. They were all entitled to the service which the government provided. The performance requirements to stay on the program, aside from those necessary to protect the program from outside pressures, were minimal. This represented a major concession by the staff, which tried, for the first few years, to require major "therapeutic progress" or adherence to a "straight lifestyle," to use the street phrase. About the only requirements were that the addicts account for failure to show up at therapy groups, take prescribed medication, and not have too many "dirty urines," i.e., urine tests indicating drug use. The number of permissible dirty urines grew over the period of our research. At last count (1974), as many as 25% of the members had dirty urines during a week's testing.

4. The staff and patients agreed that the nature of the treatment at the N.A.U. involved staff efforts to induce and persuade the patients to give up the junkie way of life. In return for the protection of the N.A.U., the patients agreed to the legitimacy of these staff demands. This does not mean that patients were morally obliged to give up their lifestyle, but only that they had to make some sort of pretense of doing so. Some

negative sanctioning by clinicians was allowed in pursuit of this goal, but it was limited.

5. Correspondingly, punishments for the above violations were to be decided on jointly by patients and staff. This provided a basis for continued negotiation about the particulars of the program's expectations.

It is apparent immediately that these moral premises are inappropriate to both the medical and outlaw models of what the N.A.U. should be like. Likewise, this accommodation differs markedly from institutionalized assumptions about the sick role. We have called this accommodative pattern the "welfare model" because we believe that the central patterns of this accommodation bear a close similarity to the institutionalized patterns through which contemporary government provides aid to the society's poor. In fact, if we can free ourselves of the implications of the term "clinic," the N.A.U. begins to closely resemble the operation of the contemporary welfare agency. In both cases, the condition of a class of people is taken to be sufficiently morally troublesome to society as a whole that a delivery system for some sort of public assistance and control is created. Whether or not that assistance is truly remedial is, in a sense, irrelevant, since it is the aggravation that produces the delivery system, not the actual condition of the recipients. As long as the assistance appears to alleviate the aggravation, the program will be considered a success.[12]

The specific similarities between welfare practice and the welfare-model accommodation come in the first three elements of that accommodation. In a welfare program, societal pressures are used to justify limits on what the caseworker can provide the client and to require certain behaviors from the clients. Likewise, the assumption is prevalent that both caseworker and client want to assure that the client has enough money to survive and thus that service to the client is continued. Finally, the entrance requirements into the program are minimal, and the client is required to *do* very little in order to receive assistance.

The accommodation at the N.A.U. differed from the operation of a welfare agency only in the last two elements of the

accommodation. These two elements involve the legitimacy of
staff efforts to persuade and induce lifestyle changes, and joint
staff-patient control over those sanctions. This seems to be
something of a second-level accommodation based on the existence of the first three elements and the relative large amount
of resources available to the N.A.U. as an experimental program. It is our definite impression that in the larger and less
well-funded programs in other cities, staff-addict consensus
concerning both of these typifications was substantially reduced
or absent.[13] Thus, in spite of some residual components of a
psychiatric-medical role relationship between staff and patients,
we believe the characterization of the clinic as based in practice
on a welfare accommodation is justified.

Two leading medical figures in drug treatment, Vincent Dole
and Marie Nyswander, recognized this nationwide trend in a
review of the first ten years of methadone maintenance,
although they held the view that the pressure toward bureau-
cratization was simply a response to increased intervention by
the federal government. They write (1976: 2119):

> the physician is made to feel as defensive as the addict and is left
> with no real authority in his clinic. . . . In a recent survey that we
> made in jails and on the streets, the reasons most often given by
> addicts for rejection of treatment were their perception of cynical
> and uncaring attitudes in the staff of programs, unreasonable rules,
> rigidity, and lack of respect.

Finding this similarity between the programmatic models of
public assistance and the N.A.U. gives us an important clue
about the basic source of the particular accommodation that
emerged at the clinic. The simple fact is that, with the exception of the legal machinery, welfare (and other similar forms of
public assistance) is the model of governmental intervention
with which the patients and most of the staff were most
familiar. Fully 47% of the patients were receiving public assistance while they were members of the program, and it is safe to
say that almost all of the others had either received some
assistance in the past, or had known others who had been on

welfare. Indeed, black and lower-class white cultures provide members with rather detailed moral typifications about what a welfare agency is like, how it operates, and what is the appropriate way to deal with it.

The same, of course, can be said for most of the ex-addict clinicians, since they had all grown up in lower-class urban environments and many had received welfare at one time or another. Even among the senior staff, many of the psychiatric social workers and clinical psychologists had previous work experience in government public-assistance programs. Only the nurses, physicians, and the few psychiatrists on the staff had never had any substantial experience with public assistance, and it was precisely these members who were the most uncomfortable with the emergent accommodative model at the N.A.U.

"Total Institutionalism" as a Countervailing Force

While the "welfare program" was the prevailing schema of moral typification throughout the N.A.U., the various programs differed somewhat in the substance of their accommodative models. Some programs, like methadone maintenance, required very little interaction between patient and staff (as little as several hours a week), while others, like Zeta House, required nearly continuous patient-staff interaction. In fact, Zeta House, organized in a radically different manner, fits Goffman's usage of the term *total institution* almost perfectly. Since the welfare model is most appropriate in situations where staff-client interaction is temporally and spatially isolated from ongoing routines of work, recreation, and sleep, its applicability is markedly attenuated in the context of a total institution. The staff-patient relationship at Zeta House was radically different from the rest of the N.A.U. for the above reasons and also because the patients were in a much weaker position at Zeta House for two reasons. First, all of the House staff were ex-addicts, which meant that they had much less need for the information which patients could use as a bargaining tool in the other programs. And second, most of the patients in the House were in serious trouble with the courts, which meant that they were under considerably more pressure to submit to staff demands than patients in other programs. These factors seemed to produce an accommodation which was much less favorable to the patients' ideology. Consequently, very few applicants to the N.A.U. would voluntarily accept House membership, which tended to reinforce those conditions which skewed the accommodation in favor of the staff in the first place.

We cannot describe this accommodation here in detail. We do, however, want to make clear that the welfare model as we have described it is contingent on numerous situational factors and is not the inevitable result of a need to cooperate between outlaw-mandated and treatment-mandated actors.

NOTES

1. It is probably the case that in other more populous geographic locales, a somewhat more varied range of addict-clinician interaction took place in institutional contexts ranging from free clinics to hospital detoxification wards. On the basis of literature cited throughout this chapter, we have concluded that the N.A.U. was broadly representative of most government-affiliated treatment programs in the United States during the late sixties and early seventies. Still, it must be remembered that alternative clinical models were experimented with in other locations.

2. Even here, the evidence of accommodation is quite clear. See, for example, Gresham Sykes's brilliant work, *The Society of Captives* (1958), and Erving Goffman's equally brilliant essay, "The Underlife of a Public Institution" (1961).

3. The ability to "gloss over" the differences between "working" and "ideological" realities was an important characteristic of *all* of the most successful participants at the N.A.U.

4. For a description of Zeta House, see Gould et al. (1974), Chapter 10.

5. Toward the beginning of the Drug Crisis, this was true of virtually all treatment programs. By the end of the crisis, however, a cadre of trained professional workers had been produced.

6. See Etzioni's discussion of the ramifications of "overmeasuring" in formal organizations (Etzioni, 1964: 9-10).

7. There has, of course, been considerable criticism of this mode of analysis as a general basis for medical sociology (Friedson, 1970), but for the present purposes it is quite fruitful.

8. Cf. Matza's (1964) observations on juvenile delinquents' objections to innovations in the law.

9. The difficulty of maintaining self-respect for both staff and clients in drug treatment programs has been recognized by Dole and Nyswander (1976: 2119), among others.

10. Some of this first group of patients had been private patients of the psychiatrist while the N.A.U. was in the process of gaining funding.

11. The label "ex-addict" is a specific term employed by most participants in the N.A.U. It does not mean that the designee is no longer addicted to anything, since many were acknowledged to be addicted to methadone; but instead, the label was used to designate anyone who (1) had once been addicted to heroin, (2) had undergone the appropriate transition rituals to signify occupancy of the new status, and (3) was making professional use of his previous involvement with heroin. The role and status of the ex-addict seems to have emerged across America during the Drug Crisis. See Johnson (1975) for an extended discussion of drug treatment and the ex-addict.

12. One important and interesting difference between contemporary welfare programs and the accommodative model which evolved at the N.A.U. is that most of the political pressure on welfare programs is to keep the number of clients as *low* as possible, whereas the pressure on the N.A.U. was to keep the client population as *high* as possible.

13. For instance, Schwartzman and Kroll (1977: 498) report, "For a certain number of individuals seen as incapable of abstinence, methadone maintenance is seen as the optimal goal. There is very little therapeutic intervention with these clients as long as they do not indicate any illegal drug use."

Chapter 6

THERAPEUTIC CONTROL

Ideologies and Professions

In Western civilization, two of the oldest and most venerated vocations are law and medicine. In contemporary America, these vocations have developed highly complex and specialized subsystems which function in the domain of social control, criminal law, and psychiatry. Even these subsystems are now so complex that we can no longer speak of criminal law being "done" by the judge, or psychiatry being "done" by the doctor. Instead, we are forced to speak of law being done by the legal system and psychiatry being done by the psychiatric system. Over the, last century and a half, psychiatry and criminal law have developed moral typifications of their proper functions in society and the proper procedures for fulfilling those functions, which are very closely tied to the ideologies we described in Chapter 3. Contemporary criminal law has adopted the punishment ideology, and contemporary psychiatry generally subscribes to the treatment ideology. While discrepancies can easily

AUTHOR'S NOTE: This chapter was coauthored by Lansing E. Crane, Esq.

be shown between aspects of both of these systems and their respective ideologies (Blumberg, 1967; Matza, 1964; Scheff, 1966: Ch. 4; Goffman, 1961; Mechanic, 1962; Szasz, 1961), for the most part the normative structure of each system can be seen as an articulation of the principles and assumptions of its mandating ideology.

While the last two chapters concentrated on intraorganizational and interactional analysis, this chapter will discuss the development of an intersystem collaboration based on the accommodative schema we have called "therapeutic control." While technically therapeutic control is an accommodative schema in the sense described in Chapter 4, the collaboration went far beyond the tentative and temporary agreements that are usually implied by the term accommodation. Indeed, the accommodative schema became so deeply ingrained in both systems that we will be forced to ask whether it might not be more appropriate to think of therapeutic control as the governing schema of a single control system which takes place in two different settings. While the other accommodative schemas were essentially hidden from the public and largely private to their members, therapeutic control, or at least part of it, was publicly acknowledged and even acclaimed. Serious efforts were made during the crisis to legitimate this accommodative model as the appropriate institutionalized system model. For this reason, this chapter will focus on these more general issues and deal with the intraorganizational and interactional problems only as they are relevant to the institutional questions.

Law and Medicine

Traditionally, law and medicine as systems of social control have been radically separated from each other. This separation can be seen, for example, in the ideological status of information and in the normative information gathering processes in each system. In the punishment ideology, the veracity of information is taken to be relative to the interest of contending parties, and the normative information-gathering procedure in the legal system mandates the collection and consideration of information from all interested parties. One of the central elements of the constitutional right to "due process" is that the courts take no irreversible action against a citizen without first giving that citizen the opportunity to present the truth of the matter—as that citizen understands it (Mullane v. Central Hanover Bank and Trust Co., 1950; Freedman, 1975).

This may be compared with the medical system. In the treatment ideology, only one truth is recognized: objective truth. In the normative medical system, everyone (patients, families, nurses, x-ray technicians, and so on) is supposed to assist the doctor in discovering the objective truth about the affliction at hand. One of the central elements of "professional ethics" is that the doctor disregards his or her personal interests in the diagnostic and treatment process (Parsons, 1951).

It is important, of course, to note that various aspects of these systems are somewhat "at odds" with the resident ideologies. Physicians' overdependence on the pharmaceutical industry and plea bargaining are examples of structural arrangements which demonstrate considerable variation from the ideological position (Blumberg, 1967). There is no sociological surprise in discovering that many legal and medical practices are essentially ideologically unjustifiable, but on the whole these two systems are excellent examples of social activities organized with reference to specific ideologies.

Ever since the use of certain drugs was identified as constituting a social problem—which is essentially a twentieth-century phenomenon (Musto, 1973)—there has been considerable uncertainty and ongoing debate about whether the rectification of the problem is in the domain of the medical or the legal system (Schur, 1962; Musto, 1973; Lindesmith, 1965; Kuskey and Krasner, 1973). For the most part, this debate has been conducted in terms of which ideology is the appropriate framework for conceptualizing the abuse and control of drugs. For the first two decades of this century, the problem was put in the hands of the medical system (with the full cooperation of the then emerging pharmaceutical industry). In 1919, in Webb et al. v. U.S., however, the Supreme Court asserted the primacy of the legal system's claim over the problem and signaled an end to the medical maintenance of drug users. In that decision, maintenance of a patient's drug habit by a physician was stripped of its "treatment" character and the general medical profession was permanently excluded from maintaining addicts.

The drug problem remained in the domain of criminal law from the 1920s until the early 1960s. While the appropriateness of the legal control of drug abuse was questioned from time to time (Lindesmith, 1965; Schur, 1962), the medical system gave no evidence of any serious interest in drug abuse during this period. So the punishment of drug users by the legal system continued unabated until the early 1960s. At that point, medicine reentered the field in the form of *psychiatric* treatment of drug users, which, unlike the earlier medical maintenance system, sought to abolish drug abuse. The stage seemed set for another major battle.

Ideological Conceptions of Drug Control

Both the punishment and treatment ideologies are programmatically capable of generating drug-control programs. A punishment program would center on the conception of the entire system of drug use as a series of willful acts, which should be repressed through the use of just punishment as a deterrent. A treatment-ideology program would center on the conception of drug abuse as symptomatic of personality or organic pathology, which should be remedied through positive clinical intervention. The ideological discongruity of these two positions must not be minimized: in the legal ideology, the drug user is a *willfully immoral* person who must be punished; in the treatment ideology, the drug abuser (like the cancer patient) is the *victim* of a misfortune, who must be helped.

To a certain extent, the debate concerns the utility of punishment in the control of drug abuse. The punishment ideology (as the name implies) prescribes the use of punishment to uphold morality and deter further deviance, while the treatment ideology is scornful of punishment, prescribing instead positive therapeutics to ameliorate the deviant's condition, thus permitting him to resume morally acceptable activities. Although the utility of punishment is the central point, the ideological conflict involves a variety of other issues, including: (1) what information is pertinent, (2) how should it be gathered, (3) how should the deviant be expected to respond to the intervention, (4) what should the intervention termination criteria be, (5) what activities is the deviant to be held responsible for, and (6) what conditions are conducive to this form of deviance.

Since the punishment and treatment ideologies generate different and often conflicting answers to these questions, we would expect to see considerable conflict between the medical and legal systems. And a careful examination of the history of drug-abuse control efforts in this country will disclose that such conflict has been endemic, from the jailing of doctors in the 1920s through the efforts of clinicians in the 1960s to "protect" their patients from legal forces (Musto, 1973; Lindesmith, 1947, 1965; Swanson, 1975).

There are, of course, some noticeable instances of institutionalized psychiatric-legal cooperation outside of the drug area, such as the treatment orientation of Juvenile Court (especially prior to the decision In re Gault, 1967), the insanity defense, and the rhetoric of the corrections system since the latter half of the nineteenth century. These areas of cooperation suggest that neither system is anxious to totally exclude the other, but this cooperation has also been subject to considerable ideological criticism (Hakeem, 1958; Gould and Namenwirth, 1972; Matza, 1964). Among other things, it has been argued that this cooperation has seriously jeopardized both the "due process" tenets of the law and the "medical ethics" of the clinicians (Szasz, 1963). Thus, while intersystem accommodations have emerged, they have often become the foci of considerable intrasystem debate. Further examples of uneasy medical-legal relationship can be found in the current controversies surrounding alcoholism and homosexuality.

In the mid 1960s, the psychiatric system began showing renewed interest in the control of drug abuse. Vincent Dole's development of a new theory of addiction, methadone as a new "positive" therapeutic regime, and the development of the concept of "therapeutic communities" provided psychiatry with fresh approaches to a problem which had come to be regarded as largely insoluble. The federal government, through HEW, was expressing renewed interest in funding medical research into drug abuse, and research and clinical personnel responded to the availability of funds. However, it is important to realize that, whereas the older medical model of addiction assumed that addiction was incurable and thus required medical maintenance, the new psychiatric interest in addiction (Dole and Nyswander notwithstanding) saw addiction as a treatable personality disorder (Glasscote et al., 1972). There was, however, no diminution of the legal system's control efforts. Indeed, the arrest rate for drug-abuse crimes increased rapidly in the 1960s.

Theoretically, this set up a potentially conflictual situation, with two extremely powerful "control" systems laying claim to the same "social problem." While most of the discussions of this conflict were directed to a limited public, each system generated considerable criticism of the other's approach to the problem. Law enforcement personnel were often skeptical about the "soft" approach of most medical therapy, while clinicians were scornful of the effects of punishment on the drug user (Morganbesser, 1974: 215; Swanson, 1975). Neither system was sure that it would be able to fulfill its mandate in the presence of the other. Yet a close accommodation developed. This development went through three successive states: hostility, live and let live, and active cooperation.

The Development of a Compromise:
Stage One—Mutual Hostility

When the N.A.U. was first opened in Riverdale in 1968, there was tremendous uncertainty and anxiety among clinicians concerning the treatment they could expect from the local police and courts. Having some familiarity with the legal system's monopoly over drug control, the clinicians feared that the clinic would be closed, or at least kept under constant surveillance, and they themselves might conceivably be arrested. Thus, for example, substantial parts of at least three staff meetings in the first year of the N.A.U.'s existence were given over to discussion of defensive measures to be taken against the prospect of the N.A.U. being raided or closed down. These measures included plans to destroy patients' files, having legal research done to determine the confidentiality of such records, developing political alliances within city government, and direct negotiations with the police. At that time, it seemed very reasonable to expect the police or courts to subvert the clinical process in order to further their own interests. Surveillance of the clinic by the police in order to apprehend (or at least discover) previously unknown drug abusers was not considered such a farfetched idea in clinical circles. Indeed, during the first year patients reported numerous instances in which they were stopped by the police and "pumped" for information about the program, and one detective allegedly told a patient not to "count on the N.A.U. being around too long," a statement that several N.A.U. staff members took as a threat.

Another source of this defensive posture was the previous experience of the two most senior clinicians below the director of the N.A.U., who had been fired from a previous job because of political pressures outside the agency they worked in. Their belief that the police would destroy the program in Riverdale was great, and not without precedent. The experience of ideological conflicts undermining social control was pervasive throughout the history of efforts to control delinquency, as Walter Miller's excellent study (Miller, 1962) clearly shows.

We know less about the early anxieties in the Riverdale legal system because some lessening of those anxieties was necessary for our observer to be admitted to that system in the first place. However, the early experiences of our observer (who, however neutral he thought himself to be, was seen initially by the police as a representative of the N.A.U., by whom he was employed) indicated some of the hostility. Some notes from the second day of observation follow:

> Things are going better. They started giving me hell about the clinic. DiMattes told me about their arresting Bobby Walters when he was over on the floor (in the Mental Health Center as a day patient) and the stink Suber raised with the press. They think that since they had an arrest warrant they had the right to take him off the floor. They see this as one of several instances that prove that we are going to protect criminals. Smith went on at length about Boss (then a research assistant to our street observer). He told me that Boss was prostituting his "old lady" for years and that indicates what sort of guy he is. Smith asked: "What sort of chance do you think you have of reforming a guy like that? I'll tell you. None." I pointed out that Boss had been on the program six months and he was clean. DiMattes said that he had heard that Boss was drinking a lot and smoking grass.

While there was no feeling that the clinic would be able to close the court down, there was a common conviction that the N.A.U. would make the police and the court's work ineffective by allowing addicts/criminals to escape punishment by hiding behind the skirts of naive clinicians (Swanson, 1975). Many of the legal system personnel knew the addicts who made up the first patient cohort, and they "knew" these addicts would prove resistant to the therapy they were being offered. While, as we noted above, our data is sketchy here, we believe that the law enforcement community's first response to the clinic was to assimilate it into their own competitive-adversarial relationship with the addicts (see Ch. 5). While they did not see the clinicians as doing anything directly illegal, they saw them as being on the other side in a polarized conflict situation.

Stage Two—Live and Let Live:
First Steps Toward Accommodation

Whatever their rivalries, though, the legal and medical systems shared a common element: they both processed the same people. This made some sort of interaction between the systems virtually inevitable, although, as Miller (1962) has shown, this does not make very much cooperation necessary.

During the first year, the N.A.U. took a controlled adversarial position vis-à-vis the courts. Clinicians would go to court *for* their patients, trying to forestall the possibility of the court taking punitive action. The clinicians were trying to argue in court for the primacy of the doctor-patient relationship. In a sense, they were proceeding along pure ideological grounds; trying to show their communality of interest with their patients, and at the same time trying not to lose patients to anything as irrational as the penal system. But by their presentation to the court that they would "take care of this guy," they implied that the court had some interest in successful treatment.

Once it became clear that such an argument could serve as a defense, defense lawyers began to request that the N.A.U. send down a spokesman whenever one of its patient's would appear in court. This was the first sustained pattern of cooperation in Riverdale between any court personnel and the clinic. From this point, it was only a short step for defense attorneys to begin sending their clients to the N.A.U. to get treatment. By the time our observers began systematically observing court and probation work in early 1970, this pattern was already an established defense (Gould et al., 1974: 130-136).

The use of the clinic by defense attorneys must be examined further, because the use of treatment rhetoric by legal system personnel was a significant step in the process of coalition. If these lawyers and their clients agreed on anything, it was that imprisonment was just about the worst possible disposition for a criminal case. Thus defense lawyers and their clients argued for treatment primarily because they saw that as more favorable than prison. They were still seeing this primarily as advantageous to their clients vis-à-vis the punitive system of the court. It was simply a good bargain. As one defense attorney put it to his client: "Well you don't have to go over to the N.A.U., but I got to tell you that the case looks bad and it's your best

defense." Rafalsky's formulation of defense strategy shows how
the treatment ideology began to be raised in court (1972: 409):

> A lawyer should acknowledge that his client is addicted, should
> show that the crime in question is related to the addiction and
> should demonstrate that the client is being treated for his addiction
> and is being rehabilitated. If a favorable disposition of the case
> cannot be obtained in that way, the attorney can then proceed
> according to normal defense strategies.

An important feature of the defense use of treatment is that
the position was raised in the course of plea bargaining sessions,
not in the course of formal proceedings (Gould et al., 1974:
104-105). The judge was simply asked to accept what the
prosecution and defense had already agreed on, namely, that
probation which would allow treatment to continue was more
useful than a prison sentence. The institution of plea bargaining
as the context for this decision is important because it sidesteps
many aspects of legal procedure. The distinctions between the
presentation of evidence, determination of guilt, and sentencing
are foregone, and all three elements are interwoven in the
undifferentiated process of negotiating a disposition *acceptable*
to both the defense and prosecution (Gould et al., 1974: 133).
Thus plea bargaining loses the ideologically presumed adversarial character of formal courtroom confrontation and acquires a
communality of interest character similar to economic contract
negotiation.

By raising support for treatment goals in the course of plea
bargaining, then, the defense was able to disregard the points of
conflict between the punishment ideology of the formal court
and the treatment ideology of the medical system. Since both
defense and prosecution sought expedient dispositions and plea
bargaining was a less restricting methodology for selecting dispositions, plea bargaining became the procedure for the conduct
of discussions which would have been inappropriate in the
course of formal proceedings. The formal courtroom proceedings merely ratified the previously agreed-upon disposition, so
the entire process was never entered in the record and was

largely beyond the scope of judicial review of any sort (Rosett and Cressey, 1976).

When we look at these earliest legal-medical interactions, then, we see that each side was simply trying to use the other to reach its own ideologically mandated goals. There was uneasy cooperation, but both systems were responding to the other as an *external* threat or resource.

We have now described the first two stages of the development of therapeutic control, hostility and live and let live. However, before we can describe the final cooperative accommodation known as therapeutic control, we must make a detour and talk about why the live and let live accommodation was unsatisfactory. This involves both a description of the crisis-produced pressure for results and a description of the practical problems that the various court and treatment role occupants had with addicts which made therapeutic control look like a good solution.

The Need for Therapeutic Control:
The Perception of Crisis

By 1970, it was becoming clear that there were serious questions about the adequacy of either ideological framework to cope with the developing drug crisis. The problems facing the punishment ideology were:

(1) Classic penal punishment was apparently not effectively deterring individual drug users (Georgetown Law Journal, 1972: 667-668; Kleeman and Posner, 1971; Kassis, 1972). The courts were "seeing" the same drug defendants over and over again, in what was sometimes called the "revolving door" of drug use and penal sanction. Of course, the court's perception of a crisis may not have reflected any real increase in recidivism. The demand for increased police pressure and more arrests meant the stepped up surveillance on those addicts the police knew, resulting in those addicts showing up in a court more often. But to law enforcement personnel, the situation appeared to be deteriorating.

(2) In the process of applying increasingly severe penal sanctions (which is the classic legal response to ineffective deterrence), the penal facilities available to the courts were apparently becoming seriously overloaded with "drug crime" convicts. Here again the perception of crisis emphasized the problem. At no point during the crisis were more than one-third of the prisoners in the Riverdale State Jail arrested for drug crimes, but in the context of the Drug Crisis they stood out as a special cause of crowded prisons. Without a single exception, every policeman, probation officer and lawyer we observed expressed the belief that drug cases were overcrowding the jails.

(3) The penal response of the legal system was apparently ineffective in combating the perceived spread of drug abuse. Punishment ideology justifies punishment as a deterrent not only to the offender who is punished, but also to the "potential" offender. In the face of the widespread perception that the incidence of drug abuse was increasing dramatically, legal-system personnel were almost forced to conclude that the penal sanctions were an ineffective deterrent for the population at large. Court personnel, like other members of the society, saw drug use as a threat to their neighborhoods and their children. While for a public consumption they maintained that their efforts would solve the community's problems, among themselves they had doubts. As one detective told our observer: "I don't know, Chuck, it's a tidal wave. Maybe we'll have to give up and let them get their junk from a clinic." In that context, cooperation with a clinic that promised to treat rather than just maintain an addiction seemed acceptable.

(4) The final problem the courts had was more subtle. Like the clinic, court personnel learned about drugs from the addicts. Using the tried and tested excuse-making techniques described by Matza (1964), the addicts tended to describe their drug use to the law enforcement personnel in terms of uncontrollable needs. While the police greeted such claims with unmitigated skepticism, court personnel were uneasy. Only one of the six assistant prosecutors we observed expressed no serious reservations about punishing addicts. Given their perception of their own lack of expertise when dealing with heroin, the prosecutors

found it hard to reject the expertise of the clinicians and the addicts who claimed that the addict "needed" treatment.

Two examples from our field notes should clarify this pattern:

> DeJean [the prosecutor] and I were talking and waiting for Nelson [a defense attorney] to finish talking with his client when some jive cat came up.
>
> "Excuse me, you're the prosecutor, aren't you?"
>
> "Yeah."
>
> "Can't you and me settle this thing without him? (pointing to the P.D. on the other side of the court)"
>
> "What's on your mind?"
>
> "Well, I mean, you're not going to send me away, are you?"
>
> "Why shouldn't I, you were dealing weren't you?"
>
> "Yeah, man, but I had a big habit to support. Where else was I going to get $75 a day. Besides, what good is it gonna do to send me away? I need treatment."

Admittedly, it was unusual for an addict to do his own bargaining, but defense lawyers often made similar arguments. Thus the following interaction:

Prosecutor:	"What about Jones?"
Defense Attorney:	"He's an addict. I'm gonna send him to the Mental Health Center."
Prosecutor:	"He's been arrested eight times before."
Defense Attorney:	"Yeah, but he's a *junkie.*"

At the same time, some major problems were becoming evident in the treatment system.

(1) While applications to drug treatment programs had not yet begun to decline, senior clinicians believed that there was a large segment of the "drug abusing population" who "needed help" but were not seeking treatment on their own (Gould et al., 1974: 205-207).

(2) Patients who applied for admission to treatment programs were all too likely to terminate treatment against the advice of the clinicians. In the language of the clinic, there were perceived to be too many "splitees." As we saw in Chapter 5, this largely resulted from conflicting ideas about what the clinic should be on the part of the addicts and the clinicians (Dole and Nyswander, 1976). Many addicts wanted to use the clinic as a way of reducing their drug habit, getting out of family and school troubles, and as a short-term way around the courts. The clinicians could not accept such a use of the clinic (Gould et al., 1974: 157-158).

(3) Clinicians were beginning to believe that patients were not sufficiently cooperative in their treatment. Clinicians (and legal-system personnel) were worried that patients were selling their methadone on the black market (rather than consuming it as medication), that patients were not foregoing various criminal activities that were supposed to be foregone by patients, and that patients were not participating wholeheartedly in therapy programs.

(4) Like the court personnel, the clinicians were faced with addicts who could plausibly claim to know a great deal more about addiction than the clinicians did. The message that they got from the addicts lead them to believe that it was a naive belief that most addicts would accept treatment without court pressure.

So the medical system was having troubles of its own, although clinicians managed to keep most of their concerns out of the public discussion of the effectiveness of the treatment programs.

By 1970, the import of these inadequacies in both control systems was apparent to both legal- and psychiatric-system personnel. The crisis of drug abuse provided a key context for the evaluation of these inadequacies in several ways. First, it was perceived by both clinic and court personnel that there would be no shortage of "drug abusers"[1] available to either system. Since drug abusers were to be the "raw material" of both systems, a scarcity might have led either or both systems to aggressively lay claim to the entire source. With a surfeit of drug abusers on hand, however, both systems could easily afford to recognize the legitimacy of the other's intervention.

The second way in which the Drug Crisis provided an important context for the evaluation of intervention strategies was through the mobilization of external pressure. Both clinic and court personnel felt themselves to be under considerable pressure from the public (and from the clinicians from Washington) to do something about the crisis. These pressures were more concrete than they might seem. The clinic felt that a favorable public image, both locally and nationally, was fundamental to their ability to get continued funding from the National Institute of Mental Health and to be able to expand in the future (Gould et al., 1974: 204-207). Major fights with the local law-enforcement community were thought likely to come to the attention of the project officer in Washington and damage the program's image. The law-enforcement community, and particularly the prosecutor's office, was thoroughly enmeshed in local politics. Political sense told them that conflict with the Mental Health Center, and thus the University Hospital, would not look good in the newspapers.

At the end of the live and let live period, the relationship between the law-enforcement community and the clinic began moving towards increased interdependence. Each system perceived the other as able to provide certain specific solutions to the other's endemic problems. The advantages of cooperation were seen by various role incumbents in both systems. Defense attorneys, as we already noted, tended to favor some cooperation because "treatment" was generally perceived by both them and their clients as a more acceptable disposition than incarceration. Of course to the clients it was a less acceptable disposition than simple probation, but judges were extremely reluctant to grant simple probation to "drug offenders," especially "repeaters." Some defense attorneys told our observers that they preferred "treatment" to simple probation because they felt that clients with a "drug problem" required some sort of intervention before they ended up with a case which would require incarceration.[2] However, as the interdependence of the legal and medical systems became routinized, some of the more civil libertarian lawyers began to get uncomfortable. But since the most repressive acts of that system occurred outside the courtroom context, the defense attorneys were rarely involved.

From the prosecution's point of view, the main advantage of a symbiotic relationship with the N.A.U. was that it facilitated plea bargaining. Especially in the lower courts in Riverdale the docket was always jammed. The prosecutors' biggest problem was to keep cases moving without "giving away the court" (see Chapter 4). In the context of the Drug Crisis, drug cases were seen as a major cause of the overloading of the docket, and a simple disposition which required little of the court's time was a major help in clearing the docket. Not all these cases involve violations of narcotics-control laws. Many involved "the kinds of crimes that addicts typically commit to support their habit" (Sudnow, 1965). In these cases, the defense usually claimed that the defendant's "drug problem" was at the core of the case and the prosecutor could easily dispose of the case by sending the defendant to the N.A.U. (Gould et al., 1974: 129). For the prosecution to even "get through" these "swollen" dockets required some form of plea bargaining. From the prosecution's point of view, successful plea bargaining involved an agreement to a less severe, but essentially just, disposition. Thus even if the prosecutor was not at all convinced of the ultimate efficacy and preferability of treatment as opposed to punishment, he found treatment to be a useful disposition because it significantly increased his ability to manage a large docket.

The probation officer's role in the hybrid system was particularly important because he was given the responsibility for invoking the punitive sanctions to support treatment. His reasons for taking on this role, therefore, are particularly important. Traditionally, probation is neither purely treatment nor purely punishment mandated. As the enforcer of the sentence which the judiciary hands out on the basis of the seriousness or nonseriousness of the crime, the probation officer is an arm of the criminal law. However, probation officers frequently come from social-welfare backgrounds and often espouse the treatment ideology. As an organized profession, probation officers are heavily committed to treatment (Diana, 1960).[3] Thus most of the probation officers in Riverdale were strongly predisposed to cooperate with treatment agencies.

Furthermore, being a probation officer in Riverdale was a frustrating job, as it is in many other jurisdictions (Diana, 1960). While they were supposed to "supervise" the probationers and see that they stayed out of trouble, the most idealistic of Riverdale's probation officers saw supervision as a form of therapy, a chance to "do some good." But with case loads of 120 probationers per officer, there was little prospect of ideologically meaningful success (Gould et al., 1974: 140-141). Their other major job, doing presentence investigations to aid the judge in sentencing, was equally frustrating because, almost without exception, sentences in Riverdale were agreed upon by the prosecution and defense and the judge simply ratified it (Gould et al., 1974: 147-148). Thus the chance to be a part of a treatment program that seemed likely "to make a difference" was irresistible. One might argue whether or not therapeutic control helped any addicts, but there is no question that it helped the morale of the probation officers who were assigned to handle the drug cases.

From the clinical staff's point of view, the advantages of cooperation came from the coercive sanctions available to the courts. The clinicians' interest in coercive sanctions was first generated by problems of recruitment. After the N.A.U. had been operating for about a year, senior clinicians became convinced of two "facts": that they could help only those addicts who wanted to stop using drugs *prior* to their application to the clinic, and that the principal reason why any addict would want to give up heroin is because of "real world" pressure—primarily from the police and the rest of the legal system, but also from family, school, or other systems.

It follows from these two "facts" that the N.A.U. could best fulfill its mission if the police were exerting the maximum feasible pressure on street addicts (or, as they were occasionally known in clinical circles, "prepatients"). To be sure, clinicians never, to the best of our knowledge, actively aided the police in pursuing any particular street addict,[4] but clinicians were effectively able to communicate a "you catch them, we'll treat them" posture to the police. The implication of this philosophy—which was not fully realized until several years later—was that clinicians viewed their roles as complementary to the constellation of legal roles, rather than antagonistic, or even orthogonal, to them.[5]

The second advantage some clinicians saw in cooperative relations with the legal system dealt with the ongoing problem the clinic had with patients leaving against the advice of clinicians. This was a source of continuous frustration to clinicians, who typically saw treatment as a lengthy process (generally several years in duration), while patients often wanted to terminate treatment after a few days or weeks. Since most of the treatment regimes relied on in-program peer pressure, a constant turnover of the patient population drastically reduced the effectiveness of group dynamics. Yet when program participation is wholly voluntary, the clinicians had no effective resource to sanction patient withdrawal.[6]

The clinicians believed that this problem would be greatly mitigated if many of the patients were on probation, with continued participation in a particular program given as a condition of probation at the time probation was granted. Then, if and when a patient thought about withdrawing from the program, he would know that he would have to serve the prison sentence which had been suspended when probation was granted (Gould et al., 1974: 143). From the clinician's perspective, this scheme had the benefit of building coercive sanctions into the treatment system, with the added advantage of having those sanctions administered by someone who was not technically part of the clinic. This added advantage was important, since it permitted clinicians to impress on their patients their "helping" role without tying that to a "punishing" role (Kahn and Nebelkopf, 1979).

It should be noted that in the early stage of the therapeutic control relationship between the courts and the clinic, clinicians did not intend to use the coercive sanctions made available to them to regulate interaction within the boundaries of the clinic. From their point of view, the coercive sanctions would be applied only to those who were *not* patients in the clinic. They considered the addict who had not applied to the program and the addict who had left the program both to be "fair game." At this stage, their interest was in emphasizing the "safe harbor" character of the clinic by stirring up storms outside that harbor. Only when this preliminary system failed to solve all of their problems with patients was this final step to therapeutic control taken.

Therapeutic Control

As symbiotic relationships between court and clinic personnel were regularized, both "sides" saw the advantages accruing, and the disadvantages—which seemed largely to involve mere compromises of ideological principles—were less than apparent. The courts were able to process more and more "drug offenders," and the N.A.U.'s treatment rolls expanded nicely. An accommodative schema began to emerge, the major elements of which were shared by both court and clinic personnel. That moral schema can be summarized as:

(1) Illegal drugs present a critical threat to the society and to the health of the patient.[7] Both the clinic and law enforcement agencies have a duty to respond to it.[8]

(2) Use of drugs indicates and causes both legal and medical problems.

(3) Therefore searching out and identifying drug users is in the best interests of both society and the individual.

(4) Preventing further drug use is more important than administering punitive sanctions for drug use, and rehabilitation treatment is thus the preferred response to drug use.

(5) Addicts cannot always be expected to see their interests in treatment and may have to be coerced into treatment.

(6) The importance of the problem is so great that anyone with a drug problem who is found to be guilty of almost any crime should be sentenced to some form of treatment.

(7) Since treatment is not a punishment, legal technicalities of guilt are less important for the court's decision than the "having" of a drug problem.

(8) The court should use its power to enforce compliance with clinical demands and the clinic can use this as a resource in both framing and securing compliance with clinical demands.

(9) The clinic has primary responsibility for determining the appropriate treatment program for the individual[9] and keeping the court, in the person of the probation officer, apprised of patient participation.

(10) Punitive sanctions are appropriate in enforcing compliance with universalistic performance standards and only those standards. A person with a drug problem who has demonstrated his inability to benefit from treatment deserves incarceration.

Discrepancies Between the Accommodative Schema and the Ideologies

The pragmatic consequence of a shared accommodative schema is that it provides a symbolic basis for stabilizing interactions which are ideologically problematic. In this case (as in the others described in this book), there are some notable discrepancies between the accommodative schema and the mandating societal ideologies.

One particularly instructive example may be found in the systematic attempt to blur the distinction between "drug use" and "drug abuse." Strictly speaking, "drug use" refers to an *act* (or series of acts) which may be in violation of the law, while "drug abuse" reflects a personal *condition* which psychiatry considers unhealthy. Ideologically speaking, this constitutes a significant distinction, since it is at least conceptually possible that experimentation with drugs might sometimes spring from healthy motives (Weil, 1972). Thus while the legal ideology supports a rather unambiguous determination of whether or not the proscribed act occurred, the medical ideology requires a clinical diagnosis of the condition of the agent.

In the emergent accommodative schema, these two criteria were mixed to the point where there was no clear conception of what was being responded to—act or agent. Court personnel broadened their criteria of culpability to include the condition of the agent.[10]

Thus, for example:

Prosecutor:	We've got two burglaries and a possession bust on him.
Defense Attorney:	Yeah, but the drug bust is no good. They didn't find it on him, and they had no warrant.
Prosecutor:	Well maybe, but there's no sense in fighting it. You know one of them (the charges) is going to hold up. Besides, he's a junkie.
Defense Attorney:	I think I can get him to go to methadone.
Prosecutor:	I don't know if Calloway (the judge) would accept that, he's had a half dozen before and he's already been in methadone once. Would you go for Zeta House?

The defendant's status as an addict is clearly central to the disposition.

On the other hand, the clinicians clearly felt it appropriate to include the commission of criminal acts as a major diagnostic criterion. The screening and evaluation unit continually used the existence of charges against the criminal/patient as a major criterion in deciding the seriousness of the problem and what sort of treatment would be appropriate, (see Gould et al., 1974: Ch. 8).

To a certain extent, this ambiguity was institutionalized by the adoption of the phrase "to have a drug problem," which was part of the common vocabulary of court and clinic personnel (Gould et al., 1974: 128). Anyone who had an ongoing involvement with illegal drugs and who had been or could be apprehended by the legal machinery was eligible for the typification "has a drug problem." Whether the person *abused* drugs (in the psychiatric sense) was not crucial, nor was it crucial that the individual be apprehended for *acts* in violation of drug control laws.[11] The typification "worked" perfectly well in identifying those people who were of concern to both the courts and clinics, but it was only marginally related to any ideologically legitimate categories, either psychiatric or legal.

This systematic ambiguity concerning the focus of attention relates to comparable problems in the accumulation of pertinent information. Both the legal and the medical ideologies assume that the actions taken with regard to the criminal/patient must be based on "historical" (in the sense of biographical) information. Of course, the legally relevant information pertains to the character of the *act,* while medically relevant information pertains to the character of the *agent*; and since that distinction was largely collapsed in practice, the criteria for selecting relevant information reflected more practical considerations.

Traditionally, the law assumes that the state may have collected systematically biased information or reached systematically biased conclusions, while the medical model assumes that it is in everyone's interest for the diagnostician to have unbiased (accurate, objective) information. In the law, the "purity" of information is reached by insisting on an adversarial relation between the parties, while in the treatment model the purity of information is assured by the assumed concordance of interests. So, for instance, in American law the defendant is not required to make available self-incriminating evidence, while in American medicine the patient is expected to disclose the full measure of his problem.

Needless to say, these ideologically legitimated information-gathering processes come into potential conflict when the agents of the law are not clearly differentiated from clinical personnel. The accommodative schema circumvented this problem by deemphasizing the punitive outcome of the criminal proceedings and emphasizing the state's interest in therapeutic rehabilitation of the criminal/patient. In some jurisdictions, the entire matter was handled under provisions of the civil law, in which case the ideological compromises did not appear to be as dramatic, but in Riverdale this option was never exercised. Of course, the adversarial relationship mandated by the punishment ideology had been seriously eroded by the widespread practice of plea bargaining in Riverdale well before the N.A.U. entered the system, so little further information-gathering compromise in the court was required by the new arrangement.

However, whatever legal justification there may have been for deemphasizing due-process requirements of adversarial information gathering because treatment is not punishment disappeared with the introduction of forced compliance with clinical demands. The agreed-upon procedure in Riverdale was that after acceptance of the defendant's guilty plea, the defendant was sentenced to prison for between one to five years, and that sentence was suspended and a one to three year probation imposed with the condition that the defendant receive treatment for his drug problem (usually at the N.A.U.). In the event that the criminal/patient did not participate in the program (i.e., voluntarily self-terminated or was terminated by the clinicians), the clinic should notify his probation officer, who should then "violate" the probation and ask the court to issue an arrest warrant. If and when that warrant was served, the criminal/patient should then be taken into custody and sent to prison to serve the original prison sentence.

In practice, particularly in the first year or so of the therapeutic control system, the consequences were usually not as repressive as it might seem from the above description. The N.A.U. was not always bureaucratically well organized enough to report the "splitee" to the probation department. Even when reported, though, the probation officers would sometimes not "violate" the probationer because he thought the probationer had tried, or he thought the program "too strict," or he thought that the probationer was "clean," or whatever (Gould et al., 1974: 143). Other times the probation officer would simply insist that the criminal/patient reapply to the N.A.U. Increased communication between the N.A.U. and the courts beginning in

1972 lessened both of the above problems. However, the main stumbling block was that the police did not serve the warrants for violating probation. Both the probation officers and our observers tried to find out why. The answer that the detectives gave both questioners was the same, it just wasn't a "good pinch." Thus violation of probation cases usually came before the court only when the probationer was arrested for other crimes. The violation of probation charge was usually dropped as part of the plea bargain. However, this did not mean that the prospect of having his sentence reimposed did not seem like a heavy threat to the addict thinking about dropping out of treatment.

In spite of the practical problems, the use of the threat of penal sanction to secure compliance with clinical demands was popular in both the courts and the clinic. It is important to note that penal sanctions were never linked to any *specific* clinical demand (criminals/patients were never told, "Drink your methadone or else you'll go to prison") except for continued participation in the program, but as one clinician told us, "Patients are more cooperative with the threat of jail hanging over their heads." Thus the ideologically assumed communality of interest between the sick and his healer was supplemented by the coercive power of the state. But since both court and clinic personnel believed in the "compelling" character of illegal drugs (especially, of course, heroin), it was felt that the criminal/patient was not really competent to judge his own "best interests." Consequently, some form of coercive control was a practical necessity.

One final element of the accommodative schema which is illustrative of the nature of the accommodation is the development of universalistic and standardized criteria for assessing patient participation. In a strict treatment ideology, a patient's clinical status depends on the extent to which his condition has changed relative to some notion of a desired state. In a strict punitive ideology, a convict's criminal status depends on the extent to which the prescribed punishment has been administered. According to the accommodative schema shared by court and clinic personnel, though, a criminal/patient's status depended on the length of time that the criminal/patient had stayed in "good standing" in the clinic. In order to stay in "good standing," a program member had to do several things: take the prescribed "medication," attend most of the required therapy sessions,[12] be employed or in school or else be able to give acceptable reasons for the lack of employment, not sell any medication (methadone) "on the streets," stay out of trouble with the police (which was easier than it sounds, since the police gave program members a bit more leeway than most people with "drug problems"), not sell drugs in the clinic, and not use physical violence in the clinic.[13] A criminal/patient who continually met these criteria could maintain "good standing" indefinitely (Gould et al., 1974: 196-197).

This is a perfectly reasonable set of criteria, given the context, but no reference is made to any concept of "making progress toward a state of good health." In fact, when we look at these criteria closely, all they require is that a criminal/patient (1) take "medication," (2) show up for therapy, and (3) stay out of trouble (Ruiz et al., 1977). To be sure, these requirements make a good deal of practical sense, since one of the elements of the accommodative schema assumes that illegal drug use causes troublesome behavior, so requiring the criminal/patient to stay out of trouble is essentially requiring him to not act like a typical addict. But beyond this common-sense notion, the criteria of performance demonstrated the court and clinic personnel's inability to agree about how a "cured" addict would be recognized. If the object of a program were to maintain social control over a group, then requiring the participants to stay out of trouble would make perfect sense. But when the object of a program is to improve the psychological health of a group of people, then these criteria seem less germane.

None of this is to assert that clinicians did not want to see the condition of their patients improve. To the contrary, they were genuinely and continually interested in the "progress" of their patients. They were elated when a patient got a job, good grades in school, or responsibly fulfilled an obligation; and they were disappointed when a patient lost a job, was thrown out of school, or did not discharge a responsibility. But these concerns on the part of clinicians lacked structural support and remained personal "concerns" rather than organizational "criteria." It would have been absurd, for example, to consider terminating treatment for a patient who failed to show up for a scheduled speaking engagement.

Actually, the N.A.U., like most treatment programs, was continually hampered by an inability to specify treatment objectives. To some clinicians, the maintenance of a "drug free life" was the obvious goal toward which patients and clinicians should work. But supporters of methadone argued that standard treatment of various diseases—for instance, diabetes—involves the ongoing administration of chemotherapy, so that was certainly clinically viable. Furthermore, since many clinicians used marijuana or alcohol themselves, an agreement to exclude these from the successful patient's behavioral repertoire was difficult to obtain in spite of the insistence of Zeta House clinicians. Thus the problem became one of "where to draw the line." Other clinicians proposed psychological or psychosocial criteria of adjustment, but these proved difficult to specify, in part because so many of the patients were poor blacks and the clinicians had a great deal of trouble believing that it was healthy for a poor black to adjust to a racist society.

Thus the accommodative moral schema which emerged with the symbiosis of the court and clinic was not in and of itself responsible for the truncation of clinical goals. That model did, however, provide an organizational rationale for the operation of a system which processed "clients" without clear institutionalized clinical goals.

The Court-Clinic Continuum

Throughout this chapter, we have viewed the "processing" of addicts as falling within the scope of two relatively distinct institutionalized systems—law enforcement and the clinic. Where members of those two systems interact, we have used various terms which specify types of relationships between differentiated elements: accommodation, cooperation, symbiosis, and so on. These terms, and our analysis to this point, tacitly assume that it is the interaction across system boundaries that is problematic, while the basic institutional differentiation can be taken for granted. In this respect, we have accepted the position of the treatment and punishment ideologies, which assumes that the *practice* of treatment is fundamentally and qualitatively different from the *practice* of criminal law.

Our analysis has brought us to the point, however, where we must at least raise the question of whether the interactive system we have been describing might not best be analytically considered a unitary system with differentiated parts (police, court, clinic, probation, etc.) rather than as two distinct systems which deal with overlapping clientele. To put it another way, did the accommodation between the two systems, under the pressure of the drug crisis, proceed so far that drug control is appropriately viewed as accomplished by an independent system? While this question is cumbersome, it has some importance if we are to go beyond an elaboration of common-sense conceptions of the systems of social control in contemporary America. We must proceed with some caution here not only because it is analytically complex, but because the boundaries between the treatment and punishment ideologically mandated professions are highly charged. The level of cooperation between the two has already been subject to more or less polemical attacks from both sides.

While sociological theory is, as yet, unable to provide us with unequivocal criteria for the identification of social systems, much theoretical attention has been paid to their boundary-maintaining and goal-directed character. (Parsons, 1951, Buckley, 1967). Both of these analytic concepts point to the nature of the integration of the system, which is the theoretical problem we face in analyzing the interaction between court and clinic personnel in Riverdale.

While the term boundary maintenance has been used in a variety of theoretical contexts, constraints and restraints on communication are particularly salient in social systems. And as macrostructures, law and psychiatry have both established restraints on the flow of information between the two systems. With the exception of some well-institutionalized points of contact, such as malpractice suits, insanity defenses, competency hearings, and forensic psychiatry, the flow of specific information between the two systems is rather deliberately restrained by the concept of "confidentiality," which is widely supported in both systems. Confidentiality is essentially a boundary-maintaining device, serving to protect the intimacy of the practitioner-client interaction by preventing third-party access to the flow of information between the two. Traditionally, both the doctor-patient and lawyer-client relationships are privileged and private interactions. The doctor should not divulge material to the court that might be detrimental to his patient without the patient's consent. The lawyer should not divulge any information learned from his client unless he has at least implied consent from his client and it is in the client's interest to do so.

If it were the case, then, that clinicians and court personnel felt restricted in their interaction by obligations of confidentiality, then we would have to conclude that a significant structural boundary between the two components was being maintained, and that the interactive system in question was really a composite of two systems. Specifically, if clinicians had felt that the integrity of the clinician-patient relationship were violated by divulging the substance of their exchange, or if defense attorneys had felt a similar need to protect the substance of their exchanges with the defendant, then we would have had some evidence that the systems were functioning autonomously with regard to the criminal/patient.

Empirically, in Riverdale during the period of observation, principles of confidentiality were considerably "relaxed." Clinicians felt it imperative that they keep track of their patients' legal status (both pre and posttrial), and most court personnel felt it appropriate information for the clinicians to have access to. Similarly, defense and prosecuting attorneys and probation officers felt they could not properly handle a "drug case" without knowing the defendant's clinical status, and often,

prognosis. In many jurisdictions, including Riverdale, this information was given in a formal report. One defense attorney has
described the practice in one New York City jurisdiction
(Rafalsky, 1972: 407):

> [the treatment counselor] should be contacted [by the defense
> attorney] in order to discuss the treatment plan that has been
> formulated for the client. . . . [T] he attorney should arrange to have a
> written report describing his client's progress delivered to the court
> on the appropriate date. . . . This process should continue until the
> criminal matter has been disposed of and, *ideally until the client has
> graduated from the rehabilitative program*" [emphasis ours] .

At least during the period of observation, though, channels of
communication in Riverdale were never fully regularized. Often
the criminal/patient was used as a go-between, reporting his
legal progress to the clinicians and his clinical progress to his
lawyer or probation officer. It was not at all unusual to hear an
applicant in screening asked, "Did your lawyer tell you to get
into treatment" by one of the intake clinicians, nor was it
unusual for a probation officer to ask a probationer for an
account of his or her clinical activities for the preceding week.
In addition, the director of the N.A.U. had many occasions to
share views with the chief of the city police, both as members
of the Mayor's Council on Drug Abuse and in private conversa-
tions. Most of the judges in the lower and superior courts had
had some contact with some N.A.U. clinicians and administra-
tors, and defense attorneys could call the clinic to check on the
clinical status of their clients when the client's report was
insufficient in some way.

Much of this information was, of course, communicated with
the "consent" of the patient. Every patient who "had a legal
problem" when he entered the N.A.U. was asked to sign a
consent form allowing the N.A.U. to report his clinical status to
the probation office. This, in theory, was a freely given consent,
but since the criminal/patient would not be admitted to the
N.A.U. without it and the alternative was jail, its legality was
questionable (Kaimowitz v. Department of Mental Health,
1976).

Perhaps the biggest compromise of confidentiality was from the clinic to the probation department. Almost from the beginning of the N.A.U., an N.A.U. clinician held biweekly meetings with probation officers to discuss patients. When the ideals of the therapeutic control system were being implemented, probation officers attended clinical meetings several times a week at the N.A.U. This was justified by treating the probation officers as part of the treatment "team," but since they were also officers of the court, this must be thought as a major breach of the boundary between court and clinic.

We must recognize that the flow of information between court and clinic personnel was *far* from unimpeded. There were relatively few informal points of contact between court and clinic personnel: they almost never "lunched" together, and "after-hours" social contact was rare and purely serendipitous. In addition, some personnel (primarily, but not exclusively, lower-echelon clinicians and police personnel) opposed the liaison for either personal or ideological reasons, and would not cooperate wholeheartedly. Clinicians never felt it proper to keep track of exactly what motions would be offered in court, just as court personnel seldom asked for intimate details of clinical exchanges. Furthermore, some formal boundaries were maintained. Defense attorneys usually did not tell the clinic what they knew about their client's life, although the clinic rarely asked. The clinicians never went so far as to testify against a former patient in court. Consent to release information was always obtained even if its legal validity was questionable.

Thus the evidence concerning the flow of information and the maintenance of boundaries is equivocal. It suggests that the generalized social boundaries which are maintained between the law and psychiatry were greatly relaxed, but not dissolved, in the specific area of drug control. Judging from the flow of information, we are led to suspect court-clinic interaction was more integrated than the generalized systems relations, but that each "side" still maintained some boundaries.

Another aspect of the boundary problem involved the relationship between the drug-control specialists and their professional associates not in the drug-control business. Here the boundaries were greater in the psychiatric area than in the court. In court, the same lawyers handled drug cases and non-drug cases for both the prosecution and the defense. The drug cases were not sent to special courts. However, in late 1972, drug cases in Superior Court began to be dealt with all on a specific day of the week. This rule was not strictly observed, but the large majority of drug cases were dealt with on that day. Another specialization within the law-enforcement system that developed during the crisis was that the probation department created three special probation officers to handle drug cases. Their case loads were cut to approximately one-third that of the other officers, and they were directed to cooperate more closely with the clinic. The Riverdale police had always had a special squad to deal with narcotics, gambling, prostitution, and liquor violations. However, none of these other functions were dropped during the crisis, and when a new unit was created specializing in undercover work it dealt with organized crime as well as narcotics.

In the Psychiatry Department of the Medical School, the N.A.U. was quite isolated. The main N.A.U. headquarters occupied a special building two blocks from the rest of the Mental Health Center. The teaching functions of the N.A.U. faculty were sharply limited to drug-abuse treatment, and very few students did residency training there. Informal contact between N.A.U. staff and the rest of the Mental Health Center's staff was very limited. Furthermore, the N.A.U. had its own administrative personnel who were minimally supervised by the administration of the Mental Health Center. Perhaps most important, the rest of the Department of Psychiatry "looked down" on the N.A.U. Several members of the department expressed the opinion that the faculty recruitment standards of the N.A.U. were unacceptably low, and indeed, only the director of the N.A.U. was given tenure at the University. To the best of our knowledge, no N.A.U. staff left to work in another program in the Department of Psychiatry. On the other hand, N.A.U. records were, with some difficulty, integrated into the general medical records. Methadone patients did spend their first two weeks on an inpatient ward in the general Mental Health Center. Nonetheless, in general, the social boundaries between the N.A.U. and the rest of the Department of Psychiatry were quite sharply delineated.

Another common characteristic of social systems which are relatively well integrated is a broad, if general and nonprogrammatic, agreement among members on system goals. Within the systems of law and psychiatry, the legitimacy of the vague goals of "justice" and "psychological health," respectively, has rarely been challenged. As the complexity of the system increases, those goals necessarily become more abstract and generalized, but regularized interaction seems to require some interpersonal agreement on what the collectivity is "supposed to be doing." Clearly the concept of a "division of labor," upon which so much sociological theory and data is based, implies that there is some common goal which unites differentiated components (Durkheim, 1933).

When we speak of the law and psychiatry as differentiated, one of the tacit assumptions we make is that within each system, activities are at least minimally consistent with regard to purpose, but that when compared holistically, the systems will be "doing" different things. One system regulates the kinds of acts which occur throughout the society, while the other system remedies deficiencies in the makeup of the members of the society. As was discussed in Chapter 3, the activities and makeup of a person are clearly analytically related, but the ideologically given assumption is that these two systems are "directed" toward different ends.

Thus we are offered another possible empirical criterion for deciding whether we are dealing with a unitary system or the interaction of two systems. If there is systematic disagreement between clinicians and court personnel concerning "what we are trying to accomplish," then we can conclude that we are dealing with two intersecting systems, while if there is broad agreement, then the data would suggest a unitary system.

Our analysis of the emergence of a widely supported accommodative schema is evidence in support of the hypothesis that both court and clinic personnel agreed on the cooperative nature of their response to an individual with a "drug problem." It was a clear implication of the accommodative schema that, in isolation, the activities of neither the courts nor the N.A.U. were perceived as constituting a practically sufficient response to an individual's drug problem. It was also implicit in that accommodative schema that neither purely legal nor purely psychiatric efforts would be practically sufficient to cope with the societal Drug Crisis. It follows from this that the members of the functionally specific system dealing with drug problems viewed themselves as partners in an ad hoc coalition responding to a crisis situation cooperatively, and that they defined appropriate behavior on each other's part on the assumption of a community of interest.

But this conclusion does not completely supply the information we need, since the accommodative schema is silent regarding the goal or product of the system. In a purely ideological sense, the goals of the medical and legal systems can be readily identified as the maintenance of their "mandating values"—health and justice. While an exact and universal specification of the meaning of these values has never been (and probably can never be) agreed upon, each value provides persuasive and unimpeachable direction to all of the members of the respective systems. But it is also part of the treatment and punishment ideologies that each value is formally irrelevant to the other. An obvious example of this is the formal disregard a judge displays for the health of a convicted defendant in sentencing him to death. Another example would be the physician's obligation to save the life of a wounded murderer. In a sense, each value is maximized only when the other is neutralized.

This quasi-oppositional relationship of values suggests that there will be problems in integrating the activities of people maintaining allegiance to these ideologies, since they will have trouble agreeing on the appropriate goals of their joint venture.

In the face of the Drug Crisis, though, public and political pressure were sufficient to generate that integration. To the extent that a shared goal emerged, though, it was largely tacit and certainly not of the same level of legitimacy or generality as either health or justice.

While that goal was rarely mentioned, the nature of the accommodative schema and the events it generated suggest that it best be termed *therapeutic control* of a deviant group. A state of complete therapeutic control would be hypothetically reached when everyone who has a drug problem (i.e., who uses drugs illegally and has some prospect of causing trouble) is under the control of some state-recognized agency which seeks to end his or her drug abuse. Depending on how irrevocably deviant the subject is and how often he or she has been controlled in the past, the control may range from the benign and gentle intervention of a methadone program through the more obtrusive intervention of a therapeutic community to the harsh intervention of incarceration in a penitentiary. The ideal system would have all of the deviants "under control," and the harshness of the control would parallel the intractability of the subject. The essence of therapeutic control consisted in an agreement by both court and clinic personnel that "within the limits of society's need to protect itself, we are trying to help these people, insofar as they will respond to help."

Evidence of the widespread acceptance in Riverdale of therapeutic control as a system goal is pervasive.[14] The court's use of clinical evaluation in judging the criminal/patient's dangerousness and need; the clinic's use of the criminal patient's legal record to evaluate the extent of his "problem"; court and clinic personnel's agreement on the necessity of legal "pressure" to insure compliance from the criminal/patient; the willingness of the clinic to see its "treatment failures" incarcerated; the willingness of court personnel to suspend the sentence of anyone who "has a drug problem," no matter what crime he or she had been convicted of, provided she or he stayed in treatment; the emphasis on status-maintaining regulations rather than progress-indicating criteria in clinical programs; the widespread support among both court and clinical personnel (with the significant exception of defense attorneys) for vigorous police action against drug users; and the common reliance on plea bargaining to circumvent problems of "due process" all suggest that the emergent system had given priority to the very practical goal of therapeutic control at the expense of the ideologically mandated goals and procedures.

Thus there is good reason to believe that the interactions between court personnel and clinicians were guided by system goals which were implicit in the emergent accommodative schema. But, as was the case with boundary maintenance, the accommodative schema did not eclipse the older, ideologically based standards. Many court personnel were troubled by some of the injustices implicit in therapeutic control, and many clinicians were troubled by the compromises of medical ethics. Such problems became most acute around the most extreme measures. The N.A.U. director faced two minor rebellions within a six-month period when he proposed taking nonaddicted ex-addicts on parole into methadone and reporting the clinic's information on dealer networks to the police. The former proposal ran into the objection that it would addict nonaddicts and treat the nonsick (Gould et al., 1974: 207). The latter raised ideological objections that "we aren't cops." Prosecutors were continually uncomfortable about sending addicts to treatment for nondrug crimes, particularly violent ones. One former probation officer recently put her uneasiness quite well: "It seems to me that we compromised too much and got too little in the way of results."

The traditional ideologies were not simply discarded as useless. But all of the participants in this system were overwhelmed by the presence of a Drug Crisis, which they saw as presenting a grave menace to the continued existence of American society. Demands for swift and effective action were all around them, and ideological quibbles seemed to inhibit practical action.

Returning then to our analytic problem, we find that, although the dedifferentiation of the two systems was never complete, a single system of drug control evolved in Riverdale which included members who were "officially" members of either the legal or medical systems. The members of that system generally agreed to a peculiar and pragmatic set of beliefs, values, and goals which we have called the therapeutic-control schema. That moral schema largely superseded the treatment and punishment ideologies which "normally" mandate the activities of members of these systems, since the juxtaposition of these two ideologies in a single system drastically impaired the ability of the members to coordinate their efforts.

It must be remembered, though, that we have been pursuing this question only in order to evaluate the ideologically based presumption that court work is different from clinical work, and therefore that interaction between court and clinical personnel presupposes the basic differentiation of the two systems. We have tried to show only that it is equally feasible to view the participants as members of a single system, claiming membership in the legal system at one "end" and in the psychiatric system at the other.

In this particular case, the emergence of a system to realize the goals of therapeutic control appears to be linked to the larger phenomenon of the Drug Crisis. Most of the members of this system believed that the Drug Crisis presented a situation which traditional (ideological) models of control were unable to successfully remedy. The need for innovative practical action generated an accommodative model of control which varied significantly from the ideological models, but which facilitated the kind of activities which addressed the practical problem.

The notion that the societal Drug Crisis was a major source of this accommodation would lead us to predict that the accommodation occurred in other places besides Riverdale. While the evidence on this is not complete, it is very suggestive.

We have already quoted extensively from Rafalsky's (1972) description of the role of the defense attorney in drug cases in New York City. Such systems have also been described elsewhere. The concept of diverting the addict out of the criminal process provided the justification for building therapeutic control systems into the law in several jurisdictions (Martin, 1974).

Federal law, as well as state law in Connecticut, Illinois, and New York, developed such procedures early in the Drug Crisis. One commentator summarized these statutes by noting that "such procedures could develop the court system into an intake unit to channel drug addicts into treatment" (Georgetown Law Journal, 1972). Philadelphia used a slightly different system which sent the drug user to treatment prior to the determination of guilt and allowed the prosecutor to reinstitute prosecution if the addict did not stay in treatment. This procedure ran into trouble with the constitutional guarantees of a speedy trial and was not widely copied (Georgetown Law Journal, 1972). Kleeman and Posner's (1971) analysis of the Massachusetts law also shows that it was intended to facilitate "treatment in lieu of prosecution."

Several other patterns of therapeutic control were also proposed or tried. Kassis (1972) describes a proposal in California for a further differentiation of therapeutic control of drugs from other parts of the legal system by creating a drug court. Joseph (1973) describes running a methadone program out of a probation office and using probation officers as drug counselors. Finally, Morganbesser (1974) describes the use of a police officer in a Madison, Wisconsin treatment program to help overcome mutual distrust between law enforcement and treatment personnel because, as the Drug Abuse Survey Project (1972) noted, "the law enforcement process will remain a significant and probably the most important intake unit for drug dependent people for years to come" (quoted in Morganbesser, 1974: 31).

Therapeutic Control and the
End of the Crisis

It might be argued that therapeutic control succeeded in stopping the Drug Crisis. By whatever indicator one looks at, the crisis tapered off by the mid-seventies. While our analysis of the crisis does not indicate that it was based on the amount of heroin use, it seems plausible, if undemonstrated, that the development of therapeutic control reassured the American public that there was no basis for panic and undercut the basis of the crisis.

On the other hand, if one looks only at the effect of therapeutic control on addicts' use of drugs, the results are less favorable. To begin with, the data collected by Lansing Crane and presented here in Table 5 show that patients at the N.A.U. who had legal cases hanging over their heads or were on probation or parole were only slightly more likely to stay in treatment or to successfully complete treatment than were other patients.

Perhaps equally interesting are the results from a followup study of patients treated by the N.A.U. reported by Gould et al. (1975). The results of that study are complex but intriguing because they show that while the N.A.U.'s former patients were generally no longer involved with heroin and only mildly involved with other drugs, the same is true of a sample of people who showed up at the N.A.U. screening and evaluation but did not become patients in spite of eligibility for methadone treatment; i.e., they had at least one year of regular heroin use and were over twenty-one years of age.

Table 6 shows that among those who have successfully completed treatment, none currently are using heroin. However, of those who did not complete treatment or never were treated, few are still using heroin. Only two people are using heroin daily. Table 7 shows that abstinence from marijuana use is highest among former therapeutic community patients and lowest among former methadone patients, with the other two groups somewhere in between. Employment records (see Table 8) show that former patients who successfully completed treatment have better employment records, but again the differences are not overwhelming.

While the data from which these tables were drawn is complex and there are many qualifying factors, we believe they fairly accurately represent the effects of the therapeutic control system on patients' lifestyles.

TABLE 5   Legal and Treatment Status of N.A.U.
Applications through 1971

	No legal Involvement	Criminal cases pending, probation or parole	Total	Percentage
Successfully completed treatment	3.3%	3.7%		
	21	31	52	3.5%
In treatment or awaiting treatment	20.9%	26.1%		
	132	218	350	23.7%
Left treatment or while awaiting treatment	75.8%	70.1%		
	481	584	1065	72.8%
Total	634	833	1467	
Percentage	43.2%	56.8%		100%

Conclusion

The emergence of a systematic symbiosis between the punishment-oriented legal system and the treatment-oriented psychiatric system, based on the system of moral typifications which we have been calling therapeutic control, is an extremely important component of the societal response to the Drug Crisis. By glossing over the ideological compromises involved, both legal and medical practitioners who had assumed (or been charged with) the responsibility to "do something" could point to their innovative techniques for dealing with the situation. The rhetoric of therapeutic control worked well for both establishing the claim that the "system" was indeed capable of responding and justifying the increased expenditures that the implementation of the therapeutic control seemed to require.

TABLE 6 Reported Heroin Use in Last Month for
Various Categories of N.A.U. Patients

Use	None		Not Daily		Daily		Totals
Treatment Completed methadone maintenance	100%	29					29
Left methadone maintenance before treatment completed	84.4	27	9.4	3	6.3	2	32
Completed treatment in therapeutic community	100	23					23
No treatment	77.1	27	22.9	8			35
Totals		106		11		2	119

SOURCE: Data drawn from Gould et al., 1975.

X = 6.73   n.s. at .05 level

The moral typifications upon which therapeutic control was based were a result of certain crucial convergences between the punishment and treatment ideologies; specifically, that drug use is inherently bad, drug users are inherently undesirable, and society has a legitimate interest in taking steps to decrease the usage of certain drugs. When interacting, court and clinic personnel could take these moral typifications for granted. Thus interaction between these practitioners could be based on an assumption of moral consensus. But the actual implementation

TABLE 7   Reported Marijuana Use in Last Month
Among Various Categories of N.A.U. Patients

Use	None		Not Daily		Daily	Totals
Treatment	24.1%		58.6%		17.2%	
Completed methadone maintenance		7		17	5	29
	53.1		43.8		3.1	
Left methadone maintenance before treatment completed		17		14	1	32
	60.9		21.1		17.4	
Completed treatment in therapeutic community		14		5	4	23
	57.1		31.4		11.4	
No treatment		20		11	4	35
Totals		58		47	14	119

SOURCE: Data drawn from Gould et al., 1975.

X = 13.565   significant at .05 level

of this system was a much more complicated matter, since it
required sustained interaction not just between medical and
legal practitioners, but between these practitioners and addicts
as well. And, as we saw in Chapter 3, the outlaw ideology, to
which addicts clearly felt an affinity, does not presuppose these
fundamental moral typifications. In fact, the outlaw ideology
typifies drug use as morally worthwhile, drug users as valuable
people, and social control of drugs as inherently evil. Interaction between medical or legal practitioners and addicts was,

TABLE 8   Present Employment Status of former N.A.U. Patients

Employment	Unemployed		Employed		Totals
Treatment	33.3%		66.6%		
Completed methadone maintenance		7		14	21
Left methadone maintenance before treatment completed	59.9	19	40.6	13	32
Completed treatment in therapeutic community	21.1	4	78.9	15	19
No treatment	45.7	16	54.3	19	35
Totals		46		61	107

SOURCE: Data drawn from Gould et al., 1975

NOTE: Those employed by drug treatment programs have been excluded from this analysis.

consequently, not facilitated by the emergence of the thera-peutic control moral schema. To the contrary, that schema generates a moral degradation of the addict and his enterprise which is probably greater than the degradation implicit in either the treatment or punishment ideologies. So while the thera-peutic control schema provided a pragmatic moral rationale for cooperation between two potential antagonists, it did so at the expense of the third party to the interactive system—the addicts.

The description of the fairness and welfare schemas presented in Chapters 4 and 5 makes it quite clear that therapeutic control as an accommodation regulated the interactions between law enforcement and treatment personnel, but not their interactions with addicts. Thus the potential of therapeutic control (as an effective therapeutic technique or the ultimate in repressive tactics, depending on your view) could not be realized. Our analytic triad thus produced three different accommodative schemas which were not only sharply different from all of the ideologies, but also from each other.

NOTES

1. The widespread usage of this term—which, strictly speaking, implies neither criminal culpability nor medical disease—is an interesting foreshadowing of the eventual rapprochement of these two systems.

2. Given that we were employees of the local drug program, these statements are somewhat suspect. We believe that we persuaded these attorneys that we were not partisan to treatment, but our success would not be easy to demonstrate. See also the position that Rafalsky (1972) took on this subject.

3. As any reading of *Federal Probation* or any other journal in the field will show.

4. Although in 1972 there was a serious debate within the upper echelons of the N.A.U. staff as to whether to turn over to the police some information they had about dealer organizations in Riverdale.

5. See Morganbesser (1974) for an interesting variant in Madison, Wisconsin; also Swanson (1975).

6. The significant exception to this involved the addicting properties of methadone. It was widely believed by clinicians that the patient's anticipation of the withdrawal syndrome brought on by the termination of methadone maintenance was a powerful deterrent to patients thinking of "splitting" a treatment program using methadone.

7. This, of course, relates directly to the crisis atmosphere discussed in Chapter 3. However, even after the sense of crisis had lessened, this belief was justified with reference to the possibility of its recurrence.

8. For published professional claims for the necessity of some such accommodations, see Georgetown Law Journal (1972), Rafalsky (1972), Kleeman and Posner (1971), Kassis (1972), Joseph (1973), Morganbesser (1974), Drug Abuse Survey Project (1972), and Martin (1974). All these sources outline general justifications for therapeutic control or some aspect of it.

9. The court reserved a veto if the treatment program required was not sufficiently restrictive of the addict's ability to commit further crimes based on his past history.

10. This was done during the course of plea bargaining, since the Supreme Court, in Robinson v. California (1962), had ordered that it could not be illegal to *be* an addict, even if it were perfectly clear that *possessing* illicit materials could be illegal.

11. Indeed, people appearing as defendants in cases involving laws as far removed from drugs as "nonsupport of a minor child" could be said to "have a drug problem."

12. It is notable that all that was required with regard to therapy groups was attendance. There was no requirement that the criminal/patient "get anything" from these sessions.

13. Most clinicians wanted to exclude patients from good standing if there was clear evidence of continued use of illegal drugs. Unfortunately, they could never find a clear-cut way of determining if a patient was still using drugs. It was hoped that random urinalysis would provide that evidence and that a patient could be excluded on the basis of "dirty urines," but during the time of our study they never had enough confidence in urinalysis results to use them in this fashion. However, occasionally "dirty urines" plus continuous gossip that the patient was using drugs led to his or her exclusion from the program. More often the patient found himself so "hassled" by the program that he "voluntarily left."

14. The reader is heartily encouraged to see Chapters 5, 6, 8, and 9 of Gould et al. (1974) for examples. See also Kuskey and Krasner (1973).

Chapter 7

CONCLUSION: Theory and Policy

The presentation of theory, evidence, and argument in this book has been long and the path sometimes circuitous. In the conclusion, we will summarize the findings, particularly as they pertain to sociological theory. We hope this will clarify any remaining ambiguities about their ramifications. After the summary, we will discuss briefly how the findings might affect policy making both about moral crises and about the deviance validation process. Let us begin with the summary of the findings.

Summary of Findings

1. *The result of doing deviance and social-control interactions is the production, reproduction, and modification of moral schemas. Doing morality is the core activity of deviance and social control.*

This, of course, is the point that Erikson emphasized in *Wayward Puritans* and which our discussion of the heroin crisis has reemphasized. Deviance and social control function to reinforce, clarify, and change the core moral schemas of the society. The communicative work which goes on around deviant behavior is what we call *doing morality*. It creates and makes visible the moral structure of the society and allows parts of it to be supported, developed, attacked, and changed. Thus, to the degree that social behavior requires a moral structure for orientation, society cannot exist without deviance and social control. At any rate, we believe that our description of the doing of the moral crisis should demonstrate that the doing of morality is central to the existence of a society's definition of itself and that doing morality requires deviance and social control.

A corollary of this is that the phenomenon which we called a moral crisis seems to arise whenever there are deep and widely felt conflicts in the moral schemas of the society. The process of doing a moral crisis is a way of reevaluating and reorganizing these schemas. There is no reason to believe that an increase in rule breaking is the cause of or even necessarily related to the crisis. The phenomenon at hand is the reconstituting of moral schemas, not the growth and/or repression of an "objectively" threatening behavior, although, of course, the behavior may be objectively threatening. One can never understand the meaning or the organization of a moral crisis—or, indeed, deviance and social control in general—without understanding its moral context.

2. *Durkheim's theoretical apparatus for describing the moral organization of modern society is, with some modification, perfectly acceptable for the description of deviance and control processes.*

While we have not used Durkheim's terminology in this volume, we have been intensely aware that the structures we found are very similar to the ones he describes in his early work. When we described the conflicts between the institutionalized values we characterized as instrumental activism and their dialectical opposite, expressive passivism, we were describing strains and conflicts within the collective conscience of American society. It is true that we see the dialectical opposition of instrumental activism and expressive passivism as essential to the clarification of the American value structure and their conflict as deeply ingrained in the moral structure of American society, while many Durkheimians have not. But this only emphasizes the dynamics of moral structures and does not indicate a basic disagreement about the importance of moral structures.

Our concept of ideology is likewise closely parallel to a Durkheimian concept, that of occupational morality. In both concepts, the emphasis is on a moral schema which provides orientation and meaning for an activity-focused group. It provides orientation for work groups whose members see themselves as fundamentally alike. Like Durkheim, we see this moral schema as a specialization of the collective conscience which draws on a theme in the collective conscience and elaborates that theme to justify and orient the existence and activities of an activity-focused solidarity group.

2a. *Modifications: Even when Durkheimian concepts did not work and we were forced to innovate, it was possible to describe the sui generis moral schemas which regulate and provide orientations for the behaviors involved. These moral schemas are the private knowledge of the groups involved.*

Only when we get to the level of routine behavior in the presence of opponents do we find difficulties with the conceptual apparatus Durkheim constructed. Specifically, our notion of accommodative schemas which serve as the basis for the integration of interactive systems consisting of members with opposed ideological mandates is not the same as Durkheim's parallel concepts. For Durkheim, the moral structure of relationships between differentiated parts of the society is focused on the "noncontractual elements of contract." These are prescribed by the society. Thus the relationships between police and addicts should, according to Durkheim, be governed by self-interest within the normative restrictions laid down by law. Criminal procedure should regulate the relations between prosecution and defense attorney. The norms of confidentiality should restrict relations between the criminal justice and mental health systems, and finally the institution of the doctor/patient relationship should govern relations between clinicians and addicts. While none of these structures are completely irrelevant, we found that relations between these groups are largely governed by situationally created moral schemas which are partially independent of all of the societal moral structures which Durkheim described.

Although the behavior which was produced by the accommodative schemas was often "immoral" vis-à-vis both the ideologies and the societally prescribed normative regulations for the relationships, these accommodative schemas provided situationally appropriate definitions of right and wrong which served to provide meaning and justification for acts which were required if the ideologically prescribed conflicts were to be limited. These ideologies and accommodative schemas functioned at various levels. When we looked at the relationships between the law-enforcement system as a whole and the treatment system as a whole, we saw that the *patterns of relations between institutionalized societal structures were organized by these moral schemas.* When we looked at the organization of the N.A.U., which was the focus of relations between addicts and clinicians, we saw that *the structure of the organization itself reflected the accommodative schemas.* Finally, when we considered the interaction between vice-squad police and heroin addicts and other vice criminals, it became apparent that *the face-to-face interaction was oriented to accommodative moralities.* Thus we can say in summary that *the practical activities that are involved in the production of deviance and control require, at all levels, the use of accommodative schemas.*

3. *Deviance and social control are normal social phenomena and can be analyzed using the same theory as any other aspect of social life.*

We believe that our findings reinforce Durkheim's position, which Erickson has elaborated so well, that, from a sociological perspective, deviance is a normal phenomenon. This is not to say that there are no psychological differences between deviants and "normals" (or for that matter between social-control agents and "normals"). We only contend that, from a sociological perspective, this is merely a consequence of the procedures of role recruitment. It is not even important from the point of view of social organization that people who play the role of addict actually use heroin. It is only necessary that they appear to do so.

Of course, if our proposition that morality is the product of deviance and control activities is correct, and if moral schemas are necessary to social life, then it follows that deviance and social control are normal parts of any society. As far as is known, there is no society which lacks them.

However, there is another meaning to the idea that deviance and social control are normal. The second meaning is that there is nothing sociologically significant which radically separates these processes from other processes in social life. We believe that the fact that the processes of deviance and control can be described with concepts that Durkheim used to describe modern social life in general strongly supports this idea.

This is not to say that there is no difference between deviance and social-control activities and the other activities of social life. Political systems produce decisions, economic systems produce goods and services, and systems of deviance and social control produce moral schemas. These differences alone mean that deviance and social control form a discrete substantive area. But these differences are not radical. We do not need a special notion of social behavior to analyze them. We do not need a different model of the actors involved. Any and all concepts and propositions from other areas of sociology are potentially useful here. Although, for instance, we have not focused our analysis on the issues of how the differential access to resources (including power, wealth, and prestige) affects the outcome of deviance and control processes, we do not mean to imply that this and similar issues are not relevant to the sociology of deviance and control. Quite the contrary! We believe that our findings contribute to the process which Matza (1964) has described as the gradual reintegration of deviance and social control into sociology.

4. *New research on deviance must focus on the structure of moral schemas and the processes of their creation, elaboration, maintenance, and change.*

It is traditional at the end of any theoretical or empirical work to call for more research. There is no reason why this book should be an exception. However, beyond simply calling for more research, we want to outline the loci which we believe should be studied.

In many ways, the limitations of what we have reported in this volume reflect the fact that we misunderstood the problem when we designed our research. Following the interactionist and ethnomethodological research on deviance and control, we believed the control agents to be critical in the construction of deviance. We took what seemed like the ultimate interactionist position and insisted on studying both the deviants and the control agents concurrently. While we have no regrets about that decision, it made apparent the difficulties with the interactionist position which seeks to reduce social order to face-to-face interaction.

As we began to see that the actors we were studying were playing out parts already organized in previously given moral schemas (however much they were adapted, modified or combined by the actors), the moral schemas themselves began to take on increasingly central roles in what we wanted to study. Yet much of what we would have wanted to study had already receded into the past before we were aware of its importance.

If we are to study the creation and maintenance of moral schemas—that it, the doing of morality—as we studied its use, much of our research style must be modified. To begin with, at least inasmuch as we are concerned with societal-level moral schemas (aspects of the societal collective conscience), we must spend a good deal of time and energy monitoring and studying the contents of television, popular music, popular magazines, and newspapers. The meaning structures of the societal community are largely articulated and elaborated through these media in modern society, and the reinforcement and development of moral schemas for the whole society is most visible there. Had we known to look at television, for example, we probably would have seen massive increases in the concentration on drugs in the late sixties and early seventies and substantial changes in the meanings conveyed.

Another aspect of the process of doing morality that now looks more critical than it did when we started the study is the process of making law and administrative regulations. While there has, of course, been considerable work on this in political science, it has not been connected with the process of doing morality. Lemert (1970) has studied the reform of juvenile law, but beyond that the subject remains almost untouched.

Finally, we need to concern ourselves with the internal structure of moral systems. We indicated that the idea of a hierarchically arranged set of norms seemed inadequate to deal with the complexity of the moral systems that we studied. Instead we have used the concept of moral schema. This concept remains, however, little better than a useful gloss. The internal functioning of such schemas has been left unanalyzed.

Some Thoughts on Policy

While the main emphasis of this volume has been on the ramifications of our findings for the sociology of deviance, it has not escaped our notice that what we have found has important ramifications for public policy.

From a policy perspective, a simple conclusion from our findings is that the crisis was a phony creation of a variety of powerful people who felt threatened by the growth of expressive passivist beliefs in the youth culture and revolutionary

politics among blacks. It seems that there was little reality to
the belief that large sectors of the American population were
about to become addicted to heroin. Rather, the Drug Crisis was
a smoke screen for the repression of political and cultural
groups.

Likewise, for policy purposes, a simple account of our findings about accommodative models is that control agents, and
for that matter deviants, did not do what they claimed. They
conducted their business quite independently of the societal
prescription of how they ought to conduct it. Police and court
personnel routinely ignored proper procedure, and clinical personnel allowed their clinics to become little more than social
welfare agencies.

These simple conclusions, while largely correct, are not very
helpful. They reflect a certain naive approach to the political
world which is prominent in much scholarly writing. The social
scientific literature is full of denunciations of psychiatric personnel for not taking care of their patients, police and court
personnel for violating the law, and studies proving that apparent crises are not real ones. Very little has changed because of
them.

Such conclusions are interesting and important only if we
assume that there exists in the society the power to make
large-scale changes. Yet it is precisely the lack of power in any
well organized, societally responsible location that both allows
and requires moral crises to become major mechanisms of
societal change in America.

This, of course, raises the question of how to evaluate moral
crises. On the one hand, as has been obvious throughout our
discussions, moral crises are both considerably more and considerably less than simply spontaneous outpourings of outrage
about an objectively threatening event or situation. The Drug
Crisis, at least, involved much distortion of the facts by both
sides and substantial damage to the reputations and life plans of
many people. Most other moral crises seem to involve similar
costs. However, if moral-crisis production is the only way to

make changes in the structure of American life, except by concentrating power considerably more and thus increasing authoritarian control, perhaps they are not so bad. Certainly, many who would condemn the Drug Crisis as bad for American society would not wish to evaluate the Watergate crisis or the ecological crisis (that is, the mobilization of the society to respond to ecological troubles) in the same way even if they would admit that many of the same types of distortions of fact and damage to individuals were present.

Thus, in evaluating a moral crisis from the point of view of policy, we must balance the costs and difficulties associated with it with a realization that in a pluralistic society it is often the only effective mechanism for reassessing moral commitments. Nonetheless, a policy maker would do well to remember the processes that are involved in the construction of moral crises, whether in order to evaluate the validity and necessity of a heralded crisis, to promote a crisis oneself, or to defend oneself and one's commitments.

Another policy-relevant finding concerns the existence of accommodations between the various ideologically mandated actions in the deviance validation process. These are particularly important for the construction of policy because they are largely invisible. Aside from the plea-bargaining process, which has received some attention recently, these have barely been mentioned in either academic or policy literature. Because they operate in such a way as to be invisible to the formal record-keeping systems, administrative and judicial policy making tends to ignore the accommodations. Upper-level police officials, appellate courts, the National Institute of Mental Health, and others who formulate rules for regulating these interactions often make rules based on false assumptions about what are the typical interaction patterns. The results are often rules and programs that are massively mistargeted.

Just what are the ramifications of the existence of accommodations is not clear. We would need to experiment with various options for producing change before realistically suggesting specific policy options. However, many well-intentioned policies are negated or dramatically transformed by the accommodative models present at the points of implementation. Likewise, the existence of the accommodations means that policy makers must decide whether to strengthen, weaken, or destroy such accommodations.

CASES

COATES v. CITY OF CINCINNATI (1971) 402 U.S. 611, 61 S.Ct. 1686.
In re GAULT (1967) 387 U.S. 1, 87 S.Ct. 1428.
KAIMOWITZ v. DEPARTMENT OF MENTAL HEALTH (1976) "Mental Disability Law Reporter 1, 2: 147-154."

MULLANE v. CENTRAL HANOVER BANK AND TRUST CO. (1950) 339 U.S. 306, 70 S.C. 652.
POWELL v. STATE OF TEXAS (1968) 392 U.S. 514, 88 S.Ct. 2145.
ROBINSON v. STATE OF CALIFORNIA (1962) 82 S.Ct. 1417.
WEBB v. U.S. (1919) 249 U.S. 96, 39 S.C. 217.

REFERENCES

AGAR, M. (1973) Ripping and Running: A Formal Ethnography of Urban Heroin Addicts. New York: Seminar.
ANSLINGER, H. J. and W. F. TOMPKINS (1953) The Traffic in Narcotics. New York: Funk & Wagnalls.
BECKER, H. S. (1963) Outsiders: Studies in the Sociology of Deviance. New York: Macmillan.
––– (1967) "Whose side are we on?" Social Problems 14 (Winter): 239-247.
BELLAH, R. (1967) "Civil religion in America." Daedalus (Winter): 1-21.
––– (1973) Introduction, in Emile Durkheim on Morality. Chicago: University of Chicago Press.
––– (1975) The Broken Covenant. New York: Seabury.
BENTHAM, J. (1961) "The principles of morals and legislation," in The Utilitarians. New York: Doubleday.
BERBERIAN, R. M., W. D. THOMPSON, S. V. KASL, L. C. GOULD, and H. D. KLEBER (1975) "Trends in the prevalence of drug use among adolescents: 1970-1973." Yale University School of Medicine. (unpublished)
BERGER, P. (1963) Invitation to Sociology: A Humanistic Perspective. New York: Doubleday.

BITTNER, E. (1973) "Objectivity and realism in sociology," in George Psathas (ed.) Phenomenological Sociology. New York: John Wiley.

BLAU, P. (1955) The Dynamics of Bureaucracy. Chicago: University of Chicago Press.

BLUMBERG, A. (1967) Criminal Justice. Chicago: Quadrangle.

BLUMER, H. (1971a) "Social problems as collective behavior." Social Problems 18 (Winter): 298-306.

——— (1971b) "The world of youthful drug use." University of California. (unpublished)

BUCKLEY, W. F. (1967) Sociology and Modern Systems Theory. Englewood Cliffs, NJ: Prentice-Hall.

BURROUGHS, W. (1953) Junkie. New York, Ace.

CHEIN, I., D. GERARD, R. LEE, and E. ROSENFELD (1964) The Road to H: Narcotics, Delinquency, and Social Policy. New York: Basic Books.

CICOUREL, A. (1968) The Social Organization of Juvenile Justice. New York: John Wiley.

CLECKNER, P. (1977) "Cognitive and ritual aspects of drug use among young black urban males," in DuToit (ed.) Drugs, Rituals and Altered States of Consciousness. Rotterdam: Balkame.

CLOWARD, R. and L. OHLIN (1960) Delinquency and Opportunity, A Theory of Delinquent Gangs. New York: Macmillan.

COHEN, A. (1955) Delinquent Boys. New York: Macmillan.

CRANE, L. E. (1972) "Legal control of heroin users: a therapeutic model of the criminal process." Presented at the meeting of the Society for the Study of Social Problems, New Orleans.

DANET, B. (1971). "Language of persuasion in bureaucracy: modern and traditional appeals to the Israel customs and authorities." American Sociological Review 36 (October): 847-859.

DIANA, L. (1960) "What is probation?" Journal of Criminal Law, Criminology and Police Science 51 (July-August): 189-204.

DOLE, V. and M. NYSWANDER (1976) "Methadone maintenance treatment: a ten year perspective." Journal of the American Medical Association 235: 2117-2119.

DOUGLAS, J. S. (1967) The Social Meanings of Suicide. Princeton, NJ: Princeton University Press.

Drug Abuse Survey Project (1972) Dealing with Drug Abuse: A Report to the Ford Foundation. New York: Praeger.

DUPONT, R. L. and T. E. PIEMME (1973) "Estimation of the number of heroin addicts in an urban area." Medical Annals of the District of Columbia 42: 323-326.

DURKHEIM, E. (1933) The Division of Labor in Society. New York: Macmillan.

——— (1964) The Rules of Sociological Method. New York: Macmillan.

——— (1973) On Morality and Society. Chicago: Chicago University Press.

ERIKSON, K. T. (1966) Wayward Puritans. New York, John Wiley.

ERIKSON, K. T. (1977) Everything in Its Path: Destruction of Community in the Buffalo Creek Flood. New York: Simon & Schuster.

ETZIONI, A. (1964) Modern Organizations. Englewood Cliffs, NJ: Prentice-Hall.

FERRIE, E. (1917) Criminal Sociology. Boston, MA: Little, Brown.

FLAVELL, J. (1963) The Developmental Psychology of Jean Piaget. New York: Litton.

FRANK, J. (1936) Law and Modern Mind. Princeton, NJ: Princeton University Press.

FREEDMAN, A. (1975) Comprehensive Textbook of Psychiatry. Baltimore, MD: Williams and Wilkins.

FRIEDSON, E. (1970) Professional Dominance. Chicago: Atherton.

GARFINKEL, H. (1956) "Conditions of successful degradation ceremonies." American Journal of Sociology 61 (March): 420-424.

——— (1967) Studies in Ethnomethodology. Englewood Cliffs, NJ: Prentice-Hall.

GEERTZ, C. (1973) The Interpretation of Cultures. New York: Basic Books.

Georgetown Law Journal (1972) "Addict diversion: an alternative approach for the criminal system." 60, 3: 667-668.

GIBBS, J. (1966) "Conceptions of deviant behaviors: old and new." Pacific Sociological Review 9: 9-14.

GLASSCOTE, R., J. N. SUSSEX, J. H. JAFFE, J. BALL, and L. BRILL (1972) The treatment of drug abuse. Washington Joint Information Service of the American Psychiatric Association and the National Institute of Mental Health.

GLENNBY, L. (1968) "Cops crush communes," in J. Hopkins (ed.) The Hippie Papers. New York: Signet.

GOFFMAN, E. (1961) Asylums. New York: Doubleday.

——— (1974) Frame Analysis. Cambridge, MA: Harvard University Press.

GOODE, E. (1969) "Multiple drug use among marijuana smokers." Social Problems 17 (Summer): 48-64.

GOULD, L. C. (1969) "Who defines delinquency: a comparison of self-reported and officially reported indices of delinquency for three racial groups." Social Problems 16: 325-336.

——— and Z. NAMENWIRTH (1972) "Contrary objectives: crime control and the rehabilitation of criminals," in J. Douglas (ed.) Crime and Justice in American Society. New York: Bobbs-Merrill.

GOULD, L. C., A. L. WALKER, L. E. CRANE, and C. W. LIDZ (1974) Connections: Notes from the Heroin World. New Haven, CT: Yale University Press.

GOULD, L. C., R. M. BERBERIAN, S. V. KASL, W. D. THOMPSON, and H. D. KLEBER (1975) "Final report on Grant DA4PG007—five year follow-up of methadone maintenance patients." (Available from Dr. Leroy Gould, Institution for Social and Policy Studies, Yale University.)

——— (1976) "Reported sequential patterns of multiple-drug use among high school students." (Manuscript available from Dr. Leroy Gould, Institution for Social and Policy Studies, Yale University.)

GOULD, L. C., W. D. THOMPSON, and R. BERBERIAN (1977) "Biasing factors in the measurement of trends in heroin use." Addictive Diseases 3 (2): 151-176.

GREENE, M. H. and R. L. DUPONT (1974) "Epidemiology of drug abuse." American Journal of Public Health Supplement 64 (December): 1-56.

GUSFIELD, J. A. (1963) Symbolic Crusade: Status Politics and the American Temperance Movement. Chicago, IL: University of Illinois Press.

HAKEEM, M. (1958) "Critique of the psychiatric approach to crime and correction." Law and Contemporary Problems 23 (Fall): 650-682.

HOPKINS, J. [ed.] (1968) The Hippie Papers. New York: Signet.

HOROWITZ, I. L. (1964) The New Sociology. New York: Oxford University Press.
HUGHES, P., R. PARKER, and E. SENAY (1974) "Addicts, police, and the neigh-
    borhood social system." American Journal of Orthopsychiatry 44 (January):
    129-141.
HUNT, L. and C. CHAMBERS (1973) The Heroin Epidemic. New York: Spectrum.
INCIARDI, J. A. (1974) "Drugs, drug-taking and drug-seeking: notations on the
    dynamics of myth, change and reality," in J. Inciardi and C. D. Chambers (eds.)
    Drugs and the Criminal Justice System. Beverly Hills, CA: Sage Publications.
JACKSON, B. (1967) "Exiles from the American dream: the junkies and the cop."
    Atlantic Monthly 219 (January): 44-51. Boston
JETTE, P. and F. MONTANINO (1978) "Face to face interaction in the criminal
    justice system." Criminology 16: 67-86.
JOHNSON, G. (1975) "Conversion as a cure: therapeutic community and the
    professional ex-addict." Contemporary Drug Problems 5: 187-205.
JOSEPH, H. (1973) "A probation department treats heroin addicts." Federal Proba-
    tion 37: 35.
KAHN, R. and E. NEBELKOPF (1979) "The other side: counselor roles." Interna-
    tional Journal of the Addictions 14: 1047-1052.
KASSIS, R. L. (1972) "Drug rehabilitation: is a separate drug court the answer?"
    Pacific Law Journal 3: 595.
KESSEBAUM, G. C. and B. O. BAUMANN (1965) "Dimensions of the sick role in
    chronic illness." Journal of Health and Human Behavior 6 (Spring): 16-27.
KIRK, R. (1955) Introduction, in John Stuart Mill's On Liberty. New York:
    Gateway.
KITSUSE, J. and A. I. CICOUREL (1963) The Educational Decision Makers. Indian-
    apolis: Bobbs-Merrill.
KITSUSE, J. and M. SPECTOR (1973) "Towards a sociology of social problems:
    social conditioning, value judgments and social problems." Social Problems 20:
    407-419.
——— (1975) "Social problems and deviance: some parallel issues." Social Problems
    22 (June): 584-594.
KLEEMAN, N. and A. I. POSNER (1971) "The comprehensive drug rehabilitation
    and treatment act: treatment in lieu of prosecution." Massachusetts Law Quar-
    terly 56: 171.
KRAEPLIN, E. (1902) Clinical Psychiatry: Textbook for Students and Physicians.
    (Abstracted and adapted from the sixth German edition of Kraeplin's "Lehrbuch
    der Psychiatrie" by A. R. Defendorf.) New York: Macmillan.
KUPFERBERG, T. (1968) "How shall we survive," in J. Hopkins (ed.) The Hippie
    Papers. New York: Signet.
KUSKEY, W. and W. KRASNER (1973) "The eyes of the beholder: the drug addict
    as criminal, patient or victim." Contemporary Drug Problems 2: 565-578.
LeMar, editors of (1969) "Down with prohibition," in E. Goode (ed.) Marijuana.
    Chicago: AVC.
LEMERT, E. (1951) Social Pathology. New York: McGraw-Hill.
——— (1962) "Paranoia and the dynamics of exclusion." Sociometry 25: 1.
——— (1967) Human Deviance, Social Problems and Control. Englewood Cliffs, NJ:
    Prentice-Hall.
——— (1970) Legal Action and Social Change. Chicago: AVC.

LEVI, E. (1949) An Introduction to Legal Reasoning. Chicago: University of Chicago Press.

LEVI-STRAUSS, C. (1967) "The myth of Asdiwal," in E. Leach (ed.) The Structural Study of Myth and Totemism. London: Tavistock.

——— (1969) The Raw and the Cooked. New York: Harper & Row.

LIDZ, C. W. (1974a) "Law, morality and the social order." Ph.D. dissertation, Harvard University.

——— (1974b) "The cop-addict game: a model of police-suspect interaction." Journal of Police Science and Administration 2: 1.

——— and V. M. LIDZ (1976) "Jean Piaget's psychology of intelligence and its place in the theory of action," in J. Laubser et al., Essays in the General Theory of Social Sciences. New York: Macmillan.

——— (1981) "Towards a deep structural analysis of moral action," in I. Rossi (ed.) Structural Sociology: Theoretical Perspectives and Substantive Analysis. New York: Columbia University Press.

LINDESMITH, A. R. (1947) Opiate Addiction. Bloomington, IN: Principia Press.

——— (1965) The Addict and the Law. New York: Vintage.

LIPSET, S. M. (1963) The First New Nation. New York: Basic Books.

LOMBROSO, C. (1918) Crime: Its Causes and Remedies. Boston: Little, Brown.

MAINE, H. (1863) Ancient Law. London: J. Murray.

MANNING, P. (1973) "Survey essay on deviance." Contemporary Sociology 2: 123-128.

MARTIN, G., Jr. (1974) "The courts, the heroin addict and the administration of justice." Contemporary Drug Problems 3: 45-60.

MARX, K. (1963) "The Eighteenth Brumaire of Louis Bonaparte." New York: International.

MATZA, D. (1964) Delinquency and Drift. New York: John Wiley.

——— (1969) Becoming Deviant. Englewood Cliffs, NJ: Prentice-Hall.

MEAD, G. H. (1918) "Psychology of primitive justice." Amer. Journal of Sociology 23 (March): 577-602.

——— (1934) Mind, Self and Society. (C. W. Morris, ed.) Chicago: University of Chicago Press.

MECHANIC, D. (1962) "The concept of illness behavior." Journal of Chronic Diseases 15: 189-194.

MEISEL, A. (1977) "The expansion of liability for medical accidents: from negligence to strict liability by way of informed consent." Nebraska Law Review 56, 1: 51-152.

MERTON, R. K. (1968) Social Theory and Social Structure. New York: Macmillan.

MILLER, W. (1958) "Lower class culture as a generating milieu of gang delinquency." Journal of Social Issues 14, 3: 5-19.

——— (1962) "The impact of a 'total community' delinquency control project." Social Problems 10 (Fall).

MILLS, C. W. (1956) Power Elite. London: Oxford University Press.

——— (1967) Power, Politics and People: The Collected Essays of C. Wright Mills. (I. Horowitz, ed.) New York: Oxford University Press.

MONROE, H. (1968) "Take tea and see/take L.S.D. and be," in J. Hopkins (ed.) The Hippie Papers. New York: Signet.

MORGANBESSER, M. (1974) "Role of police officers in a drug treatment program." Contemporary Drug Problems 3 (Summer): 213-220.

MUSTO, D. (1973) The American Disease. New Haven, CT: Yale Univ. Press.

NELSON, J. W. (1976) Your God is Alive and Well and Appearing in Popular Culture. New York: Westminster.

NEWMAN, D. (1956) "Pleading guilty for considerations." Journal of Criminal Law, Criminology and Police Science 46: 780-790.

O'DONNELL, J., H. VOSS, R. CLAYTON, G. SLATIN, and R. ROOM (1976) Young Men and Drugs: A Nationwide Survey. NIDA Monograph, Series 5. Washington, DC: Printing Office.

PACKER, H. L. (1968) The Limits of the Criminal Sanction. Palo Alto, CA: Stanford University Press.

PARSONS, T. (1937) The Structure of Social Action. New York: McGraw-Hill.

——— (1951) The Social System. New York: Macmillan.

——— and R. FOX (1952) "Illness, therapy and the modern urban family." Journal of Social Issues 8: 31-44.

PARSONS, T. and R. F. BALES (1955) Family Socialization and Interaction Process. New York: Macmillan.

——— (1964) "Evolutionary universals in society." American Sociological Review 29, 3: 339-357.

——— (1965) "Full citizenship for the negro American: a sociological problem." Daedalus (November): 1009-1054.

——— (1967) Sociological Theory and Modern Society. New York: Macmillan.

PIAGET, J. and B. INHELDER (1958) The Growth of Logical Thinking. New York: Basic Books.

PICKNEY, A. (1976) Red, Black and Green: A History of Black Nationalism in America. New York: Cambridge University Press.

POLLACK, F. and F. MAITLAND (1968) The History of English Law, Vol. 1. Cambridge: Cambridge University Press.

QUINNEY, R. (1970) The Social Reality of Crime. Boston: Little, Brown.

RAFALSKY, T. (1972) "The addicted client: rehabilitation as a defense strategy and the role of the attorney in the rehabilitation process." Contemporary Drug Problems 1: 399-411.

RAY, T. (1975) "The client oriented service delivery system with the methadone maintenance program." Contemporary Drug Problems 5: 449-458.

REICH, . (1970) The Greening of America. New York: Random House.

RICHMAN, A. (1974) "Epidemiological assessment of changes in the onset of narcotic addiction." Presented at the Thirty-Sixth Annual Meeting on the Problems of Drug Dependence, Mexico City.

ROBINS, L. N. (1975) "Alcoholism and labeling theory," in W. Gove (ed.) The Labeling of Deviance: Evaluating a Perspective. Beverly Hills, CA: Sage Publications.

ROSETT, A. and D. CRESSEY (1976) Justice by Consent. Philadelphia: Lippincott.

ROSS, E. (1959) Social Control and the Foundations of Sociology (E. Borgatta and H. Meyer, eds.). Boston: Beacon.

ROSZAK, T. (1969) The Making of a Counter Culture. New York: Doubleday.

ROTHMAN, D. (1971) The Discovery of the Asylum. Boston: Little, Brown.

RUBENSTEIN, J. (1973) City Police. New York: Farrar, Straus & Giroux.

RUBINGTON, E. and M. WEINBERG [eds.] (1973) Deviance: The Interactionist Perspective. New York: Macmillan.

RUIZ, P., J. LANGROD, J. LOWINSON, and N. MARCUS (1977) "Social rehabilitation of addicts: a two year evaluation." International Journal of the Addictions 12: 173-181.

San Mateo County Department of Health (1974) "Student drug use survey." (Pamphlet available from the San Mateo County Department of Health, San Mateo, California.)

SCHEFF, T. (1966) Being Mentally Ill: A Sociological Theory. Chicago: Aldine.

SCHUR, E. (1962) Narcotic Addiction in Britain and America. Bloomington: IN: Indiana University Press.

SCHUTZ, A. (1967) Collected papers, Vol. 1. (M. Natanson, ed.) The Hague: M. Nimhoff.

SCHWARTZMAN, J. and L. KROLL (1977) "Methadone maintenance and addict abstinence." International Journal of the Addictions 12: 497-507.

SHILS, E. (1969) "Ideology: The concept and function of ideology," pp. 66-76 in D. Sills (ed.) The Encyclopedia of the Social Sciences, Vol. 7. New York: Macmillan.

SINGLE, E., D. KANDELL, and B. JOHNSON (1975) "The reliability and validity of drug use responses in a large scale longitudinal survey." Journal of Drug Issues 5: 426-443.

SKOLNICK, J. (1966) Justice Without trial. New York: John Wiley.

SLATER, P. (1968) The Pursuit of Loneliness. Boston: Beacon.

SMART, R. and D. FEJER (1974) "Changes in drug use in Toronto high school students between 1973 and 1974." (unpublished)

SUDNOW, D. (1965) "Normal crimes: sociological features of the penal code." Social Problems 12: 255-276.

SUTHERLAND, E. H. (1934) Principles of Criminology. Philadelphia: J. B. Lippincott.

SWANSON, G. (1975) "Law enforcement and drug rehabilitation: is a bridge of trust possible?" Contemporary Drug Problems 4: 493-501.

SYKES, G. and D. MATZA (1957) "Techniques of neutralization." American Sociological Review 22 (December): 664-670.

——— (1958) The Society of Captives. Princeton, NJ: Princeton University Press.

SZASZ, T. (1961) The Myth of Mental Illness. New York: Harper & Row.

——— (1970) "The rhetoric of rejection," in T. Szasz, Ideology and Insanity. New York: Doubleday.

——— (1974) Ceremonial Chemistry: The Ritual Persecution of Drug Addicts and Pushers. New York: Doubleday.

TANNENBAUM, F. (1938) Crime and the Community. New York: Columbia University Press.

TARDE, G. (1912) Penal Philosophy. Boston: Little, Brown.

TAYLOR, I., P. WALTON, and J. YOUNG (1973) The New Criminology. New York, Harper & Row.

THOMAS, W. I. (1923) The Unadjusted Girl. Boston: Little, Brown.

WALKER, A. L. (1972) "Treatment vs. punishment: the view from the outside." Presented to the annual meeting of the Society for the Study of Social Problems, New Orleans.

WALLWORK, E. (1972) Durkheim: Morality and Milieu. Cambridge: Harvard University Press.

WALSH, J. L. (1975) "Police career styles and counting coups on the beats–the sources of police incivility." Presented to the American Sociological Association, San Francisco.

WEBER, M. (1958) The Protestant Ethic and the Spirit of Capitalism. New York: Scribner.

WEIL, A. (1972) The Natural Mind. Boston: Houghton Mifflin.

WEINER, H. (1975) "Methadone counseling: a social work challenge." Journal of Psychedelic Drugs 7: 381-387.

WERTHMAN, C. and I. PILIAVIN (1967) "Gang members and the police," in D. Bordua (ed.) The Police: Six Sociological Essays. New York: John Wiley.

WHITE, W. (1961) Beyond Conformity. New York: Macmillan.

WHITEHEAD, A. N. (1926) Science in the Modern World. New York: Macmillan.

––– (1933) Adventures of Ideas. New York: Macmillan.

WILLIAMS, M. (1975) "The search for information: procedures for seeing evil in everyday life." Department of Sociology, University of California at Santa Barbara. (mimeo)

WILLIAMS, R., Jr. (1970) American Society: A Sociological Interpretation. New York: Knopf.

X, M. (1976) The Autobiography of Malcolm X. New York: Ballantine.

Yale Law Journal (1967) "Interrogations in New Haven: the impact of Miranda." 76: 1519-1648.

INDEX

The following notations appear in this index:

n. after a reference number denotes that the item occurs in an endnote.

ff. after a reference number denotes that the item also occurs on one or two pages following the reference.

bis after a reference number denotes that the item is alluded to twice quite separately on the same page of the text.

passim after a set of reference numbers denotes that the item is referred to several times throughout the pages cited.

ABOUT THE AUTHORS

Charles W. Lidz is Assistant Professor of Psychiatry and Sociology at the University of Pittsburgh. He received his Ph.D. in sociology from Harvard in 1974. He is coauthor of *Connections: Notes from the Heroin World* and has published numerous articles in scholarly journals on deviance, sociological theory, paranoia, and other topics. He is currently completing research on the impact of legal regulation on the practice of psychiatry.

Andrew L. Walker is on the faculty of the Division of Social Sciences at Stephens College. He received his sociology Ph.D. from Harvard in 1974. His scholarly publications include papers on professional crime, field methods, and deviance theory. He is also coauthor of *Connections: Notes from the Heroin World.* He has been the Director of the Center for Conceptual Studies at Stephens. He is currently doing research on the Mayan Calendar.

Leroy C. Gould is a Senior Research Associate with the Institution for Social and Policy Studies, and a Lecturer in Sociology at Yale University. He received his Ph.D. in sociology from the University of Washington in 1964. His principal areas of research are crime and delinquency, drugs, and energy. A coauthor of *Connections: Notes from the Heroin World,* he is working on a new book, *Too Hot to Handle: Social and Policy Issues in Radioactive Waste Management.*